D1560281

A ZIONIST AMONG PALESTINIANS

A
ZIONIST
AMONG
PALESTINIANS

HILLEL BARDIN

FOREWORD BY

MUBARAK AWAD & EDWARD (EDY) KAUFMAN

INDIANA UNIVERSITY PRESS

Bloomington & Indianapolis

This book is a publication of

Indiana University Press
601 North Morton Street
Bloomington, Indiana
47404-3797 USA

iupress.indiana.edu

Telephone orders 800-842-6796
Fax orders 812-855-7931

© 2012 by Hillel Bardin

Manufactured in the United States of America

Library of Congress Cataloging-in-Publication Data

Bardin, Hillel.
  A Zionist among Palestinians / Hillel Bardin ; foreword by
Mubarak Awad and Edward (Edy) Kaufman.
  p. cm.
  Includes index.
  ISBN 978-0-253-00211-2 (cloth : alk. paper) —
  ISBN 978-0-253-00223-5 (ebook)
  1. Arab-Israeli conflict—1993—Peace. 2. Arab-Israeli
conflict—Social aspects. 3. Conflict management—Israel.
4. Palestinian Arabs—Civil rights. 5. Peace-building—Israel.
6. Nonviolence. I. Title.
  DS119.76.B37   2012
  956.9405′4—dc23   2012005739

1 2 3 4 5 17 16 15 14 13 12

TO MY WIFE, *Anita*

TO MY COMMANDER, *Shammai Shpitzer*

TO MY FRIEND, *Jalal Qumsiyeh*

CONTENTS

FOREWORD

Mubarak Awad and Edward (Edy) Kaufman

The timing of this publication is particularly important. The wave of non-violent struggle in the Middle East and northern Africa for democracy, human rights, and dignity has already resulted in regime change in a few countries. While authoring these lines, we have been deeply interested in the possibility that Palestinians in the West Bank and Gaza might join in the struggle. If that happens, what will be the reaction of Israeli Jews? Will they work across the divide with Arabs who share such values? The personal story of Hillel, whom we know from the days of the First Intifada, is not only a testimony, but also a source of inspiration for both our societies. At the same time, the human dimension of the experiences he describes should move not only those in the Arab and Jewish diasporas, but all others keen to understand the obstacles and potential impact of nonviolent struggle in one of the world's most protracted and aggressive conflicts.

For the sake of transparency, we should mention that this foreword has been written by a Palestinian and an Israeli, both of whom have been involved in furthering the nonviolent struggle to end Israeli occupation and search for a just peace. Since the First Intifada, we have spent a considerable part of our lives in advancing this strategy: Mubarak worldwide, as chair of Nonviolence International and as a teacher; and Edy in academic scholarship, applying the results of his research through activism in human rights organizations and by facilitating conflict transformation workshops. We both befriended Hillel and were participants in some of the stories covered in this book.

Moving from the individual to the collective narrative, we humbly believe that our contribution can best serve the reader not just by adding our personal experiences, but by also illuminating the wider context within which the stories in the book took place. From the June 1967 war until the end of 1987, resistance to occupation was conducted by small groups of armed fighters who were trained outside the area and carried out lethal attacks—against civilian targets in Israel proper, the settlements in the occupied territories, and abroad (e.g., airplane hijackings and the killing of Israeli athletes at the Munich Olympics). Israeli retaliations and often preemptive punitive actions against unarmed civilians amounted at times to what could be considered state terrorism.

Not a few argue that the Palestinians have tried nonviolence before, with only partial success, during the First Intifada. If it didn't work then, what's the point in trying it again? Indeed, primarily nonviolent methods were utilized during that uprising, a most significant change compared with the previous period. Moderation was evident not only in the means of protest but also in the successful efforts by Palestinians under occupation to put pressure on the PLO to move from formulas such as "a democratic and secular Palestine" to a "two-state solution," an Israeli and a Palestinian state living peacefully next to each other. However, certain elements of the First Intifada prevented it from constituting a true and completely peaceful resistance movement. It was spontaneous, only partially organized, and had a grassroots, widely shared leadership, but it lacked a clear, top-down message of endorsement of this form of popular civil disobedience. Hence, the lessons learned from previous weaknesses should be important now that this form of action is becoming widely accepted as effective.

There are some structural reasons for the breakout of the intifada in December 1987, including the deterioration of the economic situation and growing unemployment amid the Israeli economic crisis; a generation of university graduates that could not find sources of income except in menial jobs; and the stagnation of the appeal for *summud*—steadfastness—with the policy of crippling annexation through the establishment of more Jewish settlements. The trigger was an unplanned protest against the accidental deaths caused by an army truck driver colliding with two cars in Gaza. Palestinians gathered at first spontaneously, and then became mobilized under directives into massive protests across the Palestinian territories, blocking roads and Israeli army movements. Demonstrators threw stones at the Israeli soldiers despite the tear gas and rubber-coated bullets used in return. Massive funeral processions also demonstrated nonviolent resistance to Israeli occupation. The bottom-up nature of the uprising can be recognized not only through the political parties represented in the PLO but increasingly by the emergence of NGOs advocating the organizing of resistance and nonviolent actions. Much of the story has been covered by Mary King (2007), Maxine Kaufman-Lacuste (2010), and others. What is important to our analysis is that many individuals and organizations at that time advocated the involvement of Israeli activists in their struggle. And Hillel Bardin was eagerly trying to reach out from the Israeli side.

A strong impetus for a planned peaceful resistance was triggered by Mubarak Awad, when he founded the Palestinian Center for the Study of Nonviolence and made its presence known by the then-illegal display of the Palestinian flag. A disciple of Gene Sharp, Awad delved into the nonviolent methods utilized by Palestinians: demonstrations, obstruction, noncooperation, harassment, boycotts, strikes, alternative institutions, and civil disobedience. One of the more effective demonstrations he described (Awad 1984) was the cleanup campaign organized by the youth of al-Bireh and Ramallah to protest the dismissal of mayors and the closure of municipalities. Another example of defying the Israeli army in Ramallah occurred when Palestinians blew whistles and sounded car horns to protest the closure of Birzeit University (Awad 1984: 28). They also created a Library on Wheels, translating and encouraging the reading of books about nonviolence among children across the West Bank and East Jerusalem. Acts of noncooperation included boycotts of Israeli goods, refusal to work in the military government, refusal to pay taxes, refusal to sign official forms, refusal to work on building Israeli settlements, and refusal of any other form of "Judaization." Harassment of Israeli soldiers was conceived as a psychological tactic to remind them of the role they play in the injustice.

More and more Israelis joined this nucleus of Palestinians and participated in their actions. While such methods were publicly advocated, they were only partially implemented in an organized way during the intifada. When Awad's presence in Jerusalem was declared illegal by Israeli prime minister Yitzhak Shamir (even though Awad was born there and was counted as a resident in the post-1967 census), he was imprisoned for several months. Edy Kaufman, along with other Jews and Arabs, joined Awad in a sympathy hunger strike in a parking lot in Jerusalem's Russian Compound, on the other side of the prison's wall. The Israeli Supreme Court confirmed the decision to deport Awad and he was expelled, but—as is documented in this book—he continued to dialogue with Jewish Israelis about human and national rights. An NGO based in Beit Sahour, PCR, was responsible for underground schools, the notorious tax revolt, and establishing dialogue groups with Israeli supporters of nonviolent struggle.

Unfortunately, the resistance during the First Intifada was not totally nonviolent. While many protestors participated in peaceful acts of civil disobedience, a few others threw stones and Molotov cocktails at Israelis. Although the Palestinians were outmatched by Israel's military capability, the mass Israeli perception of the Palestinian resistance was that it was violent. Stones that were thrown symbolically were seen as life-threatening rocks. Kaufman published two articles analyzing the negative perceptions of the Israeli public (1990, 1992). On the other hand, violence was often idealized as limited, nonlethal, popular, or symbolic. But taking the best from two worlds by only engaging in "limited violence," incorporating both strategies, did not produce the desired results. PLO chair Yasser Arafat praised the "children of the stones," as he had the "children of the RPGs" (rocket-propelled grenades used during the first Lebanon war against the IDF), who were now aiming rocks not only at soldiers but at civilians as well. Adding a violent dimension to a nonviolent struggle is self-defeating and a contradiction in terms. Throwing rocks at soldiers may be gratifying for an individual but it does not advance the goals of Palestinians and only provokes Israeli aggression. Sharp acknowledges that such retaliatory acts against opponents have no strategic purpose and are likely to undermine the resistance (Sharp and Raqib 2009: 488). Consequently, the breadth of support from staunch Palestinian advocates of nonviolent action, such as Faisal Husseini, Sari Nusseibeh, and Mubarak Awad, diminished. The two critical elements of a nonviolent resistance movement—uniformity of struggle in the land and the diaspora, and active top-down PLO support—were absent in the First Intifada.

In general, the world was sympathetic to the Palestinian struggle during the First Intifada, a shift in attitudes toward what had until then been considered a terrorist movement in the West. The Palestinian struggle gained international recognition, which increased the pressure on the Israelis to respond to Palestinian demands. Within Israel, the resourcefulness and imagination of some of the nonviolent techniques caught the public's eye. While they could not identify a single nonviolent leader, there was a sense that the status quo, in which Palestinians acquiesced to a "benign occupation" in return for economic improvements, was totally gone. Furthermore, the transition from passivity to massive rebellion was recognized, and the realization that the partners for peace now had to include the Palestinians—and not only established Arab states—led eventually to the Oslo peace process. Still, there was widespread criticism of nonviolent action as naïve and ineffective, and it did not shatter the "positive" results from the old violent tactics. Many on both sides continued to believe that the only language Israelis understood, the only thing that would make them relinquish power, was force—and they also believed that Arabs only understood that "might was right."

It would be misleading to end this discussion with such a mixed picture, since the positive outcomes prevailed (Abu Nimer 2006), paving the way for direct PLO-Israel negotiations. The two-state solution emerged from the struggle as the dominant view, and this was another of the achievements of the intifada. The intifada also demonstrated the Palestinian movement's ability to mobilize whole sectors of the population through networks of underground civilian resistance and communal self-help projects, challenging Israel's ability to continue ruling the West Bank and Gaza. "The pattern of daily street confrontation has dealt a moral, if not logistic, blow to the might of the Israeli army. Above all, the intifada placed relations with the Palestinians and the future of the occupied territories at the top of the agenda of all Israeli political parties" (Tamari 1990: 4).

Palestinian nonviolence was represented by the low number (in the two digits) of Israeli casualties during the First Intifada. Most were killed in the occupied territories and not within Israel itself, marking the boundaries of the two-state solution. Israeli repression, on the other hand, produced more than a thousand Palestinian deaths, marginally outnumbering the deaths during the subsequent "intrafada," when internal armed confrontations marked the end of the success story.

Within an even wider spatial and temporal context, there is a deep-rooted trauma among Israeli Jews, who fear talk as an incitement from the Arab world, as well as actual violence. Many Muslim and Arab public and popular statements and actions have not been conciliatory toward the Israelis and the Jews, including some that question the true nature of the Holocaust. The Israeli psyche has been prone to perceive the message as "We will kill you all," even if many are standing up bravely among the Palestinians to publicly condemn suicide and car bombings. *Itbah al Yehud* (Butcher the Jew) still has great resonance. True, the mirror image exists in the cry *Mavet laAravim* (Death to the Arabs), the mob's call for revenge whenever a killing of Israelis takes place; both cries, even if not acted upon, are terrifying. Similarly, for Jews, the call for jihad (holy war) rings a different bell than the struggle within oneself, which is its interpretation by pious Muslims.

Today, we know from public opinion polls that the Israeli public in general is ready to end the violence and is leaning toward conciliation with the Palestinians. But the limited coverage of nonviolent actions in the Israeli media may suggest that the Israeli public's reaction has been blunted and an extraordinary, wide-spanning breakthrough activity is necessary to gain attention.

Palestinians may legitimately ask: Where is the Israeli nonviolent movement? It may be necessary to remind them that peaceful resistance in an asymmetrical situation is an equalizing tool for the weaker side. Furthermore, the importance of security for the Jewish people is not a slogan or excuse, but the result of a long history of threats to their existence. In spite of an apparent lack of reciprocity on the part of the resistance to occupation, Hillel Bardin and other concerned Israeli citizens, albeit in decreasing numbers, have demonstrated their commitment to shared goals through their involvement in human rights and peace organizations. But the number of those refusing to serve Israeli security by only utilizing military means continues to remain negligible, and will until the time when Palestinian nonviolent empowerment obliges them to look in the mirror and within themselves and join rather than fight. "When you are talking to the enemy, to an Israeli, your own people will ask you whether you are a traitor"—"but, you cannot talk only to the world or with other Palestinians, you have to tell the Israeli what is happening" (Awad 1984: 88). Violence has been inflicted on both societies, and it is often easier to escalate than to de-escalate, but perhaps a dramatic nonviolent action can lead to a clear-cut departure from the current spiral of mutual reprisals. Perhaps it is possible to build a wide consensus, in the first stage, against the targeting of innocent civilians, which may create a call for reciprocity, namely stopping both grassroots terrorism and state terrorism. While limiting the scope of violence is not equivalent to nonviolent action, a gradual decrease can contribute to finding common ground as a means of defusing the current situation.

While majorities in both nations are ready to settle on a two-state solution, their pessimism about seeing that achieved in their lifetimes is making that goal seem to be a distant utopia. Nonviolent action has the capacity to prove that a just solution can be conducted heroically and achieved by such means. It may already be possible to see small but significant progress in the debates and limited actions toward bottom-up and top-down endorsement of Palestinian nonviolent struggle. But criticism of the militarized Second Intifada by President Mahmoud Abbas and a proactive stand in boycotting Jewish settlement goods by Prime Minister Salam Fayyad are not enough; these are efforts in the right direction but strategic planning needs to involve all vital sectors of the Palestinian government and society. At times, these steps can be enhanced by charismatic and determined leaders, like President Anwar Sadat of Egypt or King Hussein from Jordan, who were able to reach Israeli hearts. But looking at the popular revolutions in Tunisia, Egypt, and other Arab countries, a massive movement can produce results even when a Gandhi figure is not available.

Means and ends have an important correlation. Moderation in Arab aims began in 1988 at the Nineteenth Palestinian National Council, with a Declaration of Independence for the state, which included the proposal to live in peace with Israel as a neighbor. This became regionalized with the 2002 Arab Peace Initiative. If such steps can be accompanied, even indirectly, by a long-term struggle legitimated by nonviolent means, the growing support at the international level and the dissatisfaction with unchanged official policy are likely to impact Jewish public opinion and strengthen the peace camp in Israel.

Moving from the macro picture to the role of dedicated individuals, Hillel has been a well-known and pioneering figure among the advocates of nonviolence in Jerusalem, seeking dialogue and bottom-up peacebuilding. His effort to work for nonviolence while wearing the Israel Defense Forces uniform has been truly unique. On the one hand, he was punished with short-term imprisonment for doing so; but on the other hand, he has been able to identify some Israeli empathy on issues such as the right of Palestinians to call for peace. Most of the activities he describes in this book took place during the First Intifada, but he has relentlessly continued, albeit getting diminishing returns.

By sharing these stories, Hillel makes it possible to discern a pattern across the case studies, one that he summarizes in the last chapter. He has grown over the years to realize the limits of Jewish-initiated joint nonviolent peace activism as it is often carried out. Through trial and error he has come to endorse the idea of "dialogue-action groups" in which the dialogue leads to community action. He notes that a certain contradiction exists between *dialogues* that are open to people of all points of view, and *action* that is designed to affect public opinion in a particular direction. He does not favor gatherings with the sole purpose of drafting a joint statement, getting it into the press, and then disbanding. Dialogue is a necessary but not sufficient condition; he is not interested in formulating policies without implementation. In both cases, action is the added dimension that is needed in order to be both credible and effective. In Hillel's own words, "The ideal group . . . is one that combines dialogue with activities whose planning is assisted by expert consultants analyzing strategic goals. The actions tap into the strengths of the community, which are activated by the dialogue group, which is given legitimacy by a local leadership that has the long-range national goals in mind."

Looking around the region at the beginning of the second decade of the twenty-first century and seeing the empowerment of civil society in popular demands for regime change, it is difficult to predict the impact on Israel. Massive nonviolent protest and disobedience against Israeli weapons will be untenable, but no riot equipment can stop a real and sustained mass uprising. A one-person enterprise, like that of Hillel Bardin, cannot provide a full answer, but he remains a strong source of inspiration.

BIBLIOGRAPHY

Abu Nimer, Mohammed. 2006. Nonviolent Action in Israel and Palestine: A Growing Force. In E. Kaufman, W. Salem, and J. Verhoeven, eds., *Bridging the Divide: Peacebuilding in the Israeli-Palestinian Conflict.* Boulder, Colo.: Lynne Rienner.

Awad, Mubarak E. 1984. Non-Violent Resistance: A Strategy for the Occupied Territories. *Journal of Palestine Studies* 13(4): 22–36.

Awad, Mubarak E., and Edward (Edy) Kaufman. 1998. The Prospect of Non-Violent Action from the Intifada to the Israeli-Palestinian Peace Process. *Civil Society* (Cairo) (November): 16–18.

Kaufman, Edward (Edy). 1990. Limited Violence and the Intifadah. *Journal of Arab Studies* 9(2): 109–121.

———. 1992. Israeli Perceptions of the Palestinians' "Limited Violence" in the Intifada. *Journal of Terrorism and Political Violence* 3(4): 1–38.

———. 2005. Dialogue-Based Processes: A Vehicle for Peacebuilding. In P. van Tongeren, M. Brenk, M. Hellema, and J. Verhoeven, eds., *People Building Peace II: Successful Stories of Civil Society.* Boulder, Colo.: Lynne Rienner.

Kaufman-Lacuste, Maxine. 2010. *Refusing to Be Enemies: Palestinian and Israeli Nonviolent Resistance to the Israeli Occupation.* Reading, England: Ithaca Press.

King, Mary Elizabeth. 2007. *A Quiet Revolution: The First Intifada and Nonviolent Resistance.* New York: Nation Books.

Sharp, Gene, and Jamila Raqib. 2009. *Self-Liberation: A Guide to Strategic Planning for Action to End a Dictatorship or Other Oppression.* Boston: Albert Einstein Institution.

Tamari, Salim. 1990. The Uprising's Dilemma. *MERIP Middle East Report* (May–August): 4.

PREFACE

This book relates the story of my unusual experiences as an Israeli Zionist among Palestinians, especially during the First Intifada (the Palestinian mass uprising that began in December 1987). Although it is written from a personal point of view, I believe that my story sheds light on aspects of our relations with Palestinians that are unknown to most readers, including Israelis. Everything in this book is true, and the descriptions are as accurate as my perceptions and memories permit. In some cases, I've changed names to protect people's privacy.

I have been privileged to meet some remarkable Palestinians (and Israelis) who have changed my life and given it new meaning. In the course of numerous dialogues, I began to view our conflict from many added dimensions.

I was born in the British Mandate of Palestine in 1935. My father had immigrated as a *halutz* (pioneer) from Ukraine in 1919. He drained swamps in Hadera, defended Jews under Jabotinsky in Jerusalem, and then studied education in Germany, Denmark, England, and finally Columbia Teachers College, where he received his doctorate and met my mother. My mother grew up in the United States; her uncle was president of Manufacturers Bank and her father was one of the very rich (until the bank crash of 1929), but she preferred the idealism of Zionism, abandoning pampered society and moving to the physical hardships of Palestine in 1931 with my father. Both of my parents were completely convinced of the necessity for a Jewish homeland in Israel, and were committed to personally participating in its building. From them I received the Zionist commitment that remains my strongest ideology to this day.

At the same time, my parents had very liberal attitudes toward Arabs. My mother was a teacher in Haifa, with both Jewish and Arab students. After her retirement, she volunteered to teach in Arab villages in Israel. My father, who founded and directed two radically new high schools, wrote in 1940 of the need for Arab-Jewish rapprochement. Nonetheless, we all believed the traditional myths that placed almost complete blame on the Arabs, while viewing the Jewish role as purer than possible.

In 1939 we visited my grandfather in America. World War II broke out and we were unable to return to Palestine by ship. As the war dragged on, my father accepted the request of Justice Louis Brandeis to establish an institute that would train American Jewish lay leaders to strengthen American Jews' ties to their traditions and people. He continued this work even after the war, until his death. Thus I grew up in the United States from the age of four through thirty, when I finally reestablished my life with my own family in Jerusalem.

As this book relates, my initially chance encounters with Palestinians changed my entire perception of who we Israelis are and radically changed the direction of my life. Nonetheless, I remain first and foremost a Zionist who sees the necessity of the Jewish homeland as an unassailable issue.

Clarifications

The term *Zionist* is used in many different ways. For me it denotes someone who accepts the idea that just as Palestinians have a right to their national homeland, so too we Jews have a right to a homeland. This homeland can both protect us from persecution and support the ongoing development of the Hebrew culture and people.

The term *intifada* refers to the popular Palestinian uprising against Israeli occupation that began in December 1987. A very different uprising began in September 2000, which is usually called the "Second" (or Al-Aqsa) Intifada. Palestinian resistance to Israeli occupation, which followed the 1967 war (often called the "Six-Day War"), can be divided into four periods:

· From June 1967 until 8 December 1987, the resistance was carried out by small groups of armed fighters who were trained outside of Palestine. They staged lethal attacks, almost exclusively against civilian targets, in Israel, in the settlements, and abroad (such as airplane hijackings and the killing of Israeli athletes at the Munich Olympics in 1972).

· From 8 December 1987 until approximately 1993, the First Intifada was a mass movement that adopted a variety of nonviolent tactics (e.g., strikes, tax refusals) as well as lower-level violence (mostly stone-throwing, but even some Molotov cocktails) within the occupied areas. The leadership was local, not from abroad, and the use of guns and explosives was banned.

· From 20 August 1993, with the signing of the Oslo Accords, until September 2000 was the period of the peace process. These years saw killings of civilians by both Palestinians and Israelis who opposed the process.

· From the last days of September 2000 (after the failure of the Camp David summit and after opposition leader Ariel Sharon's tour of the Temple Mount/Haram a-Sharif), there began what some call the Second (or Al-Aqsa) Intifada, in which armed battles took place between Palestinians and Israelis. This period of violence ended in about 2004–2005.

A ZIONIST AMONG PALESTINIANS

Israel and the West Bank.
Based on the University of Texas Libraries.

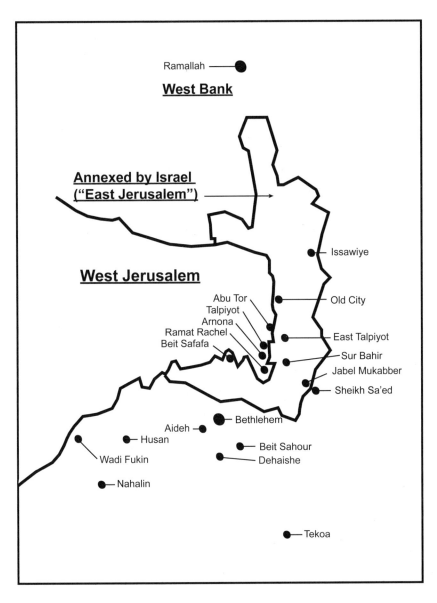

Jerusalem and environs.
Based on the University of Texas Libraries.

CHAPTER 1

Jericho I

Introduction to the Intifada

Wajiha (pronounced wa-JEE-ha) was in her twenties and still unmarried. Her impatient parents could wait no longer, so they forced her into an arranged marriage with a cousin from Jordan. But after the wedding Wajiha ran away and hid for forty days and forty nights. In the end, her opposition to the marriage succeeded; her parents had to give in. The newlyweds were then divorced, and Wajiha came out of hiding and returned home. Consequently, the groom's family was furious, and Wajiha knew that she could never go back to Jordan after insulting his family's honor.

Back in her home in the West Bank town of Jericho, Wajiha felt ill one day and started walking to her doctor's office. It was 1988. The houses in Jericho were all flying black flags in memory of Abu Jihad, Yasser Arafat's second-in-command, who had just been killed in Tunis—on 16 April—by an Israeli commando raid. As Wajiha approached the road leading from the mosque to the graveyard at the southern end of town, she saw a mass procession carrying a coffin: a mock funeral to protest the killing. The situation grew ominous because, while the Israel military authorities allowed the Palestinians to vent their anger by raising flags of mourning, the authorities would not permit a mass march to take place.

An Israeli officer called on the people to disperse. When they refused, soldiers began to fire tear gas into the crowd. Palestinians countered by throwing stones at the soldiers. Wajiha and others who were caught up in the clash escaped into a courtyard. The Israeli colonel commanding the Jericho region, a career officer, radioed orders to the reserve officers from my unit to fire live bullets at the Palestinians who were inciting the crowd. However, none of our officers would obey. So the colonel fired by himself, shooting and wounding a young man named Subhi in the leg. This clash had erupted very close to the house of Wajiha's sister Yusra. Yusra's husband, Sa'ed, rushed over with some friends and began dragging Subhi away so that he wouldn't be captured. The soldiers charged at Sa'ed. He tried to get away, but a large officer, a man with a black mole, chased after him.

Massive confusion ensued. The soldiers charged into the courtyard where Wajiha was waiting. The Palestinians all fled, except for Wajiha, who felt too sick to run. One of our officers, Uri, pulled up in a command car. Uri's driver, Wolf, grabbed Wajiha triumphantly and pulled her into the street where Uri was sitting in the command car.

"This is the one who was throwing stones," shouted Wolf, mistaking Wajiha for a boy. His imagination running away with itself, Wolf continued, "His face was masked with a *kufiye* [an Arab man's headdress], but he threw away his *kufiye* just as we entered."

Uri was a good-natured officer, a kibbutznik, and would almost certainly have let Wajiha go, but at that moment the Israeli military governor of Jericho drove up. Hearing Wolf and not knowing, as we all did, that Wolf was an unreliable hot-head, the governor arrested Wajiha on the spot.

Uri didn't know this, but I had almost killed him—Uri—several years earlier. It was during our annual reserve training, and we were pretending to capture a fortified position. The training was taking too long, the sun was already setting, and regulations required that we carry out the exercise during daylight. But the officers wanted us to complete the practice despite the semi-darkness. Uri ran over to an empty oil drum that was meant to symbolize an enemy pillbox. He pretended to place an explosive charge next to it, and then was supposed to run back to our lines. For some reason, he remained next to the drum and crouched down, his huge olive-drab *doubon* (hooded, quilted coat) making him look, in the semi-darkness, like a rock. All the shooting had stopped, and I was sure that Uri had already run back. I was an inexperienced and eager squad commander, responsible for three machine gunners, and decided that we needed to resume fire to soften up the "enemy." I was preparing to give the command "To the oil drum: fire!" but before the first word issued from my mouth Uri moved. I gasped and swallowed hard. From then on, each year when I would see Uri while I was on reserve duty, I would give a prayer of thanks that he was still alive. Uri was a big-hearted, roly-poly man with a soft, tolerant smile. He wouldn't have taken Wajiha.

Meanwhile, Wajiha's brother-in-law, Sa'ed, ran up a dead-end alley with Doron, the Israeli officer with the mole, in pursuit. With no place to go,

Sa'ed turned and raised his hands to protect his head. To Doron it looked as if he were trying some kind of karate maneuver. Expecting to be attacked, Doron came down hard with his billy club, almost breaking Sa'ed's hand. (When we had come to Jericho a few weeks earlier, for our first reserve duty during the intifada, our unit was issued billy clubs for the first time ever, in response to a call to break Palestinians' arms and legs. But our commander had locked up the clubs in the quartermaster's storeroom. This was the first time our soldiers were carrying batons.)

Doron was new to our unit. He had served formerly in the border police. Some of my fellow soldiers related that in Lebanon his unit had beaten an Arab to death. In the ensuing investigation of this action, all the soldiers gave the same cover-up story—except Doron, who told the truth. Later, when Doron was back in his *moshav* (cooperative farm), a group of his comrades showed up to "teach him a good lesson," tying him and dragging him behind a jeep by a rope, until his skin was abraded. Consequently, he had to quit the border police and came to do reserve duty with us. He was an offbeat kind of guy, but not mean like many of the others in the border police. Two other men who joined us from the border police had put out cigarettes on the arm of a Palestinian whom they had stopped. Our commander made it clear to them that our unit didn't behave that way. But Doron wasn't cruel like that. He slept in the bunk next to mine, and we talked a lot. He had just thought that Sa'ed was about to use a karate move.

I was home on leave the morning when the mock funeral procession for Abu Jihad took place. When I returned in the afternoon to the base in Jericho (less than an hour's drive from my home in Jerusalem), I saw a row of Palestinian men sitting on the ground, waiting to be interrogated by the Shabak (the general security service). One of them was thin and short and looked, even from a distance, like a girl. This was the frail Wajiha. My commander, Shammai, told me that my job would be to guard her. Perhaps he picked me for this task because I was the oldest soldier in the unit. I was fifty-two, and even though compulsory reserve duty ended at age forty-five, I volunteered each year to continue serving with my unit, for about a month a year. Perhaps he picked me because he knew that I was not filled with hatred for Arabs.

I had no idea how a male soldier guards a Palestinian woman while respecting her modesty, her honor, and her good name. It seemed to me that propriety required our being clearly visible, so I set up two folding chairs in the middle of the soldiers' yard, and there we sat. I had my battle gear, M16 assault rifle, seven magazines with twenty-nine bullets each, and two full canteens. Poor Wajiha, looking so little and tired and miserable, was resigned to her fate. I spoke to her a bit in English, but she barely responded. I couldn't tell if she didn't know the language, or if she didn't want to talk with her captors and occupiers. I asked whether she wanted something to eat. She declined, saying it was Ramadan, the month when Muslims fast from sunup to sundown. I asked whether she wanted to drink, but she said that too was forbidden. I was surprised that such a modern-looking young woman, wearing jeans and lipstick and with her face unveiled, observed the religious laws. My big fear was that she would need to go to the toilet, and that I would have to clear the large soldiers' latrine to give her privacy. But apparently Ramadan helped me out, and she never asked to go. As the sun began to set and the desert heat changed to coolness, I told her to wait a minute and I would bring her something warm to wear. I felt confident that she would not run away. Under my bunk I found my civilian windbreaker, and then, realizing that she might be on her way to jail, added a Hemingway novel to give her something to read. She accepted the windbreaker, putting it on against the evening chill. She took the book too, although I wasn't sure if it would be of any use to her.

There is no place to lock up women in Jericho. After the Shabak interrogated Wajiha, they sent her home and told her to wait there until the police came to get her. She was not guarded. At about midnight the police van arrived from Jerusalem. The police blindfolded her, tied her to a bar in the van so she couldn't escape, and transported her to the infamous Russian Compound jail in Jerusalem.

Meanwhile, the men who had been arrested were all put into a large, barred lock-up room in the army camp, with wall-to-wall mattresses. Each evening, their wives or mothers would come to the base with home-cooked food for the men to break their day-long fast. While it must have been against regulations, our commander, Shammai, let them eat their own food, after checking to see that there were no concealed weapons. Shammai enjoyed chatting with the women, especially with Wajiha's sister Yusra, who was the leader of the women and spoke the best English. Her husband, Sa'ed, was called "the singer" by the soldiers, for he played and sang Arabic music professionally. Another prisoner was called "the photographer." He would probably be punished more severely than the others, because he had stood on a roof and photographed the riot. The soldiers from my unit spent a lot of time talking about the prisoners, the only Palestinians with whom we had any real contact. One of our radio men, Itzik, would bring them their food from the army kitchen. When he talked just with us, he would regularly curse all Arabs, but because his family had immigrated to Israel from an Arab country, he would chat with the prisoners in their own language. He was their favorite soldier.

The First Intifada had erupted four months earlier, in December 1987. At home, Israelis learned about it on the television evening news, watching scenes of stone-throwing and mobs of rebellious Arabs. When our unit arrived in Jericho for our first real taste of the intifada, the company commander of the outgoing reserve unit taught us the ropes. He said that we would find this to be an entirely different experience from anything we had done in the army. He said that he had commanded soldiers who had supported the Peace Now movement, but after they saw what was going on, they had changed their thinking 180 degrees. He showed us that he kept a bottle with some gasoline in his jeep at all times, so that if he killed a Palestinian, he could convince the inquiry that the Palestinian had thrown a Molotov cocktail. When the Palestinians closed their stores for the daily strikes called by the intifada's leaders, he demonstrated how he destroyed the front of a poor man's shop by driving his jeep through its locked front door.

But what we saw was different. Driving around in our jeeps in Jericho, armed to the teeth, we saw busloads of European tourists—British and Germans and Swedes, sunburned bright pink, girls in the briefest of attire—walking around freely and looking at the sights. Jericho is the oldest city ever uncovered, with its archaeological *tel,* a green oasis in the hot, dry, dusty desert. In the town were run-down shops selling old copper and brass pots and utensils. The tourists would shop in this market, eat in the garden restaurants, and visit the site where John baptized Jesus in the Jordan River nearby.

Shammai wasn't looking for problems. He made us drive our jeeps in pairs so that there was always enough power to keep a soldier from feeling threatened and reacting violently. He didn't park the jeeps in front of the school to draw the children into confrontations. Friday prayer days, when the mosque lets out, are known as times for trouble. But instead of stationing his troops in front of the mosque to show who was boss, Shammai had us wait on a knoll a short distance away, from which he could keep an eye on things without being noticed by the congregants. On one Friday while waiting for prayers to end, my partner couldn't get his jeep started. I drove up behind him to push him, but we locked bumpers, and my ancient jeep had lost its reverse gear long ago. By the time we had disengaged, the crowds were already pouring out of the mosque. We had begun to push the second jeep to start it when a group of Arab men, seeing that the jeep wouldn't start, laughingly came over and helped us push until it started. It was hard to understand what was going on.

Early one morning an Arab man was walking home from his night's work. We stopped him and told him to clear away a roadblock that kids had set up during the night. "But I didn't build it," he complained. We didn't relent, so he began to take it apart. There was something dignified in his manner, a simple man in the suit jacket that Arabs wear regularly (but we do not). I went over and started helping him. There was a big steel bed in the roadblock, and each of us took one end. We chatted together in English as though this were the most natural thing. Just then, the military governor of Jericho drove up. He called out to me, saying I should let the Arab do the work alone. I replied that I was just helping him. The governor then said that in Gaza, Palestinians had planted a hand grenade in rocks piled across the road, and when an Israeli soldier removed the rocks the grenade had exploded and he lost his hand. I said that if there were a suspicion of a bomb, we should call for army sappers to come and dismantle it, and not let an innocent passerby be blown up. The governor, who by definition is always an army officer in uniform, lost his patience and told me to quit. But Shammai growled firmly, "He'll do what he wants to do." The governor backed off, and the Palestinian and I finished the job together.

Although we basically did not clash with the population, two weeks into our three-and-a-half-week tour of duty there were nightly throwings of Molotov cocktails. No one was hurt, but one night an Israeli woman driving with her young child received a Molotov cocktail through her open car window. It fell on the back seat, but didn't explode. From then on, we lay every night in ambushes in the banana groves beside the main road that connects Jericho to the entire Jordan Rift and the Sea of Galilee. It was a complicated situation. We were prepared to kill children throwing Molotovs, yet were casually relaxed with the population of this rebelling Palestinian town. I was confused, but my actual contact with Palestinians was strangely reassuring.

Toward the end of my reserve duty, all the arrested men were released from the lock-up in the army base. But poor Wajiha, in her jail cell in Jerusalem, had been forgotten, and there she stayed. When we were discharged, I decided that I had to find Sa'ed and Yusra and try to understand what was going on.

CHAPTER 2

Jericho II
The Dialogues

I finished my reserve duty a day before the rest of the unit, as I had a day's leave coming to me. I found out Sa'ed's address from our office, and went to find him. Unfortunately, the only pants I had that were not olive drab were a pair of running shorts, which would look odd in Jericho. However, Jericho is a small town (population about 15,000), and I figured that I could quickly jog over to any place in it. I was a little anxious about going around alone in a Palestinian town, but I felt reassured by the familiarity achieved during the weeks in which I had driven around the town. And my own friends were still serving there in the army, so soldiers would probably not give me a hard time.

I went into town and asked a Palestinian standing in the street how to get to Sa'ed's home. The Palestinian man invited me in for coffee, but I told him that all I wanted was directions. He said that his brother would drive me, it would be better, but first I should have a cup of Arabic coffee. I said that I knew it was Ramadan and I didn't want to drink while he was fasting, but he insisted, and so I drank the coffee while he looked after me, and his brother got dressed and pulled his car out of a little garage. They continued to insist that it was best for him to drive me, and that anyway Sa'ed was the man's wife's cousin. So I rode with the brother to find Sa'ed and Yusra.

In the car, after a couple of minutes of driving, the brother said to me meaningfully, "You must know that I am a soldier also, like you." I had no idea what he was leading up to. I was dressed in running shorts, running shoes, and the windbreaker that I'd lent Wajiha, which Yusra had returned after Wajiha had been taken away. The brother continued, "I am not just a soldier, I am an officer. Frequently, I drive to Tel Aviv or to Gaza to meet my contacts in the Shabak. We are working together, you and I, for the same purpose." I was shocked. I was being driven to Sa'ed's house by a collaborator. If people knew that he was a collaborator, I would not be trusted. If they did not know, I had to be sure to do nothing to blow his cover, since he was working with our security forces. What a terrible circumstance! But before I could consider my plight, we were at Sa'ed's house. The driver led me in, and he and Sa'ed gave each other hugs and cheek-to-cheek kisses, in the Arab way. They exchanged pleasantries in Arabic, and then the driver excused himself and I was alone with Sa'ed and Yusra.

I said in English, "I've come because I wanted to talk with you, but I can understand if you don't want to talk to an Israeli, and a soldier at that. I'll leave if you wish." Sa'ed invited me in with the Arabic welcome, *Ahalan w'-sahalan.* I saw that his hand was bandaged where Doron had hit him with the club. We sat and began to talk, and then Yusra came in with a small cup of coffee. "I know that it's Ramadan," I said, "and I don't want to drink if you are fasting." "It's all right," Sa'ed replied. "I am Muslim, so I will not drink. But you aren't, and you are my guest in my house, so I would be pleased to see you drinking."

I said that it was a shame that we were always fighting each other, and wondered if they thought there was hope for a better future. Sa'ed began to talk, while Yusra sat and listened. Sa'ed said that what the Palestinians wanted was a state next to Israel, in the West Bank and Gaza, and not to destroy Israel. He spoke at length and in such a moderate way that I was amazed. This was April 1988, four months into the intifada, and before Yasser Arafat made his conciliatory pronouncements in Algiers and Geneva. From the Israeli press I had understood that the intifada was a new method for achieving the Arabs' age-old goal of throwing us into the sea. Yet Sa'ed was obviously one of the rare Arab moderates with whom we could really make peace.

We talked for a while and I enjoyed the unexpected experience of meeting an Arab with moderate political views. Everything he said seemed acceptable to me, unbelievably so. Finally, in all fairness, I had to say to him, "Sa'ed, everything I hear from you pleases me, but you should be careful about saying it so openly, for your neighbors might hear you and your life would be in danger." "Not at all," he rejoined. "This is what they believe as well." Yusra agreed. "What we all want is our own state next to Israel," she affirmed. This all seemed impossible to me, and I wondered if they were carrying on some pretense or if, indeed, something was going on in this intifada that I was just not grasping.

"If that's really so, what if I bring a group of my friends and neighbors from Jerusalem? Would you be willing to bring some of your neighbors together so that we can hear what people are really thinking?" They agreed immediately. We exchanged phone numbers so that we could coordinate a date, and they drove me back to the main highway and showed me the place, not far from the army base, where we would rendezvous so that they could accompany us to their house, to make sure that no one would throw stones at our cars. We parted, and I took an Israeli bus back to Jerusalem, excited at the extraordinary events that were beginning to unfold.

I got busy calling friends whom I thought would be appropriate for a dialogue with the Jerichoans. I told them that I had met some Arabs during reserve duty, that they seemed very moderate, and that they were organizing a group with whom we could meet. My Israeli friends asked whether it would be safe. I assured them that there was no problem, basing this more on gut feeling than on experience or knowledge. Within a couple of days I had ten willing Israelis, and so I called Yusra to set up the meeting. We drove in two cars to the rendezvous point. I worried about what we would do if no one showed up, or if an army patrol came by and asked why we were there. But there was a car with Jericho license plates waiting at the spot, with several young people who told us to follow them in our vehicles. We drove to Sa'ed's and parked in his yard. They closed the gate so that an army patrol would not notice the cars.

Inside were about a dozen Palestinians. They introduced themselves and gave us a bit of background about themselves. Several were farmers, some were students. Most appeared to be in their twenties. There were about as many women as men, modern-looking in tight jeans and casual tops. Only after Jericho became autonomous (after the Oslo Accords of 1993, when Israel withdrew its forces from Jericho and other Palestinian cities) did I learn that one of them, Abdul Karim, was a top leader in Arafat's Fatah Party in Jericho. People talked freely and openly. The lack of any hostility was remarkable, considering that these people were living under our very harsh occupation. And what we heard from them was the same theme that I had heard from Sa'ed and Yusra, namely that neither these Palestinians nor their community, which they knew so well, were trying to throw us into the sea. The goal of the intifada was to replace the occupation with a Palestinian state in the occupied areas, which would live in peace with Israel.

I felt that I had inadvertently stumbled onto a remarkable find, something that contradicted everything we Israelis understood about the Palestinians. On our way home, as we talked in my car about what had taken place, I told myself that we had to bring hundreds and thousands of Israelis to such meetings. These very real Palestinians could explain themselves in a way that was just the opposite of what we were understanding from the intifada: the violent antithesis of any desire for peace. One woman in my car said that the Palestinians had said nice things, but she didn't find them at all convincing. I was bothered by the fact that she was unimpressed, since for me this encounter was mind-boggling, but I wrote it off, thinking that there is always one deadbeat in any group. We had agreed that I would bring a new group of Israelis in a few weeks, and I found the Palestinians' friendliness, openness, and readiness to continue meeting with Israelis overwhelmingly convincing of their sincerity.

At the next dialogue I committed a faux pas. It was a *hamsin* day—a day when the east wind blows in from the desert. The temperature in the desert town of Jericho was about 105 degrees Fahrenheit. One Israeli had already canceled. The homes in Jericho did not have air conditioning, and I was afraid that some of the Israelis might become dehydrated. Sa'ed's music band was out of work, as the united leadership of the intifada had banned all parties and musical entertainment. The economic situation in the territories was so severe that I decided to bring a case of soft drinks, so people would have something to counter their thirst. Yusra was shocked and insulted. I was only beginning to learn how important a part of Arab culture it is to be good hosts. "Do you think we have nothing to serve our guests?" she asked. "I felt it was unfair to bring ten guests when times are so hard," I mumbled. Fortunately, our relationship was already strong enough to overcome my blunder.

We split among two homes, and had another excellent set of dialogues. The exact content was not always the most important thing. The atmosphere was so clearly positive, in the midst of the heat of the intifada, and it was enough to hear these Palestinian supporters of the uprising telling us so clearly that their goal was peace with us. And it was remarkable for us to see how we, as Israelis, could be sitting in Palestinian homes without concern for our security. As did most Israelis, I still had an image of Palestinians killing any of their leaders who would consider making peace with us, so the open and relaxed attitude of those who received us in their homes had a very strong impact on me and on many of the Israelis in our group.

An interesting subject came up in another dialogue at Sa'ed and Yusra's house. A Palestinian told us that someone had written on a wall in Jericho, "We Want Peace," in English. However, an army patrol had wiped out the graffiti with paint. I asked whether he would be willing to write such a slogan on his house. He replied, "Of course, but I would be arrested if I did that." I asked the other Palestinians whether they really thought that they would be arrested for such a slogan, and they were unanimously convinced that they would. The original speaker then added, "I know that I would be arrested, but I would be willing to do it anyway."

I began to conceive of a mass action. What if hundreds of Palestinians would write "We Want Peace" on their homes, and it was reported on television? Mightn't this message reach some Israelis who, like me, were unaware of Palestinian sentiment?

While I felt the Palestinians' fears were exaggerated, I nonetheless turned to the Association for Civil Rights in Israel (ACRI) and to MK (member of Knesset) Ran Cohen, who was a reserve colonel in the paratroops. The ACRI gave me a letter in Hebrew and in Arabic stating that it would provide legal defense to anyone arrested for writing "We Want Peace" on his house. After two and a half months, ACRI received a reply from the army's legal officer stating, in hedged legalese, "This slogan, by itself (without considering other factors which might prevail in the place where it was written), is *not* of the type which would affect public opinion in a way which might hurt the security of the area, the peace of the area, or the public order in it, and which would therefore require that a landlord must a priori remove, cover, or erase it; however, each case must be judged on its own merits."

But Defense Minister Yitzhak Rabin (who in those days was brutally anti-Arab, accused by some of having given the command to break Palestinians' arms and legs) sent a totally different answer to Ran Cohen, writing that the Central Command had informed him that both residents of the territories and Jewish settlers were forbidden to write slogans of any kind in Judea and Samaria (i.e., the West Bank). The IDF (Israel Defense Forces) is responsible for law and order in the area and therefore the army erases the slogans of Jewish settlers and of "locals" equally, without considering their content.

Rabin's response was infuriating to anyone who values truth. Right-wing Jewish settlers had written graffiti all over bus stops, supporting Rabbi Meir Kahane's anti-Arab Kach Party. Other slogans threatened "Death to the Arabs." The army never erased such graffiti. Soldiers of the Golani Brigade often wrote slogans praising their brigade on Arabs' homes, and warned the Arabs not to erase them.

While we did not get to implement the "We Want Peace" idea in Jericho, it would be incorporated into activities in other Palestinian communities, with considerable success.

Before the next dialogue, I suggested to Yusra that instead of having the whole conversation in their homes, perhaps we could walk about a bit in the streets and talk to people who just happened to pass by. They agreed and took us to the Hadewi neighborhood, which I remembered from my army service as an area considered to be full of troublemakers. Our Palestinian hosts took us to several homes there, and we spoke briefly with each family. In the street I also saw a teenage boy sitting lazily on a bicycle, watching us. I suggested to our hosts that we speak to him, but they said that he was a collaborator, and that he was hanging around to tell the Shabak which houses we entered.

We next came to a small, one-room hut. The walls were whitewashed, and there was a simple metal bed in one corner—the only furniture in the room. On the bed lay an ancient, withered, bone-thin, dark-brown man in a white *jalabiyye* (ankle-length shirt worn by traditional men), which looked almost like a shroud. It was hard to tell if he was still alive or dead. One of our hosts crouched down next to him and said very softly, "There is a group of Israelis here, who want to talk with us about peace."

The old man pulled himself together, and very slowly stood up. He looked like Mahatma Gandhi, only taller and more dignified. Slowly he walked over to me, put his arms around me, and kissed me. "Where have you been?" he asked us. "We have been waiting so long."

Throughout the years of subsequent dialogues in a dozen Palestinian communities, I never forgot that moment, and it never ceased to bring tears to my eyes. This simple man was so direct and so sincere. But how could it be that all the time that we believed there was no one with whom to talk, Palestinians were believing that *we* were the enemies of peace?

CHAPTER 3

Jericho III

The Black Scorpion

Before our second dialogue, Yusra called me to say that her sister Wajiha was still in the Moscobiyye, the Russian Compound jail in Jerusalem. The men held in Jericho had all been released, but no one seemed to be paying attention to Wajiha. Yusra wanted to come, with a couple of girlfriends, to visit her sister in jail. I agreed to meet them at the jail, where I would try to help, as an Israeli, to get them in. We met there, but they weren't allowed to visit. I spoke with a police detective in the "Minorities" section, but he said that Wajiha was still under investigation, and therefore no one could visit her.

We decided to go to Shammai, my commander, whom Yusra trusted, to enlist his help. Shammai worked at a laboratory a few buildings away from my office on the Hebrew University campus. We told him the problem, and he said that Wajiha should never have been arrested. He told us to wait and he would telephone the governor of Jericho. He called every hour, but each time was told that the governor was in conference. Finally, toward the end of the day, he got through and told the governor that the reserve officers had discussed Wajiha's arrest, and they all thought it was a mistake, and she should be released. The Israeli governor said that he had no problem with this, but he wanted the Palestinian mayor of Jericho to be the one to request the release.

I knew from the dialogue that Sa'ed's father had been the last elected mayor of Jericho, and had been well respected. But after he died of a heart attack, the Israeli authorities appointed a mayor to replace him. This new mayor worked hand in glove with the Israeli authorities, and was disliked by the Palestinians. He knew how to profit from his relations with the occupation authorities—for example, he arranged for a larger allocation of water for his banana fields compared to other farmers. For Sa'ed to go to him and ask for a favor would be an insult and a stain on Sa'ed's family's honor. Nonetheless, he swallowed his pride for Wajiha's sake and asked for the mayor's intercession. But Wajiha was not released. Finally, at the end of eighteen days, when regulations required either charging her or releasing her, the authorities offered to release her on bail. This was an elegant way for the government to help fund the occupation, for it was rare that a Palestinian would ever ask for the return of the bail money. So Wajiha was never tried, but she essentially paid a fine since she preferred her freedom over standing trial to regain the bail money.

A few weeks later, Yusra called to tell about a new problem. A group of young soldiers from the regular army (not reservists) was serving in Jericho. They were beating people, insulting them, and hanging around the school to provoke children into conflict. They even had called one teenage girl to come over and strip off her clothes. The girl had walked away from them and no harm had come to her, but it was an insult to Palestinians' honor to be talked to that way. The soldiers called themselves the Black Scorpion, and threatened the people that the Black Scorpion would teach them a good lesson. What could I do to help?

I had no idea how to help. I brought an Israeli journalist, Michal Sela, who gathered information and wrote an article about this unit, which she learned was the paratroopers' anti-tank unit. However, in the first year of the intifada there was so much army violence that it was unlikely that her story would have any effect.

But Michal and Yusra hit it off nicely, and Yusra confided to her that she was having trouble getting pregnant. Michal gave her the name of an Israeli gynecologist who was an expert in fertility problems, and Yusra's problem was soon solved. She subsequently had several children—so something good came of our efforts.

I also tried another tack: I wrote a description of the problem in the form of a petition, hoping that soldiers from my reserve unit would sign it and send it to the army's chief of staff. I showed the petition to Shammai. He and I both loved the army. In Israel the army has a personal name: we call it Tzahal, which is the abbreviation in Hebrew for the Israel Defense Forces. Tzahal is not the impersonal organization called "the army" about which everyone complains. It is the people's army that stood between us and destruction when we fought to create, against overwhelming odds, our Jewish homeland in Israel. Our debt to Tzahal was very great, as was our appreciation for many of the values that had gone into building this structure, of which we were but small parts. Shammai had been an officer in the paratroopers' crack reconnaissance unit, but had been court-martialed and reduced in rank to a soldier. I had heard two different rumors about why this had happened, but I figured that it was his life, and I never asked about the circumstances. He was an excellent fighter and a superb navigator who had fought many terrorists in his youth. Wounded, he carried shrapnel in his spine, which caused him to be transferred out of his select unit into our troop of simple, poorly qualified soldiers. No matter how often our unit asked him to take back his former rank, he refused to be an officer, but served in that capacity without the rank.

He read my petition, and immediately said that it had to be rewritten. He stressed that our unit had served in Jericho with firmness but understanding, and that we had succeeded in bringing quiet to the area. He called on the army to investigate the charges. I called each member of our unit, and nine soldiers agreed that their names could appear on the letter. On 13 June 1988 I sent the letter, signed by Shammai and bearing our names, to Chief of Staff Dan Shomron and to the Foreign Affairs and Defense Committee of the Knesset. The next day, I received an angry phone call from the military commander of Jericho denying all the allegations, denouncing the reservists for sending the letter, and stating that it is army policy to punish Arab communities that cause trouble. I never received an answer from either Shomron or the Knesset committee. In October I issued a press release detailing that the reserve soldiers' letter had been ignored, but to the best of my knowledge it was not published anywhere.

I learned from this that it is possible to expend enormous amounts of time trying to bring information to the public's notice, in order to change public policy. I never really learned how to get the press to pick up on a story that had no blood in it.

After several dialogues that seemed to me very successful, Sa'ed and Yusra told me that the situation in Jericho was too fraught with difficulties for them to maintain our relationship. Because Jericho is next to the bridge to Jordan, the town is full of collaborators. They would have to discontinue the dialogues. (I didn't understand this logic, but didn't see a need to clarify it.) They felt that dialogues were helpful, and suggested that I try to find some other community with which to work. And so we took a break from the dialogues in Jericho.

About a year later, when we had similar programs working in several other towns, we resumed the dialogues in Jericho. One day, Yusra called and said that I could no longer visit in their home. I met her at her work, and she told me what had happened. Sa'ed and his brother had been arrested. They were kept in cages in which they could neither stretch out nor sit up. There was, of course, no toilet. A guard came in at some point and asked who wanted to go to the toilet. Sa'ed said that he did, so the guard took him out of the cage and beat him. He learned that it was forbidden to go to the toilet. Each time that he was taken to be interrogated, he would first be beaten. Once a day some rice would be slapped down on the filthy floor of his cage.

I don't believe that he was arrested because of the dialogues. At that time Israel was trying hard to find out how money was getting to intifada activists, and my impression is that Sa'ed and his brother were being interrogated to get to the sources of the funding.

Yusra told me that when Sa'ed finally came home, he wouldn't permit any Israelis into their house. The dialogues were stopped a second time, and it was months later that I finally visited my friend again.

CHAPTER 4

Sur Bahir

The Forest

Jericho was my first experience with the intifada, but it was not my first contact with Palestinians. Like most Israelis, I avoided Arab areas, and I even had a rule that whenever I would cross the Green Line (i.e., enter the areas conquered from Jordan in the 1967 "Six-Day War") I would carry my rifle. Even though I was part of the Israeli Left in that I opposed Jewish settlement in the occupied areas and favored returning the land someday in exchange for peace, I didn't know a single Arab except for two social scientists whom I knew at work.

One day in 1978 I came home to our apartment in Jerusalem's Arnona neighborhood, and found that our son Ariel's little bicycle had been stolen. Children from the neighborhood told me that they had seen two Arab kids, who made deliveries for the grocery store, taking the bike away. I went to the grocer, who said that he had fired the kids a few days before, but he gave me their names and said that they lived in the neighboring Arab village of Sur Bahir. Sur Bahir had been part of the Jordanian West Bank from 1948 until 1967, at which time we Israelis conquered it and annexed it to Jerusalem, thereby making it part of Israel. Sur Bahir was only a mile down the road from my house, but in the six years that I'd been living there I had never entered the village, nor had virtually any of my Jewish neighbors.

I considered complaining to the police, but then for some unknown reason I decided to overcome my fear of the village and try to solve the problem directly. I left my rifle at home this time, and drove into the Arab village. At a grocery store I asked where the *mukhtar* (the chosen leader of the village or of a clan) lived. Fortunately some of the Arabs there spoke Hebrew, and someone pointed out his home. I knocked at his door, and someone sent for a teenage boy who could speak Hebrew. I asked for the *mukhtar,* and was told that he would be back shortly; meanwhile, I should sit down. The family had a large sitting room, very different in style from the Jewish living rooms I knew—theirs was completely filled with upholstered sofas and easy chairs around a long, low table. There were no bookcases or paintings on the walls, nor were the gray concrete walls plastered or painted. They brought me Arabic coffee, and the teenager sat with me in silence while they sent for his father.

Finally the *mukhtar* arrived, a short, middle-aged man. He welcomed me with *Ahalan w'-sahalan,* the Arabic greeting. I began to explain in Hebrew about the bicycle, but once he understood the problem he cut me off and said, "This is a very serious problem, and for this you must go to a different *mukhtar,* Khader Dabash." I was to learn that in a large village each clan has its own chosen *mukhtar,* and in Sur Bahir the most powerful *mukhtar,* who could handle a problem between an Arab and a Jew, was Khader Dabash. They directed me to Dabash's house, where once again I sat in a long sitting room while they sent for the *mukhtar.* Again, I drank Arabic coffee until the *mukhtar* arrived and greeted me warmly. He was a tall man, warm and self-assured. In those pre-intifada days, the *mukhtar* was the link between the Arab village and the Jewish Jerusalem municipality, so Khader seemed comfortable speaking with Jews.

I told the story about the bicycle, and mentioned the names of the boys who allegedly had taken it. He looked pensive. "They are not Israelis, like us," he said. "Their family is from Hebron. This family causes many problems. None of our own people would cause such problems; we have no difficulties with Jews." It struck me as interesting that he called the villagers "Israelis," for although they had been given Israeli resident status when we annexed their town, most did not have Israeli citizenship.

We talked for a while, and he promised to do all that he could. I left his home and the village lighthearted. Why had this village seemed so threatening? It seemed that there existed another very different culture just down the road from our neighborhood, and there were people living there who were neither murderers nor terrorists.

The next day, I received a call from Khader. He had located the bicycle, but it had been sold to someone in the northern part of the city. Still, he said, he would get it back for me.

A day later, I was in the street in front of our house when an old black taxi pulled up, the type of battered Mercedes that only Arabs drive. I was suspicious at first, until Khader climbed out. He opened the trunk and pulled out Ariel's bike. The bike had already been sold, but he had managed to find it and return it. I thanked him effusively, and he apologized for what had happened to us. We shook hands, and he drove away. I remembered other instances in which our children's toys had been stolen by Jewish kids, and we'd had no one to turn to. There was something to be said for the traditional village organization.

Seven years went by, and then one day in 1985 I looked out of our living room window and saw huge bulldozers building a road through the village's land into the valley called Wadi Zeitoun. I asked neighbors what was happening, and they said that the Jewish National Fund was planning to plant a forest on that land. I knew that the JNF sometimes plants forests to prevent Arabs from using the land, and suddenly I remembered Khader Dabash and the bicycle, and how he had been a good neighbor to me when I had a problem. I drove over to his house in the village, and was directed to the hill of Umm-Leisson where Khader was building a house for one of his sons. I wasn't sure if he would remember me. As soon as he saw me, though, he asked, "Don't tell me another bicycle has been stolen?" "No," I replied. "I wonder whether this time it's not my people who are taking something from yours." I asked whether the planned forest was of any concern to him. He told me that this subject was all that the villagers were talking about, that the JNF action would destroy the little agricultural land that was left to them, since Israel had expropriated most of their free land to build the East Talpiyot neighborhood for Jews. I promised that I would talk to some of my neighbors to see what we could do to help.

How does one help people who have the whole weight of the government working against them? I really didn't know, but I remembered that ten years earlier, in 1975, Israel had organized a civil guard to counter Palestinian terrorists who were entering urban neighborhoods to capture innocent people in their homes. Together with three neighbors I had gone from house to house in our neighborhood of Arnona to talk with the residents and try to enlist them for the guard. We explained that if each volunteer would help to guard the neighborhood one night a month, we could protect ourselves against attack. It was slow work, and people had all kinds of excuses for avoiding enlistment, but after a month's work we founded the civil guard station in Arnona, which became one of the best in the city. With this model in mind, I began going from house to house to get the residents to sign a petition to help our neighbors from Sur Bahir. In almost every house people would not just sign, but they wanted explanations and asked questions, many of which I couldn't adequately answer. When I visited the home of one neighbor, Rabbi Baruch Feldstern, we had a good talk about Jewish-Arab relations, and he pointed out several questions to which I really had no answers. What I knew at that point was that in 1970 Israel had expropriated 2,240 dunams (560 acres) of the village's land, on which it had built the Jewish neighborhood of East Talpiyot, and that the unused land from the expropriation was still being farmed by the Arabs, but would now be turned into a forest. He said that if I would learn more about the issues involved, he would be happy to sign. That seemed to me very reasonable, and I made a note to return to him in the future.

While gathering supporters for the petition, I also tried to find a group of people who would use their experience to help us. My friend Debbie Porten, who was a social worker and family therapist, sent me to see Sarah Kaminker, a city planner who had been responsible for planning the Arab neighborhoods/villages in "East Jerusalem." She also sent me to Hassan Abu-Asala, a city planner who had worked for the Jerusalem municipality under Jordan and now under Israel, and who was himself a resident of Sur Bahir. Sarah, who turned out to be my step-grandmother's niece, was one of the few Jewish officials who had tried sincerely to help the Arabs in their plight. She was always greeted warmly in the Arab neighborhoods of Jerusalem. Another insider who joined us was Shalom Amouyal, the head of the East Talpiyot Neighborhood Administration.

Our first success was in getting Jerusalem's popular mayor, Teddy Kollek, to write to the minister of agriculture. He stated, "I believe that certain sections of the land from the big expropriation of 1970 could be returned to their former owners . . . [but if that is not possible, then] I request that at this stage the villagers be permitted to continue to work the land, which for some of them is their primary income and the source of their bread."

I next tried a long shot. MK Ehud Olmert of the Likud Party (who in eight years would replace Teddy as mayor, and in 2006 would become prime minister) lived in neighboring Talpiyot. His right-wing party was unlikely to support helping the Arabs, but in Israel personal contacts are frequently more important than ideology. I called him and mentioned that his daughter Michal was in the same class as my son Noam, and that we had played together on the parents' soccer team in which Ehud had scored the only two goals against the kids. Olmert came through with a lovely letter to the Jewish National Fund (which was carrying out the plantings), saying, "The planting of a forest specifically there, even if its environmental advantages are many, is liable to severely deprive the residents and to cause damage that can be avoided."

Members of the Knesset from the Left—Mordechai Bar-On (of the Citizens Rights Movement), Amira Sartani (Mapam), and Mordechai Virshubski (Shinui)—also acted on behalf of the Arab farmers.

We then had a meeting with the district head of the Israel Lands Authority (ILA), which owned the expropriated land. I was very surprised that Hassan Abu-Asala, an Arab, was allowed to participate in the meeting, and that the Jews spoke openly in front of him. The district head explained to all of us that the purpose of planting the forest was *not* to provide a park, but for the state to assert its ownership over the land. He told us that wherever the state is not ready to develop land, it plants cheap trees that will be uprooted at a later date when the land will be developed (he meant for Jewish use). In other words, the Arabs would lose their agricultural lands and could never assert a claim to have the lands returned, as the mayor had proposed.

I now felt that I understood the situation adequately. I returned to Rabbi Feldstern, told him of this meeting, and he signed the petition.

By January 1987 we had been able to get 121 signatures on the petition. We phrased it as a letter.

To the residents of Sur Bahir:

We, residents of Arnona and Talpiyot, have heard that the Jewish National Fund is about to plant a forest on your agricultural lands that were expropriated.

Our neighborhoods have enjoyed good relations for many years. We support your right to continue to farm your lands in peace.

Most of the villagers, recognizing their lack of political strength, sought to achieve a compromise with the municipality. One family, however, who were possibly more nationalistic than the rest, insisted on challenging the expropriation and forestation in the Israeli courts. Since the Israeli courts enforce laws and policies that are designed to transfer Palestinian lands to Jewish control and use, the chance of success was extremely small. In addition, an unwritten law has generally demonstrated that Arabs who dare to challenge the Jerusalem municipality in the courts are punished and made into examples. It took almost a year for the court to reach its decision. I attended the hearing before three judges from the Supreme Court, where a learned judge stated that it was quite reasonable for the state to plant a park on the farmers' traditional lands, so that Arabs and Jews could come together for picnics and coexistence.

The moment that the decision was in, revenge was wreaked on the village. The Jewish National Fund, protected by border police, rushed in and started planting pines and cypresses wherever there was space, including in the planted wheat fields that had previously been set aside for the farmers. More than sixty young olive trees that had been planted by the villagers were uprooted by the JNF. Our hopes dashed, Khader, Hassan, Sarah, Shalom, and I met for a last gloomy time.

That night I stayed awake in bed thinking of the villagers' helplessness, and our inability to aid them. But then I remembered a discussion we'd had with a member of Kibbutz Ramat Rachel, which lies between Sur Bahir and my neighborhood of Arnona. The kibbutzniks had favored planting the forest so that the villagers could be kept at a distance from the kibbutz lands, as the kibbutz claimed that Arabs sometimes grazed sheep and goats in the fruit orchards or stole from the kibbutz. But one kibbutznik had mentioned that the Jewish National Fund was also creating a wooded strip around the kibbutz, planting olive trees that members of the kibbutz could pick for themselves. The thought hit me: Why not replace the pines and cypresses with olives for the Arab farmers as well?

The next morning, I presented the idea to my Arab and Jewish colleagues, and they all accepted it. In order to sell the idea, we brought in Philip, who had served for several years as Mayor Teddy Kollek's advisor on East Jerusalem Arabs, and was well connected with people from the JNF and the Israel Lands Authority. While his job had been to maintain control over the conquered Palestinians, he had the reputation of treating the people he controlled very decently. Philip immediately accepted our invitation to help, saying that it was folly to destroy the villagers' farms, and the government's course of action could only worsen relations. The mayor and the head of the JNF agreed to our compromise, on the condition that the Arabs themselves would not plant any of the olives since the trees must belong to the State of Israel. However, the head of the ILA, which legally owns expropriated land, refused to go along with us, claiming that the court had accepted the planting of the forest, and he would not go against the court.

I decided to call in more Israelis from the neighborhood to form a committee to organize the struggle for the compromise. I invited the people who seemed most appropriate from the petition campaign, and about twenty neighbors came to the meeting. I handed out a fact sheet that I had prepared, which included the words of the Tenth Commandment: "Thou shalt not covet thy neighbor's house . . . his field . . . and all that he has." I explained the history of the affair (which had also been discussed frequently in the press) and then threw the meeting open for discussion. After about an hour, one of the participants said that a meeting should never run more than an hour, and he recommended that we set up a committee of three people to organize the struggle and then get back to us. He suggested that the chair be a particular woman who had spoken very forcefully and was obviously excellent at organizing, and that the other two participants be people who had expressed themselves clearly. The committee of three was approved by acclamation, whereupon everyone left. I was stunned that after all the work I had devoted to this issue, no one had thought to include me on the committee, and I suddenly realized how much one's ego is involved in what seems like pure devotion to a cause. But I offered the chairperson any help that I could give her. After everyone had left, my wife asked, "How could they not have included you?"

Unfortunately, I am a very shy person who has trouble being forceful. I tend to hesitate when decisions need to be made. I found it hard to imagine why people should listen to my point of view, especially when I had no previous experience with city government or politics. Naturally, they would prefer people who were experienced in decision making. But I was still irked; so much of me was invested in this struggle that it was terribly hard to stand aside and let newcomers take over.

In addition, we'd had a number of meetings in the Arab village with respected members of that community, and I had become comfortable with the villagers and was becoming known to them. I felt that I was beginning to understand the Palestinian point of view, in contrast to the new committee members, who viewed things with a Jewish conscience but were alien to the village. (These meetings in Sur Bahir were probably what prepared me to seek out Sa'ed and Yusra in Jericho sixteen months later.)

However, there was no need to be upset. As happens often in volunteer organizations, none of the three committee members really had the time to become involved, so after a few days of waiting I let them resign and took on the leadership again. This time, we added several key neighbors to our group. One was Sammy Nachmias, who had been a high-ranking officer in army intelligence and, later, head of police investigations. He made his private detective's office in the basement of his home our headquarters for the nightly meetings we would hold over the next few weeks. Sammy was a well-liked, old-time Israeli who continued to live in the Talpiyot home that his grandfather had built.

Another key member who joined us was Dr. Veronika Cohen, the dean of students at the Rubin Academy of Music and Dance. Totally dedicated to coexistence, peace, and human rights, Veronika was an Orthodox Jewish woman who would become the leading practitioner of grassroots Jewish-Arab dialogue, and would be my colleague in many adventures with Palestinians.

Another new member was Professor Uriel Proccacia from the Hebrew University Law School. He was one of Israel's leading experts on commercial law, distinguished and outspoken, and dedicated to fighting the injustice that he saw being perpetrated next to his home. Also joining us was Yehudah Litani, the Middle East news editor of the *Jerusalem Post* and an expert on Arab affairs. Dr. Israel Cohen was the editor of a Russian academic journal. With another journalist and Debbie Porten (the social worker), Sarah, and Shalom—and the *mukhtar* Khader and Hassan from the village—we had a very respectable citizens action committee.

We decided to organize a joint demonstration to press for the olive tree compromise. Now, a joint Arab-Jewish activity of any kind was virtually unheard of in Jerusalem; this demonstration would probably be the first of its kind. The *mukhtar* and I signed the application for the police permit. In order to make it less confrontational we called the demonstration a "Meeting of Neighbors." We organized our children to place invitations into hundreds of mailboxes in Jewish neighborhoods. The Palestinians made excellent signs in Arabic, Hebrew, and English.

I had never been involved in organizing a demonstration. We invited Mayor Kollek to speak, so I rented a reasonable sound system. While I was very good at getting myself to work hard, I was not so good at pressing others to help me. Everyone was either working or studying, so I had to set things up by myself. The area that Hassan had chosen for the speeches was muddy and hard to drive into. Fortunately, young people from the village saw me setting up and came over to help organize things, and then guarded the equipment so that I could get back to the area where the Israelis would be arriving.

The police officer in charge was very tough, and said that if anyone walked on the main road, blocking traffic, he would call off the activity. We had given many of the Arab kids tags as ushers (we called them "guides") to maintain order. But at the appointed time, at 3:00 PM on 10 February 1987, hundreds of people began arriving and of course filling the road. The officer began to complain to me. I had no idea how to clear the people out of the road, but Khader Dabash suddenly appeared and dismissed the police officer with "Don't worry, everything's quite all right." And so it was.

It took until 4:00 for Mayor Kollek to decide whether it was politically better to appear or to stay away. By police estimates, we had 700 demonstrators, half Jewish and half Arab, and the atmosphere was excellent, so he came and spoke, and my rented sound equipment worked just fine. Two deputy mayors also joined our cause. The *New York Times* quoted Yehudah Litani: "'I've never seen anything quite like this,' [he said] as he watched the crowds mix, smile and exchange greetings. He said such an unusual mingling might happen occasionally in a rural area, but never here in the Jerusalem metropolis" (Francis X. Clines, "Arab and Jew Join Together to Try to Save Olive Trees," *New York Times*, 11 February 1987).

As part of the demonstration, Khader's daughter Sana and my daughter Daphna, both ten years old, together planted an olive sapling in a bucket of soil, to symbolize our ability to cooperate even while the authorities forbade planting in the earth.

The demonstration was a great success. Jews and Arabs mingled together and chatted, as had never happened before. People who participated in the "Meeting of Neighbors" were enthusiastic, and the event was written up in the Israeli press and internationally. The demonstration's success, and JNF's concern for its own image in the face of criticism and suggestions that contributors consider other charities, led to the acceptance of our proposed compromise after three months. However, it was clear that those in power were very ambivalent about giving in to the Arabs in Wadi Zeitoun, since this change of policy impinged on the traditional Zionist strategy of transferring ownership and control of land from Arab to Jew. For example, the JNF planters grumbled as they planted the first twenty or thirty olive trees according to the agreement, and refused to pull out the pine saplings they had previously planted in the same place. Consequently, both types of trees were crowded together in unnatural proximity.

Despite the promises we had received, I remained anxious as to whether the rest of the olive trees would really be planted. But as the winter planting season approached, our committee came back to life. We suggested organizing a joint planting with Jewish and Arab children on Tu B'shvat (the Jewish Arbor Day), an idea that was attractive to the municipality, which wanted good public relations. But then the JNF changed the agreement, and decided it would spread out the olive plantings over three years, planting only at the bottom of the *wadi* (the valley, which the ILA didn't really care about) in the first year and determining that olives would only be planted in those places where the pines and cypresses did not grow well. I was sure that this was a plan to keep the slopes, where Israel was considering building in the future, free of olive trees. By delaying the planting, they could diminish the public pressure. Who knew if we'd ever be able to regain our strength? (To the JNF's chagrin, its pines never took root, although the cypresses on the slope struggled along bravely.)

The First Intifada erupted in Gaza on 8 December 1987. Israelis believed that Jerusalem would not be affected by the uprising, since we did not consider the annexed East Jerusalem to be occupied territory. But within weeks, Palestinians in East Jerusalem began demonstrating in large numbers, shocking us unbelieving Israelis. Our committee's suggestion for a joint tree-planting event took on increased importance as a symbol of coexistence even as the intifada (whose full dimensions were still unfathomed by us) threatened Jewish-Arab relations in the "united" city. I remember walking around Wadi Zeitoun with Philip, the former advisor to the mayor for East Jerusalem. The morning papers had described a large stone-throwing demonstration in Jerusalem. Philip told me that his most important achievement as the mayor's advisor had been getting 45,000 Arabs to abandon Jerusalem. Otherwise, he suggested, think how many Arabs would be there to clash with our security forces! I agreed with him, thinking how lucky we were to be rid of them. It was only later that I began to think of the significance of his statement. He had worked as a municipal employee with the goal of making life so difficult for Arab residents that they would decide to leave. What kind of municipality works to discourage its residents from living in their own communities?

On another occasion, Hassan told me that there was talk in the municipality of removing land mines from the old Jordanian minefield at the entrance to the village, and building homes there for young Arab couples. I listened silently, but thought to myself, "How can the municipality want to build new housing for Arabs? Don't we have enough of them as it is?" It seemed to me almost traitorous for the Jewish municipality to encourage more Arab births by providing housing. Later, I would argue with Sarah about this, as she upheld that it was a municipality's obligation to work for the good of all its residents, regardless of ethnicity. In fact, the municipality's refusal to allow most Arabs to build homes on their privately owned lands was an attempt to achieve population control through gross overcrowding. But despite Philip's success in driving 45,000 of his wards out of the city, Jerusalem's poor Arabs continued to have very large families in spite of their lack of living space.

Returning to the problem of the JNF's refusal to plant the whole area with olive trees in the winter of 1988, I decided to confront this issue one more time. I talked with Khader, and we both signed a letter to Mayor Teddy Kollek, making the joint Arab-Jewish Arbor Day dependent on the carrying out of the original agreement to plant the whole area with olives over a single winter. I was excited by this proposal and wanted to go over it with Teddy right away. I knew that he was a very busy man, so I turned to a woman who had once been his secretary and who was a friend of a friend. How, I asked her, could I get some time to sit with Teddy? She replied that he was an early riser, usually getting to his office about 5:30 AM, at which hour he would have lots of time. So I took the letter and waited outside his office, beginning at 5:00 AM. I was sure that Teddy would view our offer as a welcome present in these tough intifada days. When he arrived, with several assistants, I stepped up and asked if he could spare a few minutes. His aides were outraged: "How can you wait like this to ambush the mayor?" He had me sit in the reception room while he read the letter. He then consulted with his assistants, and in the end he shouted at me that he couldn't do any more than what he'd already done, and that was that.

A week later I got a written reply to my letter from the head of the Municipal Beautification Department, telling me that all I knew how to do was to shout and scream without making any contribution to understanding between Jews and Arabs. The JNF then planted a thousand tiny olive saplings in the bottom of the *wadi*, where the villagers liked to plant wheat. On Tu B'shvat, Jewish schoolchildren came from the Talpiyot school, guarded by border police and private guards carrying Uzi submachine guns, and planted cypress trees in the old no-man's land in front of the minefield. The Arab children did not participate in that tree planting but, influenced by the intifada, stole into the *wadi* and pulled up all the Jewish pine and olive trees that the JNF had planted, and left the *wadi* bare of trees where the Arabs' wheat and barley were growing.

Years later, the villagers converted part of the wheat fields into a soccer field, and from my window I could see the young people playing ball, with neither help nor hindrance from our municipality.

What were the lessons of Sur Bahir? First and foremost, I realized how much potential power lies in cooperative action by Arab and Jew. Interestingly, although the vast majority of my Jewish neighbors probably favored taking as much Arab land as possible, not a single voice was heard opposing our campaign (with the exception of the JNF and ILA). The press also supported us unanimously. By working within the Israeli consensus that Jerusalem is united for the good of all its residents, we silenced the opposition. Israelis want to be decent. Israelis don't want to view themselves as oppressors. While most Israelis would probably have preferred to have the JNF quietly take over the valley, nonetheless when we worked together as good neighbors—nonviolently and within the law, for the right of poor farmers to eke out their bread, and not frontally challenging Israel's right of expropriation—it was hard to fight us in the public eye. We gave Israelis a chance to feel proud of our institutions' defeat.

But there were more lessons to be learned. Conditions in Sur Bahir were nearly ideal. The neighborhoods of Talpiyot and Arnona have a very high proportion of liberal Jews from the intellectual and established elite. We have many immigrants from the West who believe in giving the underdog a chance. The area is one of the few in which many religious Jews view their Judaism as requiring moral commitment. We were fortunate to have a group of well-respected citizens who dedicated themselves to the struggle, and the village had Khader and Hassan, who led their side with wisdom and determination. And we had the good fortune to have my prior relation with Khader, which gave us the impetus to get started.

But I learned how hard it is to fight the authorities, how powerful they are. We struggled for such a long time to achieve almost nothing. Our High Court judges preferred to roll their eyes heavenward and participate in the system that legally oppresses the Palestinians. The JNF and the ILA, supported by the enormous power of the government and police, were deterred for a moment by a freakish confluence of forces, which would be hard to recreate. Today, when I look back at that struggle, I realize that the villagers were also abandoned by their own Palestinian people, whose elites did nothing to help them in their plight.

But the seed of joint Palestinian-Israeli community action was planted in my mind, and would affect my life for years to come.

Postscript: It is 2010, and I see from my living room window that Israeli contractors are beginning to build Jewish high-rise apartment houses in the bottom of Wadi Zeitoun, east of the Green Line in East Jerusalem.

CHAPTER 5

Obeidiyah

Water in the Desert

While we were still working on Sur Bahir, and before my reserve duty in Jericho, Sarah invited me to join her and some members of the Citizens Rights Movement (CRM, or Ratz in Hebrew) to meet Palestinians from Obeidiyah, a village east of Sur Bahir. The Palestinians had a particular problem they wanted to discuss. Obeidiyah lies in the Judean desert, four miles southeast of my home in Jerusalem. I can see the village clearly from my dining room window, with the ancient Theodosius monastery and its several Muslim minarets.

We met in the office of Dr. Mubarak Awad, a Palestinian who had moved to the United States, married a Quaker, and recently returned to open a Palestinian Center for Nonviolence. This was still before the First Intifada, which he would try later to direct toward nonviolent actions. The villagers had come to Awad, who in turn had brought in Israelis from the CRM to help. The Israeli Civil Administration (part of the military organization that administers civilian affairs under the occupation) was refusing to connect the village to the piped water network, so the villagers, who lived in the desert, had to depend on cisterns and had to buy water, which was brought in tanker trucks. The reason that the villagers gave for this situation was particularly interesting.

In 1967, at the time of the Six-Day War, the son of one of the *mukhtars* was studying in Jordan. According to Israeli postwar regulations, any Palestinian who was not in his West Bank home at that time lost the right to ever return to his or her village, becoming a refugee for life. The *mukhtar* was obviously heartbroken at losing his son. Some years later, the Israeli authorities came to the *mukhtar* and offered a chance for his son to return legally and regain his permanent rights to live in the village. All the *mukhtar* had to do was help a little. One of the functions of *mukhtars* in the areas where there is no land-ownership registry is to point out the owners of each tract of land. Israel had decided to build a Jewish settlement on part of the village's land. Because of a legal problem in expropriating the Arabs' land to build Jewish housing, the government wanted the villagers to sell the property to a Jewish land speculator. All the *mukhtar* had to do was arrange for the land sale, and his beloved son would be allowed to return.

In 1977 the deal was closed, with one of the *mukhtar*'s other sons selling the 6,000 dunams (1,500 acres) of land to the Jewish land dealer, Shmuel Einav, claiming falsely to be the owner of the land. Einav then sold the land to two Israeli companies (Jumbo and Dekel), which began preparing to build the new settlement, to be called Ramat Kidron. However, by chance, someone saw an official notice relating to the registry of the land, and at the very last moment a group of villagers filed objections based on their being the true owners of the land. Since 1983 the case had been in the Israeli courts, which stood fast in blocking the fraudulent registry.

The Israeli right-wing government was not prepared to give up the fight, however. According to the villagers, pressure was put on them in many ways. The authorities gave two of the *mukhtar*'s sons weapons to carry, to protect themselves from their angry neighbors. Villagers who wanted to travel to Jordan or have relatives visit from there were told that they would first have to sign a document saying that they did not object to the land registration by the Jewish companies. The villagers set up a council (*lijna*) made up of two representatives from each clan (*hamoula*), and asked the authorities to deal with the *lijna* rather than with the discredited *mukhtar*, but of course the authorities refused to work with the *lijna* and instead harassed its members, including repeatedly arresting at least one of them. But the worst thing was that while all the other villages had been connected to piped water, Obeidiyah remained dry.

We met several times with the villagers, both in Jerusalem and in their homes. I was beginning to get more comfortable in Arab society, and was given the job of heading up the project for the CRM Party. The worst part of the task was making repeated telephone calls to the office of Brigadier General Ephraim Sneh, head of the Civil Administration. I was always told that the only problem with the water was technical, and that it would be solved when a new pipeline was built to bring more water to the Jewish settlement of Maaleh Adumim to the north. That pipeline would run right through Obeidiyah, at which time the town would be connected to it. How could I know what was true? The woman with whom I spoke was an officer, and she was always polite and sounded so reasonable. And Sneh's father had been the head of the Israeli Communist Party, which worked hard for fair relations with Arabs. Yet I had heard so many stories of unfairness from villagers whom I trusted.

The best part of the job was visiting Obeidiyah, less than an hour's jog from my home. I found a dirt road perfect for running, which led through Sur Bahir and the desert and brought me to the home of Shukri, one of the leaders of the *lijna*. On one visit I saw an old man in the desert who invited me to visit his small home. We sat together and ate *faqqous* (a delicious vegetable from the cucumber family) which he grew, and drank water from his cistern. With the few words of Arabic and Hebrew that we shared, I learned that he was a brother of Khader Dabash, the *mukhtar* of Sur Bahir. He had a home in the village, but preferred to spend time by himself in the desert. Meeting Arabs as people was slowly changing some of my opinions about them.

Shukri was a proud Palestinian in his twenties. He stood up to the authorities and was repeatedly sent to prison. When they finally put the water pipeline through to the Maaleh Adumim settlement, the authorities did a strange thing. Even though the Ramat Kidron settlement had been stopped, and the Jews who had bought plots there were organizing to sue the Jewish companies who had sold them the stolen land, the authorities laid the pipeline to the area where Ramat Kidron had been planned, rather than through Obeidiyah, which was the direct and cheapest path. It was clear that a bogus Jewish settlement was more important than an Arab village of thousands of living souls. The route to Ramat Kidron ran through an olive grove, which the authorities began ripping up. Shukri stood in front of the bulldozer and was imprisoned again. He used nonviolent methods, but they had no effect on the powerful forces of the army and government, intent on pushing forward Jewish colonization of this land.

The *mukhtar*'s son used the money he'd made from the land deal to build a villa in Ramallah. On 28 June 1987, he came back to the village with Jewish bodyguards, border police, the land dealer Einav, and the Land Registration Renewal Committee, to survey the lands for Ramat Kidron. Village farmers showed up to protest. As reported in the press, one farmer tried to block the group from entering his land. The mukhtar's son and the Jews forced their way in, villagers threw rocks, the Jews opened fire, one old farmer was killed, and six other villagers were wounded. The Jews were released by the police, but seven villagers were arrested and charged with criminal activities.

We met with the *lijna* to discuss what could be done. I asked whether they would be willing to march in the village together with Israeli supporters, under two slogans: "Peace with Israel" and "Water for the Village." Much to my surprise, they accepted the idea immediately. I couldn't believe that Palestinians would be willing to openly support peace with Israel. They told us that they had no problem with this, since they had their own prince of peace—Yasser Arafat. Driving back to Jerusalem we Israelis laughed at the idea that anyone could think of that terrorist, Arafat, as a "prince of peace." But later, when Israel under Benjamin Netanyahu rejected any reasonable peace, and Arafat pushed for the Oslo peace process, I wondered if the villagers knew something that we had missed. At the time, however, I believed that the only reason the *lijna* was willing to demonstrate with us was because they lived in an isolated, primitive village in the desert and didn't realize that other Palestinians would never allow them to publicly support peace with Israel. But they were willing, and it was only because of technical problems that we never held this joint demonstration.

The problem in Obeidiyah dragged on for several years. Finally, CRM member of Knesset Dedi Zucker arranged a meeting with General Shmuel Goren, the military coordinator of all activities in the occupied territories. I was serving on reserve duty in the army at the time. The night before the meeting, I talked with the handful of soldiers I commanded, and told them about the problem of Obeidiyah, saying that I might not be with them the next night because of our meeting. One of the soldiers, a small Yemenite bus driver, said to me, "Hillel, I [will] tell you what I believe. I believe in transfer. There's no place here for Arabs. They should all be transferred to some Arab country. But people living in the desert—they should have water. As long as they live here, they should have water. So go to your meeting tomorrow, and good luck." I attended the meeting, with Goren, MK Zucker, and Sarah, in my dirty army fatigues. Goren agreed to help get the village connected to the water line. I drove back to my army base, where my company commander drove me to join my men going out to our ambush. The Yemenite soldier who believed in transfer was happy to hear that Goren had promised to help. The same army that was trying to steal Obeidiyah's lands was helping me to cooperate with the *lijna,* whom they boycotted. And I was waiting all night in ambush to shoot Palestinian terrorists who might infiltrate across the Jordan River, while cooperating with their friends in the village.

When the First Intifada started, Mubarak Awad taught his fellow Palestinians many ideas about nonviolent resistance. One of his projects was boycotting Israeli goods and buying Palestinian produce. On the wall of his office was a poster urging Palestinians to buy their own produce. The poster had a map of Israel, the West Bank, and Gaza, with no Green Line as a border between them. It angered me that his map, just like that of the Greater Land of Israel movement, showed all of Israel and Palestine as one, implying no recognition of the rights of the other side. One day when I was patrolling with Shammai in Ramallah during the First Intifada, Shammai saw the same poster in the window of a bookstore. "Look," he said, "they aren't willing to compromise. They want all of my land." I told him that this was a poster that was calling for nonviolence. "I don't care," he replied. "They want to take away my country." He went into the store and talked to the woman inside. "I'm sorry," he said in a polite way, "but this poster is forbidden. Please take it down from your window. If you're busy now, you can do it later." "No problem," said the clerk. "I'll take it down now."

Awad's nonviolence was viewed by the Israeli authorities as a threat to the state. They used an Israeli regulation that strips any Palestinian of East Jerusalem residency rights if he or she also has foreign citizenship, and they refused Awad's request to remain in Jerusalem even as a tourist. Being an American citizen did not help him, and Awad was jailed in the Russian Compound and then deported. His friend Dr. Edy Kaufman, director of the Truman Center for Peace Studies at the Hebrew University and one of the leaders of the Obeidiyah project, slept outside the jail in protest.

Years passed, conditions changed, and Obeidiyah was finally connected to the water network. Ramat Kidron appears to be dead, doomed by Israeli courts that stood firm for justice and by Palestinian villagers who paid the heavy price of standing up to the authorities. I like to think that we in the Israeli peace movement helped a bit too.

CHAPTER 6

Beit Sahour I

Intense, Long-Lasting Dialogue

When Sa'ed and Yusra told me in 1988 that we'd have to discontinue the dialogues in Jericho, they both stressed the importance of the dialogues and encouraged me to find other communities with which we could carry on the work. I didn't know how to find such groups, but through personal contacts I learned the name of a lawyer in the village of Beit Safafa in Jerusalem. I phoned him, despite feeling somewhat uncertain, but he was enthusiastic and suggested we meet at the entrance to the Diplomat Hotel —in ten minutes! We talked for about half an hour, and I could see how open he was to the idea of a dialogue. Two days later he called back to say that many people in the village supported the idea, but others opposed it, so to his disappointment they could not embark on such a project.

After a couple of weeks a prominent civil rights lawyer, Shlomo Lecker, called me. "I met someone who might be just right for you," he said. "His name is Ghassan Andoni, from Beit Sahour." Shlomo had come up with a perfect choice. I soon met Ghassan (pronounced Ras-SAN, rhyming with "a fan") in Beit Sahour, a town of 12,000 just east of Bethlehem. I liked him right away: a wiry man in his late twenties with intense eyes, olive skin, a mustache, and a goatee. He was serious and fervent, but balanced and careful. Ghassan taught physics at Birzeit University in the West Bank. We talked about the idea of starting a dialogue, and he obviously liked the idea. He said that he would evaluate the situation after talking to several people representing all of the political parties in the town. He was very unusual in preferring to include the entire political spectrum rather than just friends from his own party.

Ghassan needed the approval of the leadership of the intifada in Beit Sahour, but within just a few days, he gave me the OK. And thus started the most intense, successful, and long-lasting dialogue that I would experience. Because I was going to be away for several weeks, we arranged to start the dialogues when I returned. Just before I left, though, I saw a notice posted by an Israeli group called End the Occupation, encouraging people to go to Beit Sahour. A young Palestinian named Edmund Ghanem had been walking home with packages from the *suq* (market) when he was killed by a large rock which hurtled from a rooftop. Israeli soldiers had been stationed on the roof. Although the soldiers later claimed that the rock had blown off the roof, the Palestinians insisted that the soldiers had thrown it at Edmund. The Israeli group was going to participate in a memorial service for the young man. End the Occupation was too radical an organization for me, which is to say that while I could agree with many of their ideas, their style seemed excessively critical of Israel. There are Jews whose sympathy for the sufferings of the Palestinians renders them insensitive to, and unmoved by, the persecutions and oppression that have pursued our people throughout our lengthy exile and that led to the establishment of the State of Israel. Nonetheless, I decided to go along with them this one time, to get an initial look at Beit Sahour before getting involved in dialogue.

The rented bus took us from Jerusalem to Beit Sahour. The organizers spotted an army jeep, and tried to drive around it on back roads to avoid being stopped, but suddenly another jeep blocked our road and the bus came to a halt. There were only two or three houses in the area. The Israelis all got off the bus and started chatting with the Palestinian family in the closest house, while the organizers began negotiating with the army officer. Finally, the army allowed ten of us to attend the memorial, but the rest of us were told to stay near the bus. Soldiers would remain to guard those at the bus, even though there was no need for this since the Palestinians appreciated our support and were very friendly.

By chance, the colonel in charge was the commander of my reserve regiment. I went up to him and introduced myself as one of Shammai's NCOs. I assured him that there was no need for concern, and that we were all responsible citizens. (It was strange that I said that, since I didn't know the other people.) The officer began treating me as a sort of liaison to the group, of which I was barely a member.

The mayor of Beit Sahour, Abu-George, arrived and led us by foot for about ten minutes to the Roman Catholic church, where Edmund's memorial service had been delayed pending our arrival. We went downstairs to the social hall, which was lit only by candles. Displayed were photos of Edmund, several large Palestinian flags (strictly forbidden in those days), and crosses. Many Palestinians were sitting silently in the semi-darkness. To me it looked like some kind of satanic assembly. Remarkably, however, everyone accepted the presence of us Israelis. After the service, someone thanked us for coming, and we walked back to the bus where the other Israelis were still chatting with the Arab families.

We started back, with an army jeep driving behind us. Several of the Israelis expressed anger at the soldiers for accompanying us. Finally, our bus stopped and the organizers talked to the soldiers, getting them to agree to let us continue without escort. I couldn't understand all this anger. After all, these were our soldiers, and they couldn't believe that we would not be in danger driving without an army escort during the intifada in an Arab town. The fury expressed at the soldiers, who were concerned for our safety, convinced me that I wouldn't participate with this group again.

On the other hand, the Beit Sahour dialogue group got off to a good start. The original Palestinian members consisted of Ghassan; Salaam Hilal, an architect with a winning smile, who was insightful, warm, and friendly; Elias Rishmawi, a pharmacist who owned a drugstore in the center of town and who had a lot of professional contacts with Israelis (he would also be the leader of the pharmacists who would challenge the Israeli government in the courts as part of the tax strike later in 1988); and Mazen Badra, a good-looking young man with a large bushy mustache, who was the head of the Business Administration Department at Birzeit University. He had studied in the United States and spoke excellent English. Also included was Jamal Salameh, a quiet man, the only shy person among a group of gregarious and outgoing men. At that time he was an insurance agent, but later he would head a cooperative society for marketing olive-wood and mother-of-pearl sculptures, which Beit Sahourians traditionally produced for sale to Christian tourists. A second pharmacist in the group was Khalil Barhoum. There was a teacher, Kamal, who was the only Muslim in the original group (the others were Greek Orthodox or Roman Catholic Palestinians); he'd had no previous contact with Jews, other than soldiers. While these men were in their late twenties and thirties, another participant, Jalal Qumsiyeh, was older, closer to my age, and we would become close friends. Like Sa'ed in Jericho, he was the son of the late, well-loved mayor of his town.

We had several very successful dialogues in my home and in Ghassan's home in Beit Sahour. The Palestinians were obviously knowledgeable, personable, and articulate. They understood the intifada from the inside, and each group of Israelis I invited to meet them came away with both a new understanding and a positive personal experience.

After the first few dialogues, I told my Palestinian friends that I would have to leave for three weeks of reserve duty in Ramallah, a large city in the West Bank. They recommended that I refuse to serve, as several other reservists were doing, to protest the occupation. But I told them that I felt it was my duty, living in a democracy, to serve, and I didn't want to leave only those soldiers who hated Arabs in charge. The dialogues continued in my absence, while I went to Ramallah, which I'll describe in the next chapter.

CHAPTER 7

Ramallah I
A Soldier's Attempt to Promote Nonviolence

Several weeks after my unit finished our reserve duty in Jericho, we received our next call-up notice, for three weeks in Ramallah in August 1988. As I participated in the Jericho dialogues, I came to realize that these Palestinians were trying very hard to send a message to Israelis and to the world, which was watching the First Intifada unfold. However, our army blocked all demonstrations, violent or nonviolent, and what finally was shown were pictures of stone-throwing and tire-burning, all of which looked quite violent. I thought to myself: How different would it be if our unit offered the people in Ramallah the chance to demonstrate nonviolently? They could show us that they are looking for peace, and show it in a peaceful way that we could understand.

I went to Shammai's laboratory on the Hebrew University campus and asked if he would be willing to let me talk to leaders in Ramallah. I suggested that we negotiate with them, saying that we would leave them alone to demonstrate peacefully if they would agree to forgo all violence while we ran their town. Shammai replied, "Take it as an order—talk to the people there and let's work it out." Shammai was by no means a leftist or political extremist. He was a middle-of-the-road Labor Party supporter. Given the green light to proceed, I was excited that this stint of reserve duty would be truly different.

But how do you find Palestinian leaders when they are subject to imprisonment if caught? And who can speak in the name of the street activists? I started by going to a Palestinian lawyer, Jonathan Kuttab. I had heard him speak at a synagogue, and had been impressed by his moderation, even though he was clearly nationalistic. We sat together, he listened to my suggestion, and he obviously liked the idea. He promised to find people with whom we might be able to work.

I assumed that Palestinians would jump at the idea of having the army give them the space to present themselves in a positive, nonviolent light. But the process was not so simple. I went to speak with Ziad AbuZayyad, a lawyer who published a Hebrew-Arabic newspaper and tried to make a bridge between the peoples. He was in court that day and so was late for our appointment. While I waited, I spoke with his wife, who told me that she was a teacher in Ramallah. I asked whether she would be willing to meet with the commanders in our unit to discuss the meaning of the intifada, as she and other Palestinians saw it. She was open to the idea, but then Ziad arrived and announced that they would not deal with soldiers of the occupying force. He vetoed both dialogue with soldiers and making any deal to ban stone-throwing.

Jonathan arranged more meetings for me. One was with Dr. Sari Nusseibeh, a leading politically involved intellectual. I told Shammai that I would be meeting him at the National Palace Hotel in East Jerusalem, in the Arab part of town. Shammai was worried about my safety. Why not invite him to the western, or Jewish, part of town? When I insisted that I was fine about being in East Jerusalem, he declared that he would wait outside in his car with his M16 assault rifle, ready to rush in and save me if anything happened. "They'll slaughter you if you meet him in East Jerusalem," he warned. But I had already attended enough dialogues in Jericho and Beit Sahour that I no longer shared this fear of Arab towns. And when I met with Nusseibeh, he listened attentively to my ideas. He said that they were interesting, but he was about to go abroad for the summer, and would not be able to be involved.

A Palestinian lawyer who practiced in Ramallah, Ahmad Assayad, helped arrange some other meetings. Later, when I was serving in the reserves in Ramallah, whenever we caught sight of each other in the street we exchanged discreet smiles, without showing open recognition. I was very careful not to reveal the identities of any of my interlocutors. Similarly, I would not talk openly on the phone, since the phones of activists are always tapped.

Once, when I was patrolling with a walkie-talkie on my back in Manara Square in Ramallah, I spotted a reporter who strongly resembled Jonathan Kuttab. I remembered that he had a brother, Daoud, who is indeed a reporter. Forgetting that I was in uniform and carrying an M16, I sauntered over, introduced myself, shook hands, and asked after his brother. Only later did I realize that it was not advantageous for a Palestinian to have a soldier from the occupying forces chat with him in public.

Another Palestinian with whom I spoke was Radwan Abu-Ayyash, a refugee from the Ramallah area, who was frequently described as the number-two local Palestinian leader after Faisal Husseini (Yasser Arafat was in exile in Tunis at that time). He listened and said he'd get back to me, but didn't. An Israeli reporter gave me the name of Dr. Hanan Ashrawi, who would later become famous as the spokesperson for the Palestinian delegation to the Madrid talks. At that time she was relatively unknown among Israelis, but the reporter said that she had tried to organize non-violent women's marches, which were broken up by the army, and that she might be interested in my idea. But she was out of the country and couldn't be reached.

A soldier named Clark was in our unit, and he was a reporter for an international wire service. We had served together in Jericho, where I'd gotten to know him. Shammai and I talked to Clark about our idea. We asked if he could use his press contacts to find street leaders in Ramallah, convey our ideas to them, and propose a meeting with us. I told him that if things worked out, there would be a good, exclusive story for him. Clark agreed to feel out his secret contacts in Ramallah.

Several years later, Clark would publicize the name of a secret army unit, Duvdevan (a code word which means *cherry*), consisting of soldiers who dressed as Arabs and infiltrated Palestinian towns to arrest suspects. There were many scandals about the use of this unit to carry out executions rather than arrests of Palestinians. Once, by accident, they shot one of their own men (whom they thought to be an Arab), who fell face down, wounded. They then went up to him and finished him off with a bullet through the head, which was their standard practice. While Duvdevan was involved in much needless cruelty, one of my son's best school chums served in that unit, a boy we had known for his whole childhood, and who would never have behaved that way, both because of the kind of person he was and because of his liberal views toward Arabs (despite the fact that his former girlfriend had been stabbed to death in the street by a Palestinian from Obeidiyah). The unit was covered in the press, but Israeli censorship forbade use of its name. When Clark included the code name in his story, the army was furious. Several days later, outside his apartment in Jerusalem, Clark was jumped by masked men who beat him very professionally. The beating injured his kidneys enough that he was hospitalized and in pain for a number of days, but no permanent damage was done.

While I usually went to reserve duty with a positive attitude, the intifada had made me ambivalent. I had never sought excuses to avoid army service. I had returned to Israel (after years in America) as an immigrant at the age of thirty-six, and had been drafted a year later. The next year was the disastrous Yom Kippur War, but luckily for me my unit served on the Jordanian front, which never heated up. After that war, Israel decided it needed to enlarge its army, so despite my lack of experience I was able to volunteer for a squad commander's course. I was almost forty years old, and my instructor was perhaps twenty. He was obviously dedicated to giving the army his best efforts, and though it was hard for him to give orders to soldiers who were his father's age, I had no trouble accepting his authority. One day we were lined up in three rows when he noticed a middle-aged soldier sitting off to the side. He called the soldier to fall into place, but the soldier said he couldn't, as he didn't feel well. My instructor turned and said, with complete conviction, "There is no such thing in Tzahal as 'I can't come.' When your commander calls you, you come running. If you can't run, then walk. If you can't walk, then crawl. But know that you're a soldier in Tzahal, and you can come." Those words stuck with me and helped form my attitude of giving my best to Tzahal.

While dealing with people in the army was often hard for me, it was only with the First Intifada that I questioned what I was doing. Protecting Israel from terrorists was by no means problematic, but suppressing a reasonable uprising of a people whom we were oppressing was something else. We had rarely come into contact with civilian Palestinians before, but that was what the intifada was all about. I did not need to serve during the intifada. From the age of forty-five, I was free to leave my combat unit for civil defense work on the home front. Yet each year I signed a form volunteering to continue to serve in my combat unit. I must have been one of the only soldiers who volunteered to serve in the intifada. I justified it to myself on two grounds. First, much as I opposed the Jewish settlements, as long as our democratically elected government approved of them, our army had to protect the settlers against violent attack. Second, I felt an obligation to be present to try to block the cruel violence that many soldiers were wreaking on the helpless Palestinian citizenry.

In the few months preceding our time in Ramallah, I felt that I had finally found a way to serve my country during the intifada, without violating my conscience. I looked forward to the challenge of this very different reserve duty. But unfortunately, none of my Palestinian contacts came through. Clark told Shammai and me that his secret contacts had said that they would not cut a deal with us; they believed that the more blood that was shed, the more it would advance their cause. So when we finally went to Ramallah, there was no deal.

Shammai was put in charge of the city, which I knew meant that the people of the town would get a fair shake. Most of my work was on foot patrols. There wasn't much to do. One of the routes that we patrolled went out to the hospital. Across the street was a large pine grove. We would walk to the grove, then relax there for a few hours, make coffee on a little gas burner, and start back to end our patrol just on time. In previous reserve duties I would have struggled for us to really patrol all the time, but in the current setting it was good to keep away from the population and not trouble them, so I went along with the other guys' laziness.

You could see the soldiers' personalities in the ways they behaved in this crazy theater called the intifada. There were those who struck macho poses—standing up in the open jeeps and daring anyone to trifle with them. There were those who tried to cover up fear, for none of us wanted to return home wounded. On one occasion while patrolling a street, there seemed to be a tense silence in the air, and our patrol commander, who had a black belt in martial arts and was an expert with guns, suddenly fired a canister of rubber bullets at nothing at all, just to relieve his tension. But I was different from the others. As a result of the dialogues, I was neither angry at the youths of the town nor afraid of them. I seemed to be immune to the fear that the unknown was implanting in my colleagues' hearts.

There was only one job that I took seriously, and that was patrolling the main highway, where settlers drove by and where they had been attacked with Molotov cocktails. I saw these patrols as legitimate, and went back to my old diligence, seeking to prevent ambushes by youths with stones or incendiary devices.

But the rest of the tasks were ridiculous. On one foot patrol through the *suq*, we came up behind a ten-year-old who was in the act of throwing a stone at our observation point on a rooftop. We grabbed him, but then all the soldiers started asking what we should do with him. We decided to take him to Shammai. Shammai asked where his father was, and we walked together to a little coffeehouse that belonged to the boy's father. Shammai turned the boy over to his father, saying, *Dir balak* (take care). From then on, whenever our patrol passed the coffeehouse, the father would run out and invite us to have tea, but we just kidded with him and never troubled him to serve us.

We slept in sleeping bags in the fenced-in courtyard of the police station in Ramallah. In the courtyard was an old black Mercedes taxi with flat tires. Whenever we arrested a suspect, we would have him sit in the taxi, which served as a lock-up, until the Shabak was finished interrogating him. Interestingly, no one ever searched the suspects, tied their hands, or blindfolded them. We simply took away their ID cards, without which they could go nowhere, put them in the taxi, and left them there without even a guard.

One day another squad commander, Levi, brought in a man of about thirty, and put him in the taxi. The soldiers asked Levi what the man had done, but in reply Levi just said, "*Hutzpah*. You've never seen such *hutzpah* [nerve, brazen audacity]." I went over to talk with the Palestinian. He was an instructor at Birzeit University, which, like all the Palestinian universities, had been closed for some time because of the students' support for the intifada. We chatted a bit; I was sympathetic to his plight. We talked about what Arafat would do at the upcoming PNC (Palestinian National Council) meeting, and he said that for Palestinians in the territories it was important that the PLO make a bid for peace with Israel. He told me that his immediate concern was that he suffered from ulcers and had not eaten anything that day. It wasn't good for him to have an empty stomach. I went to the soldiers' mess, where I found some food left from our lunch. I made him a plate and brought it to him. I had also found a *leben* (a milk product similar to yogurt) which I figured would be good for his stomach.

But I explained to him that it was important not to spill any of the dairy food on the meat plate, since that would violate the Jewish dietary rules of *kashrut* that are observed in the army. He was very careful to keep everything separated.

Some soldiers were angry with me for giving our food to the Palestinian, but I said that even prisoners needed to be fed. Two foreign women, who were somehow connected to Birzeit, came to the gate of the police station. They were worried about this prisoner. He had ulcers, and needed to eat. I tried to reassure them that he'd had lunch, and even some *leben*, but they were sure that I was making fun of them, and said cynically, "Yes, of course, you Israelis gave him food." It angered me that they didn't believe me, but then that is what our behavior causes people to think.

Levi came over and closed the windows of the taxi. I said that the windows should be left open, as it was August and even with the windows open it was terribly hot in the taxi in the sun. But Levi said he didn't want the guy running away. Although this was his prisoner, after Levi walked away, I opened the windows again, and the doors as well. Levi was from a different company in our battalion, but I had a special relationship with him, and it was particularly painful for me to be in conflict with him.

A few years previously we had done reserve duty in Sharm a-Sheikh, at the southern tip of the Sinai Peninsula, and Levi's company had been in Dahab several miles farther north. It was so beautiful and relaxed there that I invited my wife and children to come down and take a vacation at the field school in Na'ama, which was an easy jog from my outpost. I got a couple of days of vacation back home, and then we all drove down together in our car. The kids fought nonstop as we drove through the Arava desert (between Jordan and the Israeli Negev). They finally fell asleep just before Eilat. The fuel gauge showed half-full, so I decided not to fill up in Eilat but to push on to Nueiba while the kids slept. Israel was in the process of pulling back from the Sinai at this time, and when we reached Nueiba the gas station was closed. I decided we could make it to Dahab, which we did, but the gauge was now reading empty, and there, too, the gas station was closed, as the army was gradually pulling out. We wouldn't be able to make it to Sharm without more gas. We had three small kids, we were out in the desert, and we were meeting friends in Sharm who would be worried if we didn't show up.

Then I remembered Levi's company in Dahab. We drove to the army base, where Levi was in charge of the gas pumps. Of course it is strictly forbidden to put army gas in civilian cars. But Levi took it upon himself to help us out, and broke the rule. "Give a contribution to Libi [the army support fund]," he said. "It will come out the same." I really appreciated Levi's cavalier help, especially since in his place I might well have refused to break the rules without getting approval from an officer. Not only had Levi really gotten me out of a jam, but he was also the cousin of a close friend of mine who had died of melanoma. So how could I clash with him?

But Levi was religious, and he saw the Palestinians in a bad light. When we first came to Ramallah he shot at a kid who had been building a roadblock and who ran away when the army jeep approached. Shammai chewed him out for shooting at someone who was not threatening our lives. And I couldn't leave the Palestinian to swelter in the taxi, so unfortunately I made Levi angry at me several times.

What bothered me most in Ramallah was that the people would never look us in the eye. Everyone we passed would either look down or to the side. I shouldn't have been surprised, though, since we were the absolute masters of their city, and could arrest anyone who demonstrated *hutzpah*.

When we had been in Ramallah for some time, we noticed that each morning at 11:30 youths would throw stones at our observation posts. At just that moment TV crews would suddenly show up, photograph their fill of fresh intifada footage, and drive off. We decided to go on the offensive, and orders were given to the soldiers to stop every young male between the hours of 10:00 AM and noon, take away his ID card, and tell him to go to the police station at once. At the police station the men would have to stand opposite the fence in the hot sun, until an officer would finally show up with all the seized IDs and hand them back to the Palestinians, who were then free to leave. In this way we wrecked their opportunity to get intifada footage on TV. Of course, the young men were essentially banned from the streets of the city for those two hours.

One foot patrol that I particularly remember was in the relatively well-off refugee neighborhood of Kadoura. Our commander that day was Motti, a young soldier who had been a member of one of Israel's outstanding commando groups, but because of an injury had been moved to our unit. As with most of the good soldiers who joined us, he immediately lost all motivation and became lazy like the rest of our unit. Motti was a kibbutznik, but not worried about ideals. In Jericho he had enjoyed throwing rocks at cats as they climbed out of garbage cans. Also in this patrol was an older soldier from Haifa who was not from our unit, who had served many years in a crack reconnaissance unit, and who from his distinguished past and from his bearing had immediately won our soldiers' respect. He knew how to tell stories, and when he began to talk everyone fell silent and listened.

Next to a bakery was a building on which youths had sprayed graffiti in Arabic during the night. According to regulations, the owner of the house was responsible for painting over the graffiti, but in practice we would grab any Palestinian who happened by, illegally take away his identity card, and tell him that if the graffiti were not painted over by the time we returned, we'd arrest him. Every Palestinian home had a pot of paint and a brush for just such situations.

The baker was rushing to pack his hot, round, flat pita breads into an old car to distribute them to the groceries in time for the morning customers. Motti stopped him, and told him to paint over the graffiti. "But that's not my building," the baker replied. "Let the owner do it."

"You will paint it over," said Motti laconically.

"Look," said the baker, "I'll paint it over. But give me an hour to distribute my pitas while they're hot. As soon as I get back, I'll paint it over, I promise you."

"Paint it over now," answered Motti.

The baker saw that there was no use arguing, so he took his brush and pot of paint and walked across to the other building and began to work. No sooner had he walked away than Motti took one of the hot pita breads for himself. We all looked at him, but none of us said a word. Then the older soldier from Haifa spoke up: "Put it back."

"It's nothing. It costs the baker a couple of *agorot,* that's all."

The older soldier's voice shook with emotion. "Put it back!"

Motti tossed the pita back on the pile, shrugged his shoulders, and led us off to patrol, without looking back.

Birzeit University, like all the Palestinian universities, had been closed by the authorities, but it was obvious to us that something was going on in several buildings, including the YMCA, in Ramallah. One day Shammai alerted us to the probability that there would be trouble near the YMCA. "How can you tell?" I asked.

"Look at all the cars parked near the YMCA. They all have *kufiyes* spread out on their dashboards, so the guys can grab them fast and mask themselves." In the dialogues I had learned that putting a *kufiye* on the dashboard was a way of telling rock-throwing youths that the car belonged to Arabs. This was a new custom, and I didn't know whether it was secret. I felt that I couldn't tell Shammai what it really meant, but I told him that I was sure it meant nothing.

One night someone set a tire on fire in the Kadoura refugee neighborhood. Ordinarily, soldiers would respond to such an incident by banging on all the doors in the wee hours, forcing all the males outside, standing them up facing the walls, and harassing them to keep them from sleeping. But Shammai was his own man, and he preferred to create his own solutions. He drove around Ramallah in his jeep and collected four old tires. He brought them into Kadoura and set them all on fire. People came out of their homes to see what was going on. They couldn't believe their eyes—soldiers were burning tires! In the end, both the soldiers and the residents wound up laughing together over the absurd games that we were forced to play.

One of our jobs in Ramallah was manning certain roofs that had been taken over by the army as observation posts. The Palestinian families living in those buildings were forbidden to come up to the roof. One problem was that there were generally no toilet facilities on the roof. Soldiers who hated Arabs would throw feces and urine down on the passersby. I manned a roof with a soldier from the paratroops who was an extreme right-winger. After the Six-Day War he and some friends had moved into the Arab neighborhood of Beit Hanina in Jerusalem, where they continued to live throughout the intifada. He was against ever returning any land to the Arabs. But in his personal behavior, he treated Arabs with decency and courtesy. He was furious at the behavior of other soldiers who destroyed property on the roofs and insulted the population. In this respect he was closer to my viewpoint than many left-wingers who voted for liberal parties but treated Arabs with contempt.

There were many standard insults of Arabs that were accompanied by general laughter. The solution to all the problems with the Arabs was "a bullet in the head." When we were given orders concerning opening fire and the officer would say, "Then fire one bullet in the air," there were always comments from the crowd: "In the air of his lungs." Once when an observation post reported over the radio an ambulance transporting a wounded kid, we heard an anonymous comment, "So may they multiply." Such racist remarks, which are much like what antisemites say against Jews, are common in our society. Many years later, when the Jerusalem Beitar soccer team won the national championship, TV broadcasts showed the exuberant crowd chanting "Death to the Arabs," with pictures of Prime Minister Netanyahu and Jerusalem's Mayor Olmert beaming happily at the crowd.

One day there was a lot of tension in the town, although nothing concrete had happened. A commander, Tzachi, was leading our foot patrol when we came to a stone barricade. Tzachi stopped a middle-aged Palestinian and told him to remove the rocks. "I didn't put them there," answered the Palestinian.

"It doesn't matter. Clear them away."

"It's not my business," said the Palestinian. In his suit jacket he reminded me of the man who had been told to clear the barricade in Jericho. "You can put me in prison if you like, but I won't move a single stone."

I liked the man's courage, because we could have beaten him or put him in the taxi with the windows closed or sent him to prison for a long time, yet his pride gave him the strength to resist us. I was fed up anyway, so I said to Tzachi, "Let him go. I'll clear the stones for him." "Don't touch the stones," ordered Tzachi, but I didn't care anymore, so I tossed them to the side while the Palestinian man watched without emotion. When we walked back to the police station, Tzachi said to me, "This is the last time I'll go with you on a patrol. You disobeyed my order. You caused shame to Tzahal. I'm finished with you." The words stung. These were the guys I had to live and work with; if there was another war, these would be my fellow soldiers. Why had I made Tzachi so mad and hurt? What did that Palestinian mean to me, that I would destroy years of good relations with my army buddy?

The next day, things were hectic. A group of college-aged youths started throwing stones at us from the top of the hill next to the YMCA. We charged up the hill, and they dispersed and fled. It turned out that they had been set up as a diversion, and while we chased them a busload of Israeli demonstrators pulled up to the Birzeit office at the bottom of the hill. We charged back down and found that the Israelis, and some Palestinians, had put up signs protesting the deportations of several Palestinian leaders. I recognized my friends Nogah and Reuven and several familiar faces from demonstrations in which I had participated. My friends were surprised to see me in this setting, and called out to ask what I was doing there. Needing to justify myself, I replied that I was there to protect them. We joked together, but then the Shabak came and hauled away two of the Israeli leaders. Officers showed up and began handing out billy clubs and gas masks, talking about rushing the demonstrators and getting rid of them. Soldiers began putting on helmets.

In the two days of training before our arrival in Ramallah, our regiment commander, who had become friendly with me after our meeting in Beit Sahour (at the memorial service for Edmund Ghanem), explained how to break up demonstrations. I asked whether he was talking only about *violent* demonstrations, to which he replied, "Of course. We only use force against violent people." But here in Ramallah we were facing nonviolent demonstrators, and it seemed as if we were about to attack them.

As the soldiers began looking grim, I asked myself what I was really doing there. I'd failed in trying to get the Palestinians and army to agree to nonviolent demonstrations, and now when there was indeed going to be one, I was on the side that was about to violate the rules of civil liberties. What good was I doing? I was just one more pawn carrying out the orders of the occupation.

I looked at my friends who were getting ready to be charged by the soldiers, and suddenly said to myself, "I should be on their side, not the side of the army." I unloaded my rifle and took off my army shirt with the initials IDF, handed them to another soldier, and began to walk to the demonstration to join it. I realized that I was breaking the ultimate rule in the army, deserting my side and joining those whom the army considered the enemy. I had no idea what punishment I would get. I assumed it would be several years in prison. But at this point I didn't care about that. I felt that I had lost Tzahal and that I belonged on the other side of the confrontation. I felt that the shock that would be caused by an Israeli soldier deserting in this way would be sufficiently important to justify getting myself punished.

As I walked toward the demonstrators, in my T-shirt and without my rifle, Shammai came and asked what was wrong. "My place is with them, not with Tzahal," I mumbled.

"I want to show you something," he said. He put his arm around my shoulder. Under his roly-poly exterior, I could feel his steel-strong muscles. He led me away from the demonstrators and away from the soldiers in their gas masks, to a quiet corner. I kept looking to find what he wanted to show me. But there was nothing. And then I saw that there were tears in Shammai's eyes. I felt so bad about what was happening. I knew how much Shammai loved Tzahal, and how my desertion, as someone who shared his feelings, caused him pain. I thought of all the times that Shammai had come to my rescue. I remembered when the driver of my patrol vehicle ignored my warning and drove us so deep into the mud, near the Jordanian border, that only Shammai with the help of a stolen earth-moving tractor could get us out. I remembered when my men refused to enter an ambush in a *wadi* near the Jordan River, Shammai came to straighten things out. He had taken us to beautiful wilderness spots in Israel to build up our love for the country. He had invested time in the two new immigrants, Bentzi and me, to make us feel at home in Israel. I don't know whether Shammai had ever cried before, but I felt terrible for him at this point. I took back my army shirt and rifle, and stood off to the side.

I expected to be punished for having done the unthinkable, but there was no punishment. No one said a word about it. I had always been a cooperative soldier, and within my unit I was protected. The demonstrators went home, the arrested Israelis were released. I later learned that Tzachi and another soldier had told Shammai that they would refuse to participate in attacking Israeli demonstrators.

I saw an article in the paper quoting Dr. Hanan Ashrawi, which also said that she was back in the country. She was the one Palestinian whom I had been unable to contact before we were called up. One evening I sat with Doron, the officer with the mole who had struck Sa'ed in Jericho, who was now working for the Civil Administration. I said that it was too bad that we wouldn't allow Palestinians to demonstrate nonviolently. He said that wasn't true, and if they would only apply for a permit to demonstrate, the Civil Administration would be most happy to issue it, but no Palestinian would apply for a permit. I was very surprised to hear this (and I doubt today that this was correct). I decided to try to contact Dr. Hanan to see whether she would like to demonstrate with a permit.

There was a pay phone in the police station. It seemed very strange to call a Palestinian leader from within the station. I reached Hanan, and told her that I was an Israeli soldier who supported peace, and I wanted to talk to her about a possible action. She said that she would not speak with a member of the occupation army. I told her I would come when I was on vacation, and not in uniform. She said, in that case, I was welcome. So we set up an appointment, and I took a vacation day and drove from my home in nearby Jerusalem to her home opposite the Civil Administration headquarters.

Hanan was waiting with Khalil Mahshi, the principal of the Friends' (Quakers) Boys School in Ramallah. She gave me coffee and cookies, and then they told me of their pressing problem. As I had read in the Israeli papers, all Palestinian schools had been closed down by the military as being hotbeds of resistance. Several parents and teachers had started teaching their children at home, but this was banned also, and some teachers had been arrested for educating children illegally. My hosts asked whether I could help get the army to permit the children to learn. This turn of events surprised me, and I had no idea how to help them. In the end I asked whether they would like to work out a method to allow nonviolent demonstrations, either by requesting a permit from the Civil Administration or by working out a deal with our unit in exchange for suspending violent activity. They both said that they had no control over the street, so our meeting ended without any practical outcome. Nonetheless, the visit was carried out in a very friendly manner, which in itself, considering my role as a soldier, was remarkable.

Shammai began taking me with him on jeep patrols, possibly to keep me out of trouble. One time we parked the jeep near the Birzeit office. Despite the fact that the university had been closed down, there was a constant stream of students moving around. I said, "Let's do a dialogue. I'll show you what I mean." I went over to a group of students, and asked if they would be willing to talk to us. They rushed off like fish that see a predator approaching. But I found another group, and said to them that they didn't have to come over, but that we soldiers, like most Israelis, never got a chance to talk with Palestinians. Several of the students cautiously joined us, and we began to talk. We asked what they wanted for a solution, and they said, "two states for our two peoples." I saw Shammai's eyebrows go up, surprised. We talked with them for a while until they had to move on, and then we got others to take their place. This certainly beat running after stone-throwers. When our shift was over, I asked Shammai if he believed what they had said. He answered that he was surprised by what they said, but he wasn't sure if he believed them.

Two days later I was commanding a foot patrol. We walked down the road toward the hospital, but I stopped when we got to a *falafel* stand in Kadoura. There were a couple of Palestinians buying *falafel* (deep-fried balls of ground chickpeas). They spoke Hebrew and we started talking with them. Soon, Shammai came by in his jeep, and I waved him over to join the talk. Before long, our other jeep called over the radio, and someone told them to join us, so all the patrols wound up at the *falafel* stand talking with the crowd of customers, who stayed to express their opinions.

The talk continued for a long time, until someone noticed that our shift was over, so we all parted company. Before he left I again asked Shammai whether he believed them, and this time he nodded in assent.

Three days before we wound up our tour of duty, I had a day's vacation. That evening I got a phone call at home; it was a reporter named Roni Shaked, from the popular Israeli newspaper *Yediot Aharonot*. Roni asked if it was true that I had negotiated with Palestinians from Ramallah. I was flabbergasted. How could he have known? I had been so careful to protect everyone's confidentiality. I asked what made him ask, and he said that some Palestinians had told him so. I had heard Roni talking at a workshop given by Peace Now, so I felt that I could trust him. He told me what he knew, and I informed him that not all of his details were quite correct, and that in two more days I'd be finished with my reserve duty and would be able to supply the whole story correctly. But he insisted that he wanted the scoop, and couldn't wait until some other paper got the story. So I described my grasp of the issue, and told him that I had not negotiated with anyone but had presented the Palestinians with the possibility of talking with my commander, but nothing had come of it. I didn't know then that Roni, like many reporters who cover the territories, had previously served in the Shabak. He was especially interested in my meeting with Palestinians (I didn't provide their names) while I was on active duty, since that was my only violation of the regulations. I asked him not to write about anything that could get me into trouble, but he said that if I was telling the story, why not go the whole way. Since I no longer really cared about the repercussions, I told him to write what he wanted.

During the first half of each Beit Sahour dialogue, people would sit together in one large circle. For the second half, people broke up informally into small groups to mingle. At far left is Shraga Gorni of the Jerusalem planning group, at far right is Professor Jad Isaac of the Beit Sahour executive committee. 12 May 1993. *Courtesy of Debbi Cooper.*

ABOVE. Runners for Peace running together between Jerusalem and Bethlehem, past the Mar Elias monastery, to demonstrate their common desire for a peaceful end to the conflict. In the foreground from left to right are the author (with white beard), Mohammed Abu-Sroor, Mustafa 'Akel Dar el-Haj, MK Ran Cohen (with sunglasses), and Palestinian organizer Walid Abu-Sroor (with baseball cap) from Aideh refugee camp. 23 February 1990. *Courtesy of Eli Hershkovitz/Zoom 77 Ltd.*

FACING. Israelis, who have come to Nablus for dialogue, are greeted by Palestinians at the Friends of An-Najah University hall. 25 June 1993. *Courtesy of Flash-90.*

Two busloads of Palestinian families from Nablus were hosted by Israeli families in West Jerusalem. They marched together for peace through the streets of Talpiyot-Arnona, and then conversed in a hall over dinner. 29 August 1993. *Courtesy of Debbi Cooper.*

Dozens of Palestinian and Israeli families picnicked together on
Mt. Gerizim, overlooking Nablus, on the Jewish Sukkot (Tabernacles)
holiday. 5 October 1993. *Courtesy of Nahum Slapak.*

The three main players come together—the Americans, the Palestinians, and the Israelis. The U.S. consul general of Jerusalem, Edward G. Abington Jr., speaks to hundreds of Israelis from Jerusalem and Palestinians from Nablus at a festive communal dinner in Jerusalem. Left to right: Judith Green, Hilal Toufaha, Abington, Mohammed Sawalha, and Veronika Cohen. 13 September 1994. *Courtesy of Debbi Cooper.*

Hundreds of Palestinians from Nablus and Israelis from Jerusalem enjoy a meal together in Jerusalem's Arnona neighborhood, gaining an opportunity to talk together in small groups. 13 September 1994. *Courtesy of Debbi Cooper.*

CHAPTER 8

Ramallah II and Prison

The day after that phone call, I was back in Ramallah. I went out on a foot patrol, but Shammai came by and picked me up in his jeep. He said that we had to go to army headquarters. The company commander and battalion commander would join us there. I asked what was happening. Shammai handed me that morning's *Yediot,* with its front-page headline: "Reserve Soldier Conducted Private Negotiations in Ramallah." I was not especially concerned. If I hadn't been punished for almost joining the demonstration against expulsions, why would it matter that I had spoken to some Palestinians?

I said to Shammai, "But you told me to talk with the people from Ramallah."

He replied, "That was before we were activated. I never said to talk with them when you were a soldier."

He was right. I hadn't really considered the difference before I had called Hanan.

We arrived at the headquarters for the entire West Bank, in Beth El. As we walked in, all the soldiers who worked as clerks and secretaries cheered, waved, and called out words of encouragement to me. I learned later that they assumed that I must have killed a Palestinian, and was being brought in for the official investigation. We went into a very large room with army officers sitting around a fancy table. It looked like a seminar or boardroom. My commanders were already there, as well as a brigadier general and other high brass whom I didn't know.

The general told me that anything I had done before I began active reserve duty was my own business as a civilian. But meeting with a "local" while serving in the army violated regulations. In point of fact, that specific rule was part of the regulations designed to protect the occupied people from soldiers who might take advantage of them, and appeared in a section next to a rule prohibiting soldiers from buying on credit from Palestinians in the territories. But I was glad that they were not calling me a traitor, nor accusing me of talking with the "enemy" (although that was surely the way they viewed the significance of my meetings). I was still pretty relaxed, my main concern being not to get Shammai into trouble. Also, I did not want to give the army specific information about my meetings with Palestinians.

The brigadier general decided that I would be tried by a colonel for meeting with Palestinians and for talking to a reporter. A sergeant major took me to an office, where the colonel was sitting at the other end of a long table. I sat down at my end, but I noticed that the colonel seemed uncomfortable. "Did I sit down in the wrong seat?" I asked.

"Actually, you are supposed to stand during your trial," he replied with a little smile, "but it doesn't matter, you can remain seated." I must have been at least fifteen years his senior, and he realized that the situation was different from the usual trial of twenty-year-old soldiers.

We had a nice chat, in which I explained what I had done. He looked the way an officer should look: handsome, well-built, no potbelly, like someone who could lead us charging up a hill. He didn't appear angry, but was interested in our talk.

"Do you realize," he asked, "that you were risking your life, as a soldier, by entering a Palestinian house?"

I said that I knew I would be received well, and did not believe there was any risk involved. But I realized that our officers only met Palestinians as enemies, and had no comprehension that there is a normal side to Palestinian life.

The colonel asked if there was anything else I wished to say. I answered that I didn't feel that I had done any wrong, as everything I did had been intended for the good of Tzahal. I said I knew that he was the commander and I would be happy to accept whatever punishment he saw fit to give me.

The maximum penalty for my offenses was seventy days in prison, which I later learned was what some officers had wanted me to get, but Shammai had dissuaded them. The colonel was more understanding, and sentenced me to only fourteen days in prison and another seven days sus-pended (for talking to the reporter). I was surprised that I was sentenced to prison at all, but the number of days didn't seem too long.

I was transferred to army prison number 4. When I got there, the prisoner-clerk who checked me in said, "We've been waiting for you. We read in the newspaper that you were sentenced to prison. There are a half dozen of us who are here for refusing to serve in the occupied areas. Welcome."

I met interesting people in prison. One was Dr. Benny Morris, the his-torian whose book on the origins of the Palestinian refugee problem had revolutionized our way of viewing the situation. I met a young soldier who had been in the border police, who told me how in that unit the targets had pictures of Arab faces, and it was not enough to shoot the target: one had to hate the enemy as well. There was also a Druze soldier who had gone AWOL for over a year. He told me that he simply left his unit when it was harvest time on his father's farm, to help the family, and he didn't bother going back.

A young soldier whose job was like that of a social worker apologized to me for all the questions she had to ask, and said she was ashamed that I had been imprisoned. Life was tolerable for me in the prison, but it was much harder for my family, who had no idea whether I would be raped in prison (it wasn't like that at all), and struggled to get me out. My wife enlisted the help of MK Ran Cohen, who was a colonel in the reserves. My brother in the United States got some people to contact the Israeli embassy there to protest. At the same time that I was sent to prison, another soldier had brought a hunting rifle to the territories and killed a Palestinian with it, for which he got a suspended sentence. The discrepancy in punishments was embarrassing to the army.

After six days, I was called away from supper to talk with the prison commander. He asked whether I was contrite over what I had done. I said I felt that I had done the right thing. He tried repeatedly to get me to say that I was sorry, but I wouldn't. I couldn't understand what he wanted. I later learned that the OC (officer commanding) Central Command, General Amram Mitzna, had decided to pardon me, but they wanted to be able to say that I had admitted that I had done wrong.

At about two in the morning I woke up in my cell hearing one of the guards calling out the name "Bar-Tzion." The other prisoners said there was no one by that name. The guard insisted that there must be someone by that name, and he was to be released. Finally, I realized that my name in Hebrew, when handwritten, could look like "Bar-Tzion," so I got my things together and signed out. My two sons were waiting outside in our car, and took me home where we had a wonderful reunion.

After my release, Shammai filled me in on what had occurred during the last days in Ramallah. There had been an attempt by a group of Palestinians and some foreigners to stage a protest march, but Shammai had told them that they couldn't demonstrate and so they disbanded.

Another company from our battalion was located south of us near the Al-Amari refugee camp. Their operations officer, Avishai, was a friendly guy whom I liked even though we hardly knew each other. Each morning he would go running along the highway in his running shorts, with his rifle, for the exercise. One day there was a large demonstration, and Avishai was told to fire at the ringleaders below their knees, with new plastic bullets that were presumably less lethal than metal bullets. He fired at a Palestinian man's foot, but hit a girl in the head, killing her on the spot. Five years later, another soldier from his company, the reporter Hillel Cohen, recalled the incident in a critical article. Because the reporter and I have the same first name, Avishai thought that I was the writer, and sent me a bitter letter calling me a traitor to my people for having dealt with the enemy.

My experience in Ramallah left me with lots of ambivalence. I respected the reserve soldiers who went to prison rather than serve in the occupied territories. Had there been a sizable movement with a chance to change the course of the occupation, I might well have refused also. About a year later, a friend who was about to be called up asked me to help him decide what to do. Having had time to think things over, I said that if he felt that he could influence his fellow soldiers to behave more decently, then he should serve.

More recently, there has been a movement of soldiers who support the settlements and threaten to refuse orders to evacuate any settlement.

They are just as sure that God gave the territories to the Jews as I am that the occupation is immoral.

The clash of values in a democracy, where soldiers are subservient to politicians yet have their own consciences to answer to, does not make for simple answers.

CHAPTER 9

Beit Sahour II
From Dialogue to Action

After prison it was good to get back to the dialogues with our group from Beit Sahour. The first few discussions were at Ghassan's house in the evening. Across from his house was a driveway that led into an inner court, hidden from the street. There, we would park our cars so that soldiers would not see them. After several dialogues, the Palestinians decided to have each meeting at a different home, so as not to attract too much attention to any one house. For me it was interesting to be in different homes, so that I could see how people lived and meet each host's family.

One evening, toward the end of the session, Ghassan asked whether we would like to meet a man who had just been released from five months in the Ketziot prison camp in the Negev desert. We all agreed, and walked a couple of blocks to the home of Dr. Jad Isaac, an agronomist who taught at Bethlehem University. I had read about Dr. Jad in the papers. One tactic of the intifada was to make the Palestinians more self-sufficient and less dependent on the Israeli economy. This could help economically and would make it easier for people to survive the frequent curfews. Many Palestinians began growing pigeons and chickens as a local supply of protein. Jad opened a plant store and gave the urbanized population instructions about growing vegetable gardens in their backyards, similar to the "victory gardens" of World War II. The authorities saw this as weakening their control, and ordered him to close his store, which he did. Nonetheless, he was arrested and given six months' administrative detention. "Detention" may sound like house arrest, but it is in fact imprisonment in a prison, with the only difference being that the detainee does not know what he is charged with and gets no trial.

Despite his having just been released, Jad invited us into his home. He described the experience of imprisonment in the harsh conditions of a tent camp in the desert. He told how he, a middle-class professor, suffered at first from the lack of access to personal hygiene; he was used to a daily shower and shave. He described the camaraderie of the prisoners, who were all imprisoned for their activities in the intifada. Jad showed us a little sandstone sculpture he had crafted to pass the time. Despite being Israelis, we were clearly on his side.

As we left Jad's house, an army patrol saw us. The next day Jad was ordered to appear at the military governor's, where he was warned not to receive Israelis in his home.

We tried to alternate venues for the dialogues, one in Beit Sahour and then one in an Israeli home in Jerusalem. It may be hard for Israelis and westerners to comprehend this, but throughout the intifada there was no closure and Palestinians could drive freely in their cars everywhere in Israel without a permit. Many Israelis were afraid to go to a Palestinian town, so it was important that there be dialogues in our homes as well.

Dr. Veronika Cohen joined the dialogues right from the start and became one of the leaders. Veronika was at various times head of the Music Education Department, dean of students, and dean of the faculty at the Rubin Academy of Music and Dance. She had long been active in radical movements. The two of us, however, had an initial difference of opinion. I believed that 90 percent of the positive effects (on Israelis) of any dialogue would be achieved at the first meeting, especially if it was in the Palestinian community. It wasn't necessary for Israelis to return for additional dialogues, I thought, so we should emphasize getting as many one-time participants as possible. I viewed the dialogues as a sort of fear-dissipation mill—where exposure to Palestinians would allow Israelis to let go of their stereotypes. I told the Palestinians that all we needed to do was get the Israelis back alive; the rest was automatic.

Veronika, by contrast, believed that we should find a group of Israelis and Palestinians who would meet together for a series of dialogues to gain deeper understanding and trust. We solved the dispute by my organizing one-time discussion groups and Veronika organizing an ongoing dialogue, which I joined after it was established. I tried hard to bring native-born Israelis, and they were mostly male and nonreligious like me. Veronika was a leader in the politically progressive Orthodox congregation Yedidyah. Most of the people she brought were religious Jews, many of them immigrants from the West and many of them women.

There is no question that, even if one-time meetings accomplished some important changes, the ongoing dialogue added a whole new dimension. I had concentrated on the effects of the dialogues on the Israeli participants. But for the Palestinians, too, there was a need to overcome a lifetime of stereotypes—about Israelis. The ongoing dialogue forged a group of Palestinians and Israelis who would learn to trust each other and would work together for many years.

One of the key discoveries was that Palestinians could not believe that Israelis were motivated more than anything by fear of them. How could Israelis, with such a powerful army, be afraid of the weak occupied people? For a very long time, the Palestinians could not grasp this idea. I used the analogy of two people who meet in a dark alley: one has an atomic bomb and the other a knife. Who is more powerful in that situation?

A basic strategy of the Arabs, since they were unable to defeat us in 1948, has been to use terror to instill fear in our population and to get us to leave. Terrorism was effective—it created a deep-seated fear in every Israeli Jew—but it did not achieve the goal of getting us to leave in sizable numbers. Instead, it made us more adamant and defensive. It was my belief that if we could counter these fears in Israelis and reassure them, the Israelis would be prepared to take risks for peace. A great deal of my effort was spent working with our Palestinian colleagues to try to counter the damage that had been done throughout decades of terrorism. (My deep-seated convictions about the readiness of my people to compromise for peace would be sorely tested in the Netanyahu years ahead.)

My thinking about our conflict has undergone enormous changes in the twenty-two years since I began participating in the dialogues. It is almost impossible for me to remember exactly what I believed when I started. I think that, as with most Israelis, I placed almost all the blame on the Arabs. If they had accepted partition in 1947, or if Hussein had stayed out of the war in 1967, we would have done our part and they would have no real complaints against us now. They rejected compromise and peace, and so brought their own disasters upon themselves. However, like other Israelis from the Left, I was prepared to open a new page and work out a fair solution based on returning most of the occupied areas (demilitarized) to some Arab authority. I rejected the Greater Land of Israel policy of keeping all the land, and in choosing our home my wife and I were careful not to move into any area across the Green Line, even though the best real estate prices were to be found there.

In the one-time dialogues we concentrated mostly on direct personal contact and goodwill, which seemed so refreshing in contrast to the picture of the intifada that we got from the evening news. The Israeli who overcame his fears and placed himself at the mercy of the Palestinians was amazed that within minutes he felt totally relaxed. We emphasized our mutual good wishes for the future, and our hopes were quite similar. Everyone wished for peace, an end to violence, freedom, and a decent life for our children. Even if we viewed the history of the conflict from different perspectives, it was unnecessary to waste our few minutes together trying to force agreement from the other side.

There were certain sticking points that came up from time to time. We Israelis wondered if the Palestinians' willingness to accept us was based only on our strength. We worried that they would attack us if we ever became weaker than the Arabs. And if we were required to return all the land conquered in war, why wouldn't the Arabs attack us repeatedly in the hopes of someday winning, since there would be no penalty for losing a war?

In the ongoing dialogue, on the other hand, our very different readings of history and views of morality had a way of coming up. Sometimes a person would reveal a simple ignorance of facts that could be corrected to our mutual satisfaction. Ghassan told us that after the 1967 war many Palestinians stared at Israelis, looking for the tails that they truly believed we had. In one dialogue, a Palestinian teacher expressed disbelief that there had ever been a Holocaust. One of the Israelis present had lost his family in the Holocaust, and the immediacy of his reply had a convincing effect.

Sometimes Palestinians would make statements of fact, or of values, that contradicted my beliefs, yet would leave me with a measure of uncertainty. One of my fundamental beliefs was that the use of terrorism by the Arabs (what they call the "armed struggle") was absolutely wrong, regardless of their ends. I thought of the brother of a boy in my son Noam's class, who, while serving as an officer during the intifada (although he supported the peace movement), had his face burned and totally scarred by a Molotov cocktail thrown by a Palestinian. In the course of time I tried to decide if there might be situations that would justify such violence. In the extreme, the violent struggle against Hitler and his regime were certainly justified in my mind, but where does one draw the line? The Palestinians accused us of conducting "state terrorism." And I agreed that we were doing terrible things to the Palestinian population daily. The ongoing dialogue made all of us review uncertainties that were difficult to reconcile.

At the same time that my beliefs were being challenged by the Palestinians, articles were appearing regularly in the Israeli press reviewing parts of our history that I, with my good Zionist education, had understood quite differently. The "purity of arms" that I had learned was fundamental to our army's conduct was challenged by new revelations of massacres and the killing of prisoners, in all our wars, by our troops as well as by the Arab forces. Our treatment of the Palestinians who remained in Israel—we stripped them of much of their land and ruled over them with an iron fist—harshened my self-image. The writings of the "revisionist historians" made me question whether we had really been so much purer than our rivals.

The desire to assign blame comes up frequently in dialogues. Sometimes one blames the other side, and sometimes one beats one's own breast. For some, extracting an apology from the other side became an important goal. To me, one of the essential characteristics of our conflict is that both sides are right, and both are wrong. There are many analogous situations in which who is to blame is unclear. For example:

- A fire breaks out in a house, and a trapped person jumps from the third-floor window, landing on an innocent passerby below. Was he wrong to jump? Was he wrong to be so concerned with saving himself that he didn't make sure that the sidewalk was clear below? And if there were no safe landing spot, should he not have jumped?
- A soldier goes off to war and is reported killed. His "widow" remarries and has children, but her husband finally returns after years in captivity. Whose wife is she? Has someone done "wrong"?
- As a ship is sinking, people in a lifeboat refuse to pick up more survivors, fearful that the lifeboat will become overloaded and sink. Survivors still in the water fight with them to force their way onto the boat. Who is "right"?

꙰

During one dialogue session, Ghassan decided to define the First Intifada for us. He said that the intifada was the Palestinians' message of
peace. We laughed about this in the car driving home that night, just as
we had laughed at the villager from Obeidiyah who had called Yasser
Arafat their "prince of peace." It took me a long time to realize what most
Israelis do not realize to this day, that Ghassan was really right. Packaging
the message in stone-throwing and Molotov cocktails made it impossible
for us to recognize that, in fact, the Palestinian indigenous leadership and
the thoughtful Palestinian people were trying to replace the occupation
with peace—peace with Israel. When Arafat publicly recognized Israel in
1988 and vowed to end terrorism, we either ignored him or laughed at his
stupidity in thinking we'd fall for that stuff. We were sure that we knew
the PLO too well for that.

The First Intifada basically replaced murderous terror incidents—
bombs placed in buses or markets, and other attacks on civilians in Israel, carried out by small cadres of trained terrorists—with widespread
nonviolence and low-level violence against army or settler targets in the
occupied territories, carried out by the masses. Terrorism essentially
evaporated with the appearance of the intifada, and the intifada leadership forbade the use of firearms, which many people had hidden away. But
these changes went unnoticed by us Israelis, who saw the intifada solely
as a violent war to destroy Israel.

The intifada was much more than the stone-throwing that caught all
our attention. Through the dialogues, we were exposed to its nonviolent
side. Remarkably simple facts had to be told to us before we could recognize them. Much, if not most, of the intifada was in fact nonviolent.

Every day the intifada leadership called a general strike at a certain
hour. One evening I was sitting with Jalal on his veranda when a little
boy, perhaps nine years old, with his face masked, came by to give him
the latest intifada *bayaan* (instructional newsletter). People would hoist
Palestinian flags. Youths would paint slogans on buildings. Palestinians
organized into neighborhood committees to replace their dependence on
the Israeli authorities. There were committees for first aid, for cleaning
the streets, for helping families in need. There was a refusal to cooperate

with the occupation authorities, including a refusal to pay taxes. There was a demand that collaborators confess in the mosque or the church and cease their collaboration. There were secret leaders who planned strategy. And there were meetings with Israelis to talk about our joint future. All of these nonviolent activities were integral parts of the intifada, and one could go to prison for a lengthy sentence, or be exiled, for participating. The regulations forbade more than nine Palestinians from meeting anywhere for any purpose.

We Israelis viewed any Palestinian action whose goal was ending the occupation as a violent attempt to throw us into the sea. As I met Palestinians from more and more locations, I realized that, in fact, they were united in wanting to reach a true peace settlement. They were trying to send a message of peace, but the communication was coming out completely garbled, both because of our authorities' successful jamming of the message, and because the Palestinians were not speaking in a language that we could understand. One of my principal goals in the dialogues was to help those Palestinians who had a message of peace to formulate it in a way my fellow Israelis could hear.

Part of the payoff from repeatedly participating in the dialogues was an increasing ability to discern nuances in speech that might otherwise have been misunderstood. For example, while the Beit Sahourians spoke fine English, there were translation problems, as there are between any two languages. The Arabic word *haadis,* for example, means both "incident" and "accident." In one session, a Palestinian referred to the shooting of an Israeli as an "accident," which angered us, because we thought that he was denying Palestinian responsibility for it. He probably meant to refer to the "incident." The word *narvaze* means both "angry" and "nervous." Typically, a Palestinian might say, "When Israeli leaders talk that way, it makes me *nervous.*" I remember wondering why the speaker wouldn't be straight with us and say that it makes him *angry.* Why was he beating around the bush? Once, in a dialogue between Fatah teenagers from Ramallah and Peace Now teenagers from Jerusalem, a Jewish youth asked whether the Palestinians supported the intifada. I had to break in and point out that the word *intifada* means something entirely different to the two groups. To the Israelis, it means violence, hurling rocks, throwing us into the sea. But to the Palestinians, it means a mass, united uprising against the occupation. Each group was thinking something different while discussing this.

Similarly, we learned that the noun *moderate* has its own meaning for the Palestinians. We tended to think of all those who supported peace with Israel as moderates. But for them, *moderates* referred to supporters of Fatah, FIDA, and the Communist Party. (FIDA was a new party that broke off from the Democratic Front for the Liberation of Palestine, rejecting the violent struggle.) Many of the most active peace supporters in Beit Sahour supported George Habash's Popular Front for the Liberation of Palestine or Naif Hawatme's Democratic Front, which were considered "radical," and for them it was an insult to be called a "moderate."

From time to time an Israeli from a Jewish settlement in the occupied territories would come to a dialogue session. I was personally in favor of talking with anyone who could speak without being obnoxious, but both the Palestinian organizers and several Israelis objected. Nonetheless, if a settler showed up he was always treated politely by the Palestinians.

One day, Jalal told me that an Israeli from a more radical group had spoken to a meeting in Beit Sahour. Jalal said it was wonderful to listen to him, as he seemed more Palestinian than the Palestinians. But that, said Jalal, was not the point of the dialogues, and it was better to talk with Israelis who presented the Israeli points of view.

Three years into the ongoing dialogue, Ghassan addressed a crowd of some 2,000 Palestinians and several hundred Israelis. He said to the Israelis, "Do you accept coexistence? I believe many of you do. Then we are not your enemies. Your enemy comes from within your society. Your enemy is the one who blocks the way for peace." Veronika and I exchanged looks. This was a very brave statement from a follower of a radical, rejectionist party, pronounced before his own community. While few Israelis probably noticed this significant step in Ghassan's formulation of his own thinking, we two viewed it as extremely conciliatory. But immediately afterward, an old-time Israeli peace activist gave a fiery speech in Arabic, winning the crowd's love, but causing some other Israelis to tell me afterward that they felt that they had been at a PLO demonstration, not at a peace rally.

There was always a certain conflict between our wanting to choreograph the dialogue to make it more attractive and convincing to new participants, and wanting it to be spontaneous and unguided. The styles of talking and behaving, the nuances of slogans, all had an enormous influence on the way people responded. We tried to attract Israelis who would set a certain tone—those who felt a love for their own people, who were still a bit idealistic despite everything; those who could challenge other people's statements without being insulting or condescending; those who had backbone to present their viewpoints, but could listen to others.

As the dialogues progressed, we set up a planning committee that met with the Palestinian leaders to chart our course. In addition to Veronika and me, there was Judith Green, an archaeologist who taught at the Hebrew University and was also one of the leaders of the Orthodox congregation Yedidyah. At various times the planning group included Danny Orstav, an editor on the classical music radio station with a rich background in left-wing politics; Dr. Yitzhak Mendelson, a clinical psychologist who directed a program for families of Holocaust survivors, who led dialogues in Beit Sahour and later in Nablus, and was subsequently seriously wounded by Palestinian terrorists who shot randomly into a coffeehouse in Jerusalem, resuming his peace work after undergoing a series of operations; and Shraga Gorni, the chief engineer of the Physics Department at Hebrew University and a former tank commander. Danny and Shraga both spoke fluent Arabic.

The dialogues were proceeding so well that we decided to expand to public activities that would send the "peaceful message of the intifada" to a wider public. We had learned how important hosting is to Arabs, and how graciously they received us. This was just the opposite of the picture that Israelis had of Palestinians driving us out with rocks. We accordingly designed an action to present a positive message, and sent out an invitation called "A Taste of Peace."

A Taste of Peace

What will it be like when Israel and Palestine live together in peace?

A town in the West Bank invites you to tour sites in what will someday be the Palestinian state, as you would tour sites in Egypt or Cyprus, and taste today the peace of tomorrow.

In addition to the usual tourist attractions, you will meet local Palestinians to discuss our hopes for the future, and be invited to drink coffee in the intimacy of private homes.

Accept this invitation to visit and tour

NOT AS AN OCCUPIER, BUT AS A GUEST.

This idea was really radical, especially as it was announced in the first year of the intifada. We Israelis went around personally to invite both the press and the participants, traveling to their homes and offices since we were afraid that phones might be tapped. Since we were a small, relatively unknown group of Israelis, we were not sure whether important people would accept our invitation. We therefore went to Peace Now, the only really large peace group at that time (with which we all identified) and told them secretly that we were planning this activity. We would be glad for the action to appear under the organization's name if its leaders would give us their sponsorship. This was a good arrangement for both groups, and we continued our association in several other actions as well. Fortunately, no one in our group had political aspirations or cared about personal fame, nor did we have to impress any financial contributors, so we had no problem giving Peace Now the credit. Several activists in our group were also members of Israelis by Choice, a small organization of immigrants opposed to the occupation, and this organization too sponsored many of our activities.

But suddenly our plans had to change. On Friday afternoon before the scheduled activity, Ghassan called to say that we would have to call it off. In a clash in Nablus, a large number of Palestinians had been killed, and all Palestinians were in mourning. The sun was about to set, bringing in the Jewish Sabbath. Veronika and Judith were both observant Jews who could not drive on the Sabbath, so I drove by myself for a meeting with the Palestinians. I knew how difficult it was to organize a group secretly, without using telephones, and I pressed hard not to cancel the action. Finally, we decided to dispense with the tourist activities planned (which were inappropriate for a mourning period) and hold a joint meeting at the Greek Orthodox church, immediately after Sunday mass.

On the morning of Sunday, 18 December 1988, we had about fifty Israelis ready to travel, including Mordechai Bar-On, who had been the chief education officer of the army and a member of the Knesset; M K Ran Cohen, who was a reserve colonel in the paratroops; Rabbi Levi Weiman-Kelman; and Dr. Edy Kaufman, director of the Truman Center for Peace Studies. We drove in a convoy of private cars to the Mar Elias monastery, where Ghassan had said he would send a Palestinian to guide us. Instead, despite the risk of being caught, Ghassan had come himself. Meanwhile, the army had apparently learned of our planned activity, and had closed all the entrances to Beit Sahour, and was also waiting for us in front of the church.

Ghassan led us by a back road that he had learned of only that day. There was a very steep climb up a dirt road, on which Edy's car conked out, and he left it with Palestinians who lived nearby. While waiting for the last cars to make it up the difficult slope, the Israelis from the first cars talked with the enthusiastic Sahourians who lived along the road. We regrouped, and Ghassan led us into the backyard of the church, incredibly without the soldiers noticing us, as they were deployed around the remainder of the church. We walked quickly into the social hall under the church, where about 500 Palestinians awaited us.

It is hard to understand today how rare an experience this was. The Israelis were swallowed up in the Palestinian crowd, and were immediately made to feel at home. The V I Ps from each side sat on a platform. My family had asked me to keep a low profile, since our oldest son, Ariel, was waiting to hear whether he would be accepted to the air force pilots course, so I stayed off the stage. The Palestinians sang their national anthem, "Biladi Biladi" (My Country, My Country), and the Israelis were unsure whether to stand or not. (All national symbols were taboo in the eyes of the Israeli public and authorities, whom we wanted to influence positively.) A group of Palestinian teenagers was chanting in the back of the hall, "PLO—Israel No!" Salaam went back and talked with them, and then the chant changed to "PLO—Occupation No!" The mayor of Beit Sahour called on the *shabab* (young men) not to throw stones on that day, so that none of the guests' cars would be damaged. Someone called this the first truce of the intifada. Everything went better than we could have dreamed: the spirit was fantastic. After the speeches we talked in small groups in the churchyard, until the soldiers spotted us and demanded that we leave immediately, which we were ready to do anyway. The soldiers wrote down the license numbers of our cars, as though we needed to be intimidated.

The next day I called Mordechai Bar-On (what a luxury to use a phone) and thanked him for coming. "Don't thank me," he said. The veteran peace supporter added, "I must thank you. I've never had such a positive experience in all these years."

The action was reported very positively in the press. The only one who suffered was the army commander who had failed to prevent us from getting into the church. I later met one of the reserve soldiers who had served there, who told me that the army had known of our plans two days before the event, and the commander had been reprimanded.

Why did my army work so hard to block us? Why did they oppose Israelis receiving a message of peace from Palestinians? If the idea of a Palestinian state was anathema to our government and army, how did we want the conflict to end?

CHAPTER 10

Beit Sahour III

The Sleepover and the Prayer for Peace

Our group (which was still unnamed) was one of the only peace organizations sponsoring joint Israeli-Palestinian activities at that time, and possibly the only one that did not have an anti-Israeli character. Peace Now has always been divided internally between people who feel that its mandate is to work exclusively within the Israeli community, and those (usually a minority) who feel that the best results come from joint demonstrative activities.

In early 1989, Peace Now tried to hold joint meetings with Palestinians in several villages, but the army prevented them. Finally, the organization went to court and got permission to visit several villages simultaneously. That activity was scheduled for a Saturday, the one day that Israelis did not work (in those days of the six-day work week, before we went over to a five-day work week). But our group included many Jews who did not travel on the Sabbath, and this meant that we would not be able to participate in exactly the kind of activity that we specialized in. We held a planning meeting to discuss this problem.

After our analysis, I hit upon a solution that I was convinced was perfect. We would organize a group of Israelis who would arrive in Beit Sahour on Friday afternoon before sunset (the start of the Jewish Sabbath) and sleep over with Palestinian families, returning home after sundown Saturday night. The army would try to kick us out, but they couldn't force religious Jews to desecrate the Sabbath by riding, and Jerusalem was too far to walk. We would achieve the goal of *neutralizing* the army, not *clashing* with it.

Our many meetings with Palestinians had convinced me that this community could pull off such a plan. The idea would have been unthinkable for virtually any Israeli, but in our group everyone realized immediately that this was a perfect solution. Sleeping in someone's house is putting

oneself completely at his or her mercy, and is therefore a powerful symbol of a relationship between peoples, based on trust, not fear. None of
us doubted for one moment that it would work. Ghassan decided very
wisely to set a different date from that of the Peace Now meetings, so
that we would be free to work things out according to our needs, and also
not split the press coverage. I asked the Palestinians to show us where all
the host homes would be so that we could better picture how the activity
would look, but they said to simply count on them. As with every joint action that we would do, I had a certain preconception of how things would
be—and as usual, my image bore little resemblance to the actual activity
as it would unfold.

Judith ordered kosher food from a caterer, which we would transport
on Friday morning. We began secretly contacting people whom we felt
would be appropriate for the action. Danny and I went to MK Ran Cohen's
home; in his kitchen, Ran made us Arabic coffee while we described the
plan. He never batted an eye. He accepted the idea—and that meant we
weren't crazy. Perhaps the success of our previous activities had given us
the confidence to work with Palestinians. "Wait one minute," he said, and
asked his wife, Orit: "What would you think of our sleeping over, with the
kids, in Beit Sahour?"

"Sounds good," she answered without a moment's hesitation.

We told each participant where to meet, what to bring. We warned
them that under no circumstances should they speak to us on the phone.
If anything had to be discussed, the participant should set up a meeting
with one of us and speak face to face. However, our people were not used to
the conspiratorial life, and several people called and broke phone security
in the most outrageous ways.

We had decided to bring the Israelis in a bus. Through an old friend
from the neighboring village of Sur Bahir, I was directed to a man with a
bus, whose son was in prison for intifada activity, and who would not be
afraid to risk being caught. It was good that he lived close to me, for I had
to go to his home several times to make arrangements, because I didn't
want to risk using the phone.

In almost every activity, something goes wrong and requires or almost
requires cancellation. A couple of days before this action, we met for our
final planning session. Everything was set. But then Ghassan delivered

the mortal blow: a new regulation had just been announced. The governor could now replace any Palestinian's orange ID card with a green one. The green ID meant that its bearer could not cross the Green Line into Jerusalem or any other part of Israel. (In those days there was no closed border; Palestinians were free to drive their cars anywhere.) This meant that the bearer of a green ID card would lose his chance to work in Israel or to travel even to Palestinian areas (such as Ramallah, Nablus, and Gaza) that were reachable only via Israeli territory. Ghassan said, "I can't take the responsibility for causing a Palestinian to lose the chance to work and live reasonably. If we carry out the activity, the governor will find out who was involved, and the danger that he would give them the green IDs is just too great. We have to cancel this activity."

The shock was awful.

For one of the few times in my life, my mouth opened and words came out of their own accord. Without thought or hesitation, I said, "The intifada is over. The governor has won. There's no chance to do anything anymore, because Israel has a super-weapon—the green ID. Let's forget about doing anything. The occupation is here for good."

The words did the trick. Ghassan changed his mind and said that we had to go ahead with the action.

On Friday morning, 24 March 1989, Judith delivered the food and the sleeping bags. An hour before sundown, we boarded the bus. We numbered about seventy Israelis, including several families with children, a couple with a baby in a stroller, and Professor Jeremy Montagu of Oxford University, who came with his Israeli grandchildren. We had three rabbis and several academics, including the philosopher Paul Mendes-Flohr and the political scientist Yaron Ezrahi. We had decided that it would be too risky to drive into Beit Sahour, since soldiers might spot us. So the bus dropped us off at the foot of Jabel Abu-Ghneim, where Israel would later build the very controversial settlement Har Homa. We began climbing Jabel ad-Dik toward the neighborhood of Al-Iskan, where we would be hosted. After we had walked for several minutes, some young people from Al-Iskan met us and led us along a path, helping us to climb over the terraces. A committee assigned us to different homes in the neighborhood, which was slightly physically separated from the main part of Beit Sahour. Our Palestinian friends had picked the perfect place for the sleepover.

Carrying our sleeping bags, we met our hosts, moved into our new homes, and watched the sun set, which meant that it was too late for the army to evict us. We had pulled it off!

I was accompanied by my wife, Anita, and our eleven-year-old daughter, Daphna. I had assumed that Daphna and the other Israeli kids would stick with their parents but might also get to see what Arab children were like. To our surprise, our children were not the least bit shy, but immediately ran off with the Palestinian kids to a playground and had no more need of the adults. One of the outstanding lessons of this activity was the ease with which children can get along together.

The Palestinians had prepared a house in the neighborhood, whose owners were currently in Saudi Arabia, to serve as a synagogue for the religious Jews. We all, Israelis and Palestinians, had a festive Shabbat dinner together. The Palestinian members of the dialogue group had told us that they would not be able to join us because of the danger of being caught, but they could not keep themselves away, and a steady stream of Sahourians kept arriving from the main part of the town at the isolated Al-Iskan, to sit with us and talk away the evening. Finally, we went back to our hosts' homes for the night. Anita, Daphna, and I stayed with Khalil, Hana, and their three smaller children. Their oldest boy, the age of our Ariel, was wanted by the authorities and was in hiding on the opposite hill. From time to time his parents would pull out their binoculars to try to catch sight of him in his hiding place.

The following day, after the religious Jews had finished their prayers, we all walked in the beautiful olive-filled valley, past the upper monastery of St. Saba to the Shepherds' Field where, according to tradition, the shepherds saw the star heralding the birth of Jesus. We were about 200 people in the valley, and more Palestinians joined us at the field, along with members of the press. Several Palestinians and Israelis addressed the crowd. Ran Cohen told how he had grown up in Baghdad, and that once when he was a boy Arabs had organized a pogrom against the Jews. His Arab neighbors smuggled him and his family over the rooftops to save them. Today, he said, it was his turn to try to help save the Palestinians from the occupation. As he spoke, a masked boy climbed the fence in back of Ran and attached a Palestinian flag above the speaker. The Israeli press finally had something salacious to photograph and took the embarrassing picture of a member of Knesset giving a speech under the flag that to Israelis symbolized throwing us into the sea. Ran took it in stride and said that he had no problem with the Palestinian flag in Beit Sahour as long as the Israeli flag flew over Israel.

After the speeches, we were invited to the municipality to meet with the mayor and other dignitaries. We walked up the main street, but were spotted by a group of soldiers in the center of town. Their officer declared Beit Sahour a closed military area and ordered all Israelis and reporters to leave immediately. The press left, but we explained that there were many religious Jews among us and that we could not travel on the Sabbath. They didn't know what to do, so they called for Brigadier General Gabby Ophir to come. In the meantime, some of us went into the municipal building, where the important people were waiting for us. Several officers insisted on entering also; they sat down with their rifles on their laps, looking uncomfortable but determined. It wasn't clear to me whether they thought they were protecting us from terrorists, or whether they were preventing us from signing a treaty to dismember the State of Israel. In the end, Ran convinced Gabby that there was no way to get rid of us. The Palestinians put on a show of *debka* dancing for us. The chicken for lunch had spoiled, so we made do with the salad, and then we went back to our host families. Everyone was tired. We rested while we waited for the sun to slowly, slowly set and release us to go back to our homes after an unforgettable experience.

While we were waiting for the bus, Ran Cohen told me that he had to rush back to Jerusalem to repair the damage that the photographs of him speaking under a Palestinian flag—forbidden in those days—would do. His political foes would definitely try to take advantage of the situation. The Palestinians, living under occupation, had cheered the masked boy who had clambered up the fence to place their flag. He was certainly risking arrest for such an act. So this was an example of how difficult it was to find symbols that could be understood positively by both peoples. The incident of the flag would be remembered years later and would cause a proposed march in Nablus to be called off (described below). Many years later, when it was no longer illegal to fly the Palestinian flag, I tried my best to get agreement that in the annual Beit Sahour Christmas March for Peace and Freedom, Palestinians would march with their national

flag and we Israelis would march with ours—illustrating that we each
supported the other's claims to nationhood. But this was unacceptable
to their leadership: the occupiers' flag would no longer fly over their
community.

That evening, the news reported on the violence raging throughout the
occupied areas, while in one place, Beit Sahour, Israelis had spent Shabbat
as guests of Palestinians. This enormously successful activity reaffirmed
for me that if we could only neutralize the army as a destructive force, Palestinians and Israelis could work out activities that were positive for the
participants and that could project the peaceful message of the intifada.

Our group was innovative in producing unique actions. A busload
of Palestinians from Beit Sahour, with children, visited Congregation
Yedidyah to participate in a *kiddush* (a reception following the Sabbath
morning prayers), with the kids off playing together as usual. A panel of
Palestinians and Israelis answered questions during an advertised evening
at the Windmill Hotel in Jerusalem. MK Dedi Zucker appeared (twice)
on panels before large audiences in Beit Sahour, as did Professor Irwin
Cotler and attorney Mona Rishmawi on questions of international law.
Professor Elihu Katz analyzed survey data concerning Israeli public opinion. When Shmuel Toledano, who had been for many years the prime
minister's advisor on Israeli Arabs, developed a peace plan, he presented
it to a mixed Palestinian-Israeli group in Beit Sahour. All such activities
were extremely rare, if not unique, under the occupation and especially
during the First Intifada.

One of the most famous campaigns of the intifada was the tax revolt
in Beit Sahour. The people of that town refused to pay taxes to the occupation authorities. There was a long history to this campaign, but finally
Defense Minister Yitzhak Rabin (who was brutally anti-Palestinian in
those days) announced that he would defeat it. He embarked on a forty-
two-day siege and punishment of the town. No food or medicine was allowed into Beit Sahour, nor were residents allowed to leave. Tax collectors
went through stores, factories, and private homes, confiscating whatever
they could find. Soldiers beat people and dumped food from the kitchen
onto the floor. About 150 residents were arrested. All telephone service
was disconnected. The people refused to break, even though they were
suffering intensely. Fortunately, the world was shocked by daily reports of

the repression of this nonviolent form of protest, and finally Israel called off the siege. The Sahourians had won.

The tax revolt had been a Palestinian struggle. We Israelis provided a little support, especially in helping to get the news out. But when success was imminent, we met together to plan a large joint action. The town was still under occupation, even though the round-the-clock siege had been lifted. How could we find a safe place for our activity, one where the soldiers would not be able to break it up? We decided that the safest place was a church (even though in the past soldiers had on occasion entered churches). Instead of a secret political rally condemning the occupation, we would plan a Prayer for Peace event with an open invitation to all. Two of our most active members, Ghassan and Salaam, were in prison, but we carried on without them. International organizations wired their support, and Pulitzer Prize–winning columnist Anthony Lewis interviewed me by phone and ran a story in the *New York Times* about the tax revolt, mentioning our upcoming prayer. We also posted the invitation in the Israeli press.

With so much publicity about the Prayer for Peace, I couldn't believe that the army would try to block us. But Veronika, who was wiser than I on these matters, insisted that a group of us sleep over the night before in Beit Sahour, just in case. The next morning, Sunday, 5 November 1989, paratroopers were on all the rooftops around the church. The army declared Beit Sahour a closed military area and stopped the busloads of Israeli participants. (For some reason, the local and international press never fought against the military's right to exclude them from any embarrassing happening by declaring a closed military area. Not one journalist attended the prayer.) We had prepared a contingency action, and our people read Jewish, Muslim, and Christian prayers at the barricade. The army allowed only non-Jews to pass through the roadblock, and some Christian ministers refused to pass if Jews could not go as well. The highest Muslim cleric, the mufti of Jerusalem, was initially blocked by the army, until a reporter pointed out who he was. He received overwhelming applause from the Christian Palestinians. The Roman Catholic patriarch's mother had died the previous day, but his assistant was there. The Greek Catholic and Anglican archbishops attended as well. Former U.S. president Jimmy Carter sent a message with his representative. The parish priest gave a talk, part of it in Hebrew for the Israelis present. Despite the roadblock, there were more than a thousand participants.

We had planned a musical duet of the church organist and an Israeli flutist. Psychologist Yitzhak Mendelson brought the flutist Sunday morning, but soldiers stopped them at the roadblock. Yitzhak left his car and led her through the fields on foot, so the flutist made it, and the duet took place as planned.

I had prepared a speech designed to be balanced for the Palestinian audience and for the Israelis who would see it on TV. But when I realized that not a single journalist had troubled to come (they all got their story at the roadblock and went home), I threw out the speech and spoke extemporaneously, asking why my government was so concerned with blocking Israelis from hearing the Palestinians' message of peace. A minister from the Middle East Council of Churches recorded the activity on his home video camera, and he gave me a copy for the TV stations. Although exhausted from the tension, I rushed back to Jerusalem to try to interest the TV stations in what was an unbelievable story. But Israel TV told me that its technicians would go out on strike if the station showed footage that they had not filmed. I then went to an American network, where the first question was, "Is there any violence in it?" They took the film anyway, but presented the Prayer for Peace in their news broadcast as though it were another Palestinian confrontation, and not an attempt at reconciliation.

Despite our losing the Israelis and the press at the roadblock, we had been correct in assuming that holding our political action in a church would neutralize the army. They made no attempt to keep people out of the church, no soldiers entered, nor did they beat the people as they left. Once again we saw that when the army was neutralized, Palestinians and Israelis could work together effectively for peace.

One of the greatest rewards of my work in Beit Sahour was my friendship with Jalal. Each of us was the oldest in his group, and each had grown up in the shadow of a much-loved and successful father. Jalal had been a teacher under the Jordanians, but his activity in a teachers strike had led to his termination. Like most of the Palestinians in our group, he was unemployed during the intifada, which was ironically advantageous for me, because every Saturday morning (normally a workday in the Arab sector) I could jog over to his home, where we'd sit on his veranda sipping Arabic coffee and talking. Jalal had deep roots in Arab culture, and was never short of interesting stories. He was often called on to arrange *sulhas* (a traditional process for resolving conflicts between people or clans), and he would explain to me how these customs worked. We were guests at his daughter's engagement, and he brought his family to our Passover *seder.*

One of the worst times for me was when Jalal was arrested. He had chronic lower back pain, and had had all his teeth pulled recently, and I could imagine how painful it must have been for him in the tent prison in the desert at Ketziot. A wonderful lawyer, Tamar Peleg, worked hard for Jalal and finally one day she called me: "The legal officer has told me that Jalal will be released today. But don't tell his family. My experience is that they don't always follow through on these promises. Go by yourself to bring him home, so his family will not be crushed if he doesn't get out."

I drove to Shoket Junction, which is in the middle of nowhere in the northeast Negev desert. There was a wide open space with some trees for shade, with lots of Arab cars (old models) parked there. I waited among the Arab families waiting for their sons to be released. It was strange to them that a Jew would be waiting to receive a Palestinian prisoner. Someone gave me grapes to eat, and someone else brought me cookies. I hadn't thought to bring Jalal food. I wasn't used to these moments.

Finally, a bus arrived with the prisoners. Soldiers made the prisoners line up, and then removed the plastic one-use handcuffs. Suddenly, the prisoners were free. My friend was one of the last to get off, older than most, older than when I'd seen him last, tired, wearing a beard. We fell into each other's arms. He had never expected to see me there.

For prisoners who are not met by anyone, there is no arrangement for getting home. Because we had my car, Jalal was able to give a ride to three fellow prisoners who, like him, needed to get home to the West Bank. My car had the yellow license plates of Israeli cars, and we were stoned going through Halhoul, but no one was hurt. We dropped off each man at a different village, and then finally pulled into Jalal's street in Beit Sahour. "I'll wait in the car while you greet your family," I said.

Asma and the boys saw my car, then saw a bearded man approaching them from the darkness, and they assumed that he was I. Only when he reached the light from the veranda did they recognize Jalal, and it was a pleasure to see their joy.

Jalal was not embittered despite the difficult conditions in prison. He spoke about the camaraderie, how he had met Palestinians from all over, and how they had organized courses for the prisoners.

Once I jogged to Ghassan's house, which was a little past Jalal's. As I turned a corner, I saw a pile of tires waiting to be set on fire and a group of several masked youths. I was startled at the unexpected sight. Not knowing what to do, I waved at them. I was wearing a T-shirt that stated, in three languages, "We Want Peace." They waved back, and I kept on running. As I passed I could see by their eyes that they were only ten to fifteen years old. And then I saw women peeking out from the nearby store, perhaps their mothers, watching as their young heroes fired up the tires, which would summon the armed soldiers to join them in knightly combat.

Another time, I stopped at Elias Rishmawi's pharmacy in the center of Beit Sahour. His mother, Emily, introduced me to a young man who was buying some medicine. He had recently finished at the top of his class in the Talitha Kumi high school, one of the best schools in the Bethlehem area. I asked what his plans were now.

"I wanted to study at the university in Jordan. I went to the Civil Administration to get a permit to go abroad. They sent me to the Shabak. 'Captain Tony' [Shabak officers always use pseudonyms] told me it was no problem. 'You help us a little, and we'll help you.' They wanted me to collaborate. Nothing serious. A little information. I know how they work. Something harmless, like who were the guys that attended George's birthday party. Once I tell them, they can blackmail me to keep me working for them. And when they interrogate someone who was at the party, and they show him that they know everything about him, even that he was at George's birthday party, it will be easier to break him. I refused to collaborate. After a few months I went back and asked for a permit, but it was the same answer. So I won't study in Jordan this year. Maybe next year."

For an agency fighting terrorism, it may be proper to use various tricks to learn about possible secret cells. But when it leads to totalitarian control over people's most reasonable needs, like their desire to study at the university, and when gathering intelligence is more important than allowing the populace to live normal lives, something has gone wrong.

CHAPTER 11

Beit Sahour IV

Out from the Underground

Veronika and Judith went to the desert prison at Ketziot to serve as character witnesses for Ghassan and Salaam, who were imprisoned administratively. This meant that they had been confined without being charged or put on trial, the cases against them based solely on secret reports from the Shabak. Veronika and Judith succeeded in getting their imprisonments shortened, and finally all our Palestinian organizers were free.

A short time later at a planning meeting, the Palestinians told us that they wanted to end the secrecy of our activities and to emerge from the underground. They wished to operate as an open organization with an office in Beit Sahour, with a sign out front. Although it took us by surprise, we Israelis were very pleased by this decision. We agreed with them that the chances of their being arrested were not too great, and in any event the authorities pretty well knew who the Palestinian leaders were.

In order not to be closed down by the authorities, they got the Mennonite Central Committee, a Christian organization recognized by the authorities, to sponsor them. While we would have preferred a single joint Palestinian-Israeli organization, they chose to organize in parallel: they became the Palestinian Center for Rapprochement between People (in the West Bank) and we formed the Rapprochement Dialogue Center (in Israel). They were more successful than we were in getting registered; the registrar of nonprofit societies in the Israeli Interior Ministry refused to register us, and we needed the help of the Association for Civil Rights in Israel, which went to court on our behalf. After a long wait, on the day before our court hearing, we were finally registered.

We wanted to stage a really large peace demonstration, but of course that was illegal and would be blocked by the army. We therefore again decided to employ religion to protect us by neutralizing the army. Christmas was coming up, and the Shepherds' Field in Beit Sahour is a holy site. The

Palestinians told us that prior to the intifada, the people of Beit Sahour had always assembled there to light candles on Christmas afternoon. We decided to restore this tradition, but with the addition of a new dimension. Jalal gave us our slogan: "Light a candle for peace and freedom."

We decided to place an invitation in an Israeli newspaper. Jalal, who was executive director of the Palestinian Rapprochement, said that he would sign his name to the invitation. His friends burst out laughing, saying, "Jalal wants to go back to prison." After all, demonstrations for any purpose were illegal. But he believed he would not be arrested, and he was willing to take the chance—the invitation to Israelis would bear his name, which was befitting.

Once again I had no idea how this action would turn out. At 4:00 PM on Christmas Day 1991, busloads of Israelis arrived. Next to Shepherds' Field was a bonfire, with an enormous crowd of Palestinians. We lit torches from the bonfire and began to march up the main street. The Palestinians had prepared signs in Arabic, Hebrew, and English, with slogans appropriate for both peoples. The scouts' pipe and drum band led the way for some 2,000 marchers, who lit the darkness with their torches.

The Israelis were warmly received by the Palestinians, and mingled freely with them. One unexpected benefit was a brisk wind that kept extinguishing the torches. Many of the nonsmoking Israelis turned to Palestinians to relight their torches, thus breaking the ice and leading to conversations. We then marched to the Greek Catholic church for a series of speeches.

The army was sensible enough to stay away, only leaving one border police jeep parked a little beyond our march to keep an eye on what was happening. When we finally broke up and started walking to our buses, the border police arrested two young Palestinian boys. I had no idea of the policemen's motive—whether they were simply being mean and showing that they ran the place, or whether the boys had been caught doing something. I had wanted the evening to pass without confrontation with the army, and would have ignored this incident, but a large group of Israelis descended on the border policemen, lashing out at them verbally. The police released the boys, giving credence to the probability that the boys had done nothing. I realized that the Israelis had been right to intervene with the policemen, even though none of us knew what had happened.

The tradition of a joint Palestinian-Israeli peace march on Christmas was established and was observed annually for several years, with the exception of one year when outside circumstances forced its cancellation. The Israeli press consistently ignored these peace marches, even though several thousand people participated.

Perhaps the toughest time for the dialogues occurred when Saddam Hussein invaded Kuwait (2 August 1990). The Palestinians had no sympathy for the corrupt Kuwaiti regime, and opposed Western attacks on Iraq. We Israelis, by contrast, viewed Saddam as a criminal who was also a threat to Israel. The dialogues were bitter. The Israeli peace camp saw our erstwhile Palestinian partners turning to our enemy with the hope that he would flatten us. Yossi Sarid, a leader of the civil rights movement, said that from now on the Palestinians could seek him out—he would no longer initiate contact. Despite the anger, we managed to keep the dialogues going, and unlike other existing groups, we didn't allow the Gulf War to put an end to our contacts. For some of us who empathized with Palestinian suffering, it was even possible to understand some Palestinians' happiness at seeing Arab missiles cause us hysterical fear.

The Gulf War (which ended 28 February 1991) was followed by the Madrid peace talks (which began on 30 October 1991) and later the Oslo Accords (1993). The Sahourians, who had presented a united front during the intifada, now began to fight among themselves; they were divided between those who supported the peace process (supporters of Fatah and, later, FIDA) and those who wanted different approaches toward peace (supporters of the Popular Front and the Democratic Front for the Liberation of Palestine). Gradually the supporters of the peace process began to drop out of the divisive meetings. Also, with the intifada fading out, people began returning to normal life, trying to rebuild their economic situations, going back to work, and investing time in family life. Worst of all—from my point of view!—Jalal got a job, which kept him busy on Saturdays, the day I had regularly visited him. For Palestinians generally, there was less energy to expend in peace activities.

When the Oslo Accords were announced, I was sure that they would end the occupation. I had been witness to the army's blocking of the Palestinians' peaceful message. Now, Palestinians would be running their own cities, without IDF interference. It seemed that nothing would be able to stop them from presenting themselves as they wished to. The decades of their frightening Israelis into rigid rejectionism could be reversed, and my people could be soothed into accepting the idea that peace was worth trying.

I was amazed to find that, finally given the chance to present a positive image to the Israelis (who held the key to their freedom), Palestinian grassroots groups completely ignored this opportunity. Peace activities became the exclusive province of governments, which achieved more in a few short months than the peace camp had been able to do in years. Palestinian priorities shifted, and Oslo essentially brought an end, at least in Beit Sahour, to the type of dialogue and joint activities that I had come to believe in during the First Intifada.

The dialogue in Beit Sahour did continue nonstop until the second, violent uprising in 2000. Ghassan succeeded in forging a large group of Palestinians in their twenties to participate in various activities, including dialogues with Israelis. But the original drive had diminished significantly, and from my perspective the group seemed content to drift without strategic design or goals.

CHAPTER 12

Jabel Mukabber

Several days after I was released from prison in 1988, I received a phone call at home from an Israeli whom I didn't know. He told me he was visiting a Palestinian friend who wanted to talk to me. He then put his friend, Jamil Salhut, on the phone.

Jamil told me that he was a neighbor of mine, from the nearby Arab village of Jabel Mukabber (which was annexed to Jerusalem in 1967). He had read about my experience in Ramallah. He wanted his little son to meet me, because up until then the only Israelis his son had met were border policemen who had frightened him. I gave him directions to my house, and they came right over. Jamil's little son, Kais, watched me with big eyes as we all had coffee and cookies. We talked about Israelis and Palestinians, about Jerusalem, and about my military service in Ramallah. I told Jamil about our dialogues in Jericho and Beit Sahour. He was interested in starting a similar dialogue in his village.

Jabel Mukabber is located behind Government House, which today is the United Nations headquarters in Jerusalem. It is directly next to East Talpiyot, which was built mostly on land expropriated from the villagers of Jabel Mukabber and Sur Bahir. As with most of the land in the expanded Jerusalem that was expropriated from Arabs, land was cheap for the Jewish contractors and East Talpiyot's apartments were sold at bargain prices, as they were designed for low-income families. These tended also to be families with strong anti-Arab feelings. Several streets were built for middle-class families, some of whom were more liberal in their attitudes. It was natural to match Jabel Mukabber with the people of East Talpiyot because of proximity. One possible subject for discussion could be the issue of reconciliation between those whose land was expropriated and those who lived on the expropriated land, adding spice to the relationship.

I visited Jamil, who was a teacher and a writer, in his home to try to set up the process. When he was five years old, another kid had thrown a rock at him and Jamil had lost an eye. He was called the "red sheikh" by his neighbors, because as a boy he had studied Islam and achieved the rank of sheikh, but later had abandoned religion and joined the Communist Party. His wife, Halima, was also a writer, having published a book of Bedouin stories she had learned from her grandmother. Halima had an inner quiet, a patience, a long view of life. Unlike most Muslim wives, she would often join us when we would sit and talk. Jamil, with his communist connections, had supported peace with Israel for a long time. We agreed that each of us would bring several people to start a dialogue.

I tried to find Israelis who had not been part of the Beit Sahour dialogues, in order to expand the circle of Israeli participants. I found several liberal Jews who lived close by. One family I turned to was that of Rabbi Benjy Segal and his wife, Judy, whom I had read about in the newspaper. They lived on a street of "cottages" (i.e., townhouses with little gardens) that bordered on the village of Jabel Mukabber, and they had recently (this was during the First Intifada) had rocks thrown through their living room window. I felt that it was good to have people who would present facts from a different point of view. I described the dialogue group that we were starting, and they consented to take part. They said that they had never been in the village, and would welcome an opportunity to meet its residents in more favorable circumstances than when they'd had their windows smashed.

At the appointed hour, some Arab youths met us at the border between the Jewish neighborhood and the village and led us to Jamil's house. It was only a 500-meter walk to his house, yet the Israelis commented that it had seemed like the end of the world before, and they had not believed that they could be safe walking in Jabel Mukabber.

Jamil brought several of his neighbors: an electrician, some builders, a lawyer, and a journalist. The Israelis were put at their ease, and we began talking quite easily. At one point an Israeli referred to the problem of youths from the village throwing rocks at Israeli homes. Jamil glossed over this in the very polite Arab fashion, explaining that the stories in the press were misleading, the children were throwing stones at the police, and a stone had missed its goal. However, Judy Segal spoke up and said that the home that was hit was *her* house, and the kids had definitely been aiming at her window. Jamil accepted her correction, and the dialogue went on without any problem. I was pleased by this exchange, because I felt that it pointed out to everyone that it is possible to be open and honest in talking, and even unpleasant facts do not have to be hidden. When there is goodwill among participants, the dialogue can tolerate some unpleasantness.

We were fortunate that Jamil was a leader in his community and an active nationalist in East Jerusalem political circles. He also understood us Israelis well enough to know how to talk with us. Our problem was to find Israeli leadership for this new dialogue. I wanted the group to become self-sufficient, without needing help from Veronika, Judith, or me. At about this time we were trying to start other new groups in new communities. Judith formed a dialogue in her own neighborhood of Abu-Tor, one side of which is Jewish and the other side Palestinian. Veronika was working with the family of one of her music students in the Christian Quarter of the Old City. Unfortunately, it was hard to find Israelis with enough free time, commitment, leadership ability, and genuine interest in dialogue to take over the leadership of the Israeli side.

After several successful dialogues, we spoke to Jamil about organizing an activity that would carry our message, via the press, to a larger audience. He was pleased to try this. I had told Veronika about my idea, from Jericho, to write "We Want Peace" on Palestinian homes. Veronika improved the slogan to state "We Want Peace between a Free Palestine and a Secure Israel," utilizing the chief goal of each people. We asked Jamil whether residents of his village would be willing to put up such signs. He assured us that they would. We therefore worked out an action in which we would start at the *mukhtar*'s house for some speeches, and then would walk from house to house, giving the people stickers with the slogan to paste on their entrances. We asked Peace Now if it would sponsor the activity under its aegis, which was accepted, and Professor Galia Golan agreed to speak for the Israelis.

The action took place on 23 January 1989. In our press release, we said simply that a Palestinian community thirty minutes from Jerusalem was inviting us to meet each other. This tactic was meant to throw off the police, so that they could not close off the area. The Israelis met at the Liberty Bell Park parking lot. Just as we were about to leave, a police van pulled up, and an officer asked where we were going. I was startled by this unexpected appearance, and was not sure which lie to tell, but the Peace Now spokesman, Professor Amiram Goldblum, simply told the truth, "We're going to Jabel Mukabber." The policeman thanked him and drove off. I was sure that they would stop us, but it may have been that the policeman was simply curious and had no real interest in us. Because Jabel Mukabber is in the expanded Jerusalem, Israeli law applies there, unlike Jericho and Beit Sahour in which occupation regulations, which deny all civil rights, apply (and where General Amram Mitzna had forbidden Peace Now to demonstrate). In any event, there was no police presence or interference. At the *mukhtar*'s house we saw more TV crews than I have ever seen at any of our other activities. Two photographers almost got into a fight over the only remaining parking spot. Kids from the village held up our stickers and smiled the most photogenic grins you could imagine; the cameramen were having a great time. Galia and the *mukhtar* gave speeches short enough not to bore anyone, as did MKs Ran Cohen and Haim "Jumas" Oron. Other celebrities included Assad Al-Assad (head of the Palestinian Writers Association), Professors Uriel Simon and Michael Ardon, and the politically active Moshe Amirav. This was the first joint activity in Jerusalem since the intifada had reached the "united" city.

After the speeches we all sat, Bedouin style, on mattresses spread on the floor next to the walls in the *mukhtar*'s large sitting room, where we drank coffee together. We then got to the part that Veronika and I were waiting for, when we would walk from house to house to see if people would, in fact, display the stickers for peace on their homes. Several Israelis from the dialogue group were ready with the stickers, but suddenly all the Palestinians were worn out and left us to our own resources. One of the Palestinians, the journalist Mohammed Sbeh, saw that everyone had disappeared, and stayed with us. We went from house to house, in the light winter drizzle, and Mohammed asked each homeowner if it was all right to put the sticker on his gate. One woman said she didn't like stickers, but everyone else accepted them. But this part of the action, which had seemed to us the most important, which put the villagers' acceptance of peace with Israel to the test, did not interest any of the press, and we made our rounds alone.

As we wended our way slowly from house to house, we noticed a border police command car about fifty meters behind us, driving slowly in pace with us. We wondered what they were planning to do. I said I thought that they were concerned for our safety. We walked over to them, Veronika gave them a sticker, and I told them that there was no need to protect us, as we were with a resident of the village. They smiled and drove off, but parked where they could keep an eye on us. I think it was impossible for them to accept the notion that we were perfectly safe in this intifada-supporting village.

The next day we went back to the village to see the display of stickers. We thought perhaps to add more stickers and invite the press to see them personally. But there was not a single sticker on any house. We asked our Palestinian friends why the people had removed them. They replied that kids had gone around collecting them for souvenirs. We were not completely sure where the truth lay, but decided that the next time we tried such an activity, we would place the stickers higher up where kids couldn't reach them.

Now that we had succeeded in transmitting the message "We Want Peace" in Jerusalem, we thought we would repeat it in the occupied territories. We showed a sign saying "We Want Peace between a Free Palestine and a Secure Israel" to Ghassan in Beit Sahour. He thought about the slogan for a while, and finally replied, "Why should only Israel have security? Don't Palestinians need security too? We won't put it up in Beit Sahour if it is written like that." So we changed the slogan to "We Want Peace between Palestine and Israel, Each Free and Secure." Everyone was happy, and our sticker went up on the door of the Rapprochement Center in Beit Sahour. But for various reasons which I never understood, the sticker action was never implemented in Beit Sahour. It would wait for another dialogue group, in the refugee camp of Dehaisheh, as we will soon see.

The Jabel Mukabber group flourished for a while. When Peace Now finally was able to arrange visits to Palestinian villages throughout the West Bank on a Saturday, Jabel Mukabber organized several homes for observant Jews to visit (the village was within walking distance for many Orthodox Jews, who couldn't travel on the Sabbath). Unfortunately, at least one of the hosts was uncompromising in his nationalist views, and turned off some Israelis. Nevertheless, the fact that even such an extremist was prepared to host Israelis in his home in the midst of the intifada was an important message for us.

One night at midnight I received a phone call from Jamil. That afternoon, youths had burned tires and clashed with the police. At night, the police returned and began hauling the men out of many of the village's homes, taking them to a large fenced-in yard and beating them. Even our friend Mohammed Sbeh had been taken. I ran to the holding place, but before I could enter, a policeman demanded to see my identification. Instead of showing him my regular ID card, I showed him my identification as a special policeman in the civil guard. I demanded to see where my friend was being held. The policeman lied and said it was a closed military area, and it was forbidden for me to go there. Still, I managed to get close enough to see rows of Palestinians sitting on the ground, with their hands behind their necks, just like prisoners of war. The policeman prevented me from getting closer, so I shouted, "Mohammed, it's Hillel. What are they doing to you?" I knew he couldn't answer me, but I wanted the border policemen to know that there was an Israeli around, so they might hesitate to keep on beating them. Veronika and Professor Shlomo Elbaz arrived with a few reporters, and my son Noam drove up in our car. And I did learn later that from the time we arrived, the beatings stopped.

The Palestinians were finally released, and we went home. There was an article about this event in the next day's *Jerusalem Post*. Later, I read an article in which a Palestinian criticized dialogues for being just a lot of talk, but he cited the incident of our intervention to help a colleague as something of true value.

The next day Jamil took me to see two brothers, in their forties, who had been beaten by the border police in their home. One policeman would hold a Palestinian's arm extended, while a second policeman would give him a tremendous whack on the forearm with his club. Both brothers had been to the hospital and had plaster casts on their arms. They showed me their X-rays, with identical fractures across their forearms.

The dialogue sessions in Jabel Mukabber lacked sufficient Israeli leadership, and when the lone Israeli leader left Jerusalem, the group fell apart. But Jamil and Halima remained good friends of mine, and I was always happy to see them when the occasion arose.

CHAPTER 13

Runners for Peace

As a boy I had not participated in sports. In the 1970s, jogging had become a popular adult exercise. One evening on television, the chief of staff of the army, General Raphael Eitan, called on all reserve soldiers to improve their physical fitness between calls to duty. So I began to jog to and from work, and gradually built up to being able to run the marathon several times. At some point, it occurred to me that it might be possible to combine these two interests: working for peace and jogging. It was illegal for Palestinians to demonstrate in the occupied territories, but if they had a message of peace to get across, why not run with it written on their chests? Why not organize Jewish and Arab runners to jog together, both to meet each other and to proclaim a joint message of peace?

A Palestinian friend introduced me to Samir Hazboun, a professor of economics at Birzeit University, who lived in Bethlehem and whose brother was a leader of the Communist Party there. Samir liked the idea, and said he would talk to some athletes from Bethlehem. For my part, I was concerned about getting some international support in case the Palestinians were arrested, so I talked with the heads of public relations at *Runner's World,* a large American running magazine, and they agreed to sponsor us and run a story about us. They donated T-shirts with the magazine's name printed across the top, which I hoped would help deter the army from stopping us. We printed our slogan from Jericho and Beit Sahour—"We Want Peace between Palestine and Israel, Each Free and Secure"—on the shirts in Hebrew, Arabic, and English, in the colors of our two flags.

I met several times with Samir in his home on Manger Street, near the Church of the Nativity, to plan everything. Finally, in September 1989, we organized our first run. I brought several Israelis who liked the idea, and Samir brought a few members of the Bethlehem soccer team. We met at the Star Hotel, whose owner was a friend of the group. We sat for a bit in the lobby, chatting with those Palestinians who spoke English or Hebrew, and drank soft drinks together. Each of us was given a mother-of-pearl dove as a present. Then we donned our shirts, and went into the street. We jogged together up and down the main streets of Bethlehem for about twenty minutes. Palestinian bystanders were startled to see the mixed group, but when they read the slogan they expressed their support and waved to us. Things were going better than I had hoped. The runners were all friendly and outgoing, and we actually enjoyed the activity (in contrast to standing in a demonstration, which is usually boring). The one mistake I had made was that I'd printed the shirts on the chest only, whereas most people didn't notice us until we had passed by. Before our next meeting, I took the shirts to have the slogan printed on the backs as well.

The next week we met again, chatted at the Star Hotel, and then ran again, to the approval of the people in the streets. When we got back to the hotel, however, one of the Palestinians pointed out a problem. When we had passed soldiers stationed on the roofs of buildings, we had waved to them and even called out to them in Hebrew. This was a problem, he said, for the soldiers are oppressing the people. But, we replied, these soldiers are our brothers and our children, and we can't pass by as though we are their enemies. We noted this as a problem to be recognized, but did not yet have an answer.

I met again with Samir, and suggested that since things were going so well, we should invite the local press to the next run. We agreed that the activity would be a true, ongoing running club, and not just a publicity stunt, yet it was a high-priority goal to get our message to a mass audience. I felt that inviting the three local West Jerusalem Israeli papers and the East Jerusalem Palestinian papers would be a good start. In time, as we got stronger, we could invite the national papers and television stations. Samir agreed. We named the club Runners for Peace.

The next week, I came with four Israelis. We drove to the house of the Palestinian runner who lived on the main road, who was supposed to take us to the Star Hotel. We pulled up to his house, trying not to be noticed by soldiers, but he didn't come out. I went over and asked for him, but everyone in the house was excited, and finally I understood that he had been arrested that day. I was concerned for him, but also wasn't sure how to find the hotel, and didn't really want to drive around excessively with Israeli license plates in Arab Bethlehem. Fortunately, I got us to the hotel, but before we could park, the manager came out, agitated, and said there was a problem, and we should not sit in the lobby. I noticed there was a broken window in the hotel. My plan had been for the runners to sit together and chat, and I would drive back to meet the journalists, who were to be waiting shortly at the entrance to Bethlehem. I gave the runners the shirts to put on, but as they were donning them in the street, somebody snatched away the bag with the extra shirts. I noticed soldiers on the roofs around the hotel. I left the runners to manage as best they could, and drove back to get the journalists. When we returned, everyone was eager to get started.

The photographers moved to the bottom of the street, complaining that the sun was already setting, and that in another couple of minutes there wouldn't be enough light to take good pictures. We jogged toward them, then went back and did it a second time for more photos. The photographers were now finished, so we started our run into Bethlehem with a couple of reporters jogging along and interviewing us on the fly. Things were finally settling down, and I was beginning to enjoy the run, when all of a sudden two army jeeps pulled up in front of us, officers jumped out, and a large colonel told us we couldn't run in Bethlehem. Ben Lynfield of *In Jerusalem* (the *Jerusalem Post*'s local supplement) asked his name, but he refused to give it and ordered Ben to stop writing. When Ben continued to write, the colonel began pushing him into a jeep to arrest him. Tension was high. I was concerned about Ben being arrested, and forced my way into the jeep, but the colonel pushed me out, saying *he* would decide who was to be arrested. Getting involved in an Israeli reporter's arrest was my mistake, for my real concern should have been for the Palestinian runners, who had no idea what was in store for them. One of our runners was a prominent civil liberties lawyer, Avraham Gal, and he intervened. We had to get back to the hotel, but the colonel refused to let us wear our shirts. Finally, Gal told us to turn the shirts inside out to hide the slogans, and we all walked back to the hotel, with the jeeps following us. When we reached a turn in the road, a Palestinian runner (who was concerned that the soldiers would arrest him as soon as the Israelis left) pulled me aside and told me to walk away with him; as soon as the soldiers couldn't see him, he bolted down a side street to get away. Fortunately, the Palestinians were neither arrested nor beaten. But back at the cars, I saw that my rear windshield had been shattered with a rock. As far as I can understand what happened that day, there had been a fight between communist Palestinians and those from another group. The army had also decided to clamp down on our activity.

Everyone was upset. However, the photo story came out fine, projecting our message. Samir said we should wait a bit before continuing. We waited and waited. After several weeks, I asked Samir whether the Palestinian runners wanted to continue, and he replied that the circumstances made it too dangerous. This was a setback.

Our runner-lawyer, Avraham Gal, wrote to the military governor of Bethlehem, but received no reply. I wrote to the military commander of the area, Colonel Danny Ze'evi (who turned out to be the officer who had stopped us and had refused to identify himself). He replied that in his judgment our runs put us into physical danger and therefore he required that we coordinate each run with him, and that in any event the runs could not take on a political character nor be accompanied by slogans, printed shirts, or the press. We could not accept these limitations, so we turned to the Association for Civil Rights in Israel, which began preparations to attack the limitations in the courts.

Around the same time, my friend Malik told me about a young Palestinian money-changer from Bethlehem who was well liked by an Israeli friend of hers who was a right-winger. The Palestinian, who was very outgoing and knew how to talk to Israelis of all persuasions, was interested in hearing about our dialogues. I met Walid Abu-Sroor and immediately liked him. He was a refugee living in the Aideh refugee camp behind Rachel's Tomb in Bethlehem. He offered to start a dialogue there, but first we needed approval from the leaders of the camp.

At the appointed time, I brought several Israeli friends and we drove with Walid along a run-down dirt road up to a huge wooden gate in a stone wall. They opened the gate and we drove the car into what looked to me like a fairyland—an old stone house, antique cars, and a lovely olive grove. We got out of the car. Walid told us to wait on the dirt road, and then walked away from us toward the refugee camp. We waited alone, unsure of what was about to happen. A few minutes later, a group of Palestinians appeared, walking toward us slowly and deliberately, as though in a procession. The leader was perhaps in his thirties, a solidly built man in a long *jalabiyye* and *aba'* (Bedouin cloak). Walid and several other men came with him. They greeted us formally, then brought out Arabic coffee, and we all sat and drank. The leader, Abu-Nasser, told us that the idea for a dialogue had been approved, and Walid would organize it from the Palestinian side. They took us for a walk around the camp. There was a channel in the middle of the road for the sewage to run down. The houses were built of simple, unpainted, gray concrete. My Israeli friends would comment on the drive home about how depressing the camp was, yet for me Aideh was always a beautiful place, with the houses huddled together, filled with neighbors interacting with each other.

We went back to the stone house where the car was parked. The owner, Abu-Salim, would be our host many times. An old man, a Christian Palestinian, he had a dent in his skull from a beating. His hobby had been collecting old cars, including a Morris Minor from the 1930s. Unfortunately, a soldier from a foot patrol smashed its windshield for fun. Where could Abu-Salim ever get a replacement?

Walid was a born dialogue leader. He was a proud Palestinian, but knew how to talk with Israelis of all types. We would meet in his small backyard, under the grape arbor and between the fruit trees. My wife, Anita, still remembers a dialogue that took place there one day, while just outside in the street there was constant shooting and clouds of tear gas just beyond the fence. Yet we, Israelis and Palestinians, kept on talking quietly to try to understand each other better. At the end of another dialogue, after the Palestinians had dispersed, Walid asked if we had noticed the group of teenagers who were there for the first time, who had been mostly quiet. Walid told us that they were members of the Islamic Jihad (a Muslim rejectionist group often connected with violence against Israelis), that they did not agree with his and our viewpoints, but that he had invited them because they had never met Israelis who supported peace, and he felt that it was important for them to listen to the dialogue.

To my surprise, many of the refugees spoke openly of their pragmatic willingness to give up their claims to return to their villages in Israel— on the condition that there would be a Palestinian state in the occupied territories.

After the Bethlehem joggers withdrew from the runs, I asked Walid if he could organize a group of runners from Aideh. He agreed, and we re- sumed jogging—in Aideh, Bethlehem, and Jerusalem. Walid and I signed as petitioners in ACRI's case before the Israeli High Court of Justice to allow us to run in Bethlehem. Three days later, his nephew Ahmad was waiting for us to pick him up to drive to Jerusalem for our run. An army jeep took him, the soldiers beat him up, and then they threw him from the moving jeep. The commander also threatened to kill Walid, just as he had killed Khalil (Walid's middle-aged neighbor who had been shot to death by a patrol). MK Ran Cohen lodged a complaint with the minister of defense, citing the name of the commander and the number of the jeep, but there was apparently no army investigation.

The High Court case was heard on 12 February 1990. The three justices suggested we reach a compromise, so we went into the corridor to thrash it out. The two lawyers from ACRI and I were pitted against Colonel Danny Ze'evi; an officer from the army's legal corps; and attorney Malkiel Blas from the Government Attorney's Office, which represented the Defense Ministry before the court.

I wanted the decision to state that we could run in Bethlehem without army interference. Colonel Ze'evi was furious that the army was being subordinated to a pack of lawyers and academic left-wingers. He growled angrily that our shirt, with the colors of both flags, was the "PLO flag," which he would never allow to appear in Bethlehem. I was used to military commanders being all-powerful in their struggles against us, and so was surprised to see their lawyer whisper to Ze'evi to calm him down, and then propose that we work out a compromise. The lawyers agreed that we would have to notify the army a week in advance of each run, and that the army would only withhold permission if there were a bona fide security problem. We would be allowed to wear our shirts, and the press would be permitted to attend (although if *we* invited the press, we would have to notify the army in advance so that they could keep the press out if their presence would create a security problem).

I was unhappy about the requirement to coordinate with the occupying army. The Palestinians had been concerned about our waving to our soldiers on the rooftops; how would they feel about running with army jeeps and police cars driving beside us? Our message was that Israelis were safe in Bethlehem and in the refugee camps when they came in the name of peace. How could we project that message if we could not move without the whole army guarding us?

The final problem was the army's insistence on a single approved route. I wanted us to be free to run a different route of our choosing each time. Ze'evi wanted us to run way out in the country, where no one would see us. I pulled out a map of Bethlehem and drew a proposed route: down Manger Street to the Church of the Nativity and the municipal building, back on the main market street of Pope Paul VI Street, and on the main road through the Aideh refugee camp. Ze'evi, under pressure from the government's lawyer, agreed to our running down Manger Street, but insisted we return on SOS Street, which in those days was almost completely empty, and involved a steep descent and ascent as well.

I told our lawyers that we should reject this compromise and try to convince the judges. I said how important it was that we run where the people were, and especially through Aideh, which was our refugee runners' home. Our senior lawyer looked at me as if I were feeble-minded. I realized that while she was committed to fighting for civil liberties, she could not believe that running in a refugee camp was anything but suicidal. How could she ever convince the judges if she herself didn't believe in the rationality of our claim? How could Galileo have gotten his lawyer to convince the judges that the earth was round, when his lawyer (like any sane man) knew that it was flat? Our lawyers had never been in Aideh with us, and had no idea about it other than the usual Israeli stereotype.

Israelis view all Palestinian villages and towns as jungles; refugee camps or the casbah of Nablus are regarded as treacherously barbarous encampments. Two stories will illustrate my people's view of our neighbors. Sergeant Amnon Pomerantz was a reserve soldier, like me. Returning in his car from a home leave to his base in the Gaza Strip during the First Intifada (on 20 September 1990), he made a wrong turn and found himself driving deeper and deeper into a refugee camp. Realizing his mistake, he maneuvered hurriedly to make a U-turn, but accidentally ran over two children. Faced with his duty as a driver to render assistance to the children, but with the good possibility of being lynched by the refugees, who had suffered terribly at the hands of soldiers wearing the same uniform, he decided to try to escape. Residents of the camp managed to stop him, and burned him alive in his car. The army later destroyed a number of homes in the vicinity of his killing. For Israelis, this series of events reinforced the image of Arab mobs lynching any Jew who accidentally happened by.

The second story concerns a group of Jewish settlers who took their children for an organized hike among Arab villages to demonstrate that all the land really belongs to us. Near the village of Beita, they were stoned by Arab youths. One of the guards then shot and killed an Arab. Word of the killing spread fast among the Arabs, and to get away quickly to the main highway the Jews walked through Beita, where a Jewish girl was shot and killed. That day, Israeli radio mistakenly reported that Arabs had killed the girl, making "Beita" a hated word throughout Israel and reinforcing the Israeli view that Arabs are murderers of innocent Jewish children. But the next day, the army's own investigation disclosed that Arabs had tried to protect the children, and the girl had in fact been shot accidentally by one of the Israeli guards. Nonetheless, the army destroyed many homes in Beita and punished the villagers severely.

I knew that we would be completely safe jogging with Walid and the Aideh runners on their home turf, but how could I explain this to our lawyer? And how could I convince her and the judges that placing control over the runs in the hands of a military despot, who viewed our running as a grave threat to the nation he had sworn to defend, was like sending a beaten wife into the care of her husband?

Standing in the corridor of the courthouse, our lawyers said to me that this compromise was the best we could do. If I wanted to reject it, our lawyers would have to resign and we could find someone else to represent us. I was stunned. How would it look to the judges if our own lawyers would not work with us? Who would pay for a private lawyer, and how much more time would be lost? I remembered the learned judge in the Sur Bahir case, who could accept the reasonableness of destroying the Arabs' fields in order to foster coexistence. I had been one of the founders of ACRI and had served on the first board of directors. But now I felt deserted, and with a heavy heart I agreed to the compromise.

We decided to run the next Friday, 16 February 1990, at 4:00 PM, on the approved route. This agreement was, in fact, a tremendous accomplishment, and was cited later as having been the single instance in which Palestinians were permitted to demonstrate politically in the history of the occupation. Colonel Ze'evi notified me that he would not permit more than nine runners, nor members of the press. Even though this was contrary to the agreement, I decided that for the first run we wouldn't argue. Two reporters asked when we would be running, but I replied that we would invite them another time.

We Israelis arrived in several cars at the entrance to Bethlehem at 3:30 PM and were surprised to find a military roadblock. (From the beginning of the occupation in 1967 until the Gulf War in 1991, there were no roadblocks or checkpoints between the West Bank and Israel. The closure of the occupied territories was instituted gradually and for limited durations, until it was made permanent by the Labor government after Hamas suicide bombings during the Oslo peace process.) Soldiers asked each runner whether he had a camera, for Ze'evi was banning any photographs of the run.

Danny Orstav, who edits classical music programs for radio, brought his son Dodani, who would be running. Danny's car had a press sticker, so the soldiers refused to allow them to enter Bethlehem. I argued with the soldiers for a while, then left Danny and Dodani to solve the problem. The rest of us drove into Aideh to meet with the Palestinian runners. We sat together in Abu-Salim's house, where I tried to explain the significance of the compromise. As I had expected, people were angry that the army had such a pervasive role in our run. I asked the runners to be patient, and to accept the limitations for now. About thirty runners were present, and we discussed how to limit ourselves to just nine. I finally suggested that we all go to the starting area (the Paradise Hotel), and I would propose several alternatives to Ze'evi, including running the route several times, each time with a different group of nine runners, or letting different groups of nine run different sections of the route. We agreed that if he refused, we'd pick nine runners and the rest would wait for us at the Paradise Hotel.

We finished our discussion about 4:30, and then faced a new problem. We didn't have enough cars to transport everyone to the hotel. We decided that we'd drive as many as would fit in the cars to a gas station near the hotel, and the others would walk over to join us. We drove slowly, and the others jogged along behind the cars. As we reached the gas station, we saw groups of soldiers in jeeps and other military vehicles leaving the area. I found Colonel Ze'evi, and said that we were arriving for the run. He was furious. Apparently he had organized an enormous military task force for the purpose of securing the route. He couldn't understand why we hadn't arrived promptly at 4:00, and decided that we must have gone running somewhere else, in violation of the agreement. He also saw more than nine runners, and would not give me a chance to explain our proposals to run nine at a time. The fact that some of our runners had jogged behind the cars convinced him that we were trying to make a monkey out of him. One officer who had been on a rooftop pointed me out and said that he had seen me running (even though I had been driving a carload of runners, and couldn't have both run and driven simultaneously). Another officer agreed with the first one, so Ze'evi was convinced that I had been making fun of him. He declared that we had violated the conditions of the High Court of Justice, and he would not allow us to run. He demanded that all the Israelis leave Bethlehem immediately, and that the Palestinians remove their shirts at once and return to the refugee camp. I said that we were prepared to run without delay, but if he refused, then we would run the next week at the same time. He refused to accept my prior announcement, and said that we would never run in Bethlehem.

So despite our best attempt to abide by the compromise, the event ended in disaster.

The lawyers at ACRI were not eager to return to the court to enforce our agreement. So in the meantime we answered Colonel Ze'evi by organizing a run for the next week in Jerusalem, with the press and with MK Ran Cohen running with us. Interestingly, there was no problem with us running within Jerusalem, where Israeli law applies (rather than the military regulations of the occupied territories). So we ran in areas that had been "annexed" to Israeli Jerusalem in 1967, from the Mar Elias monastery almost to the Armenian monastery. We had the largest group of runners ever, and were photographed with our shirts by several TV crews and news photographers. We then continued running in Jerusalem for several weeks, each time in both Jewish and Arab neighborhoods (e.g., Jabel Mukabber and East Talpiyot, or Sur Bahir and Talpiyot-Arnona), and we drank and talked in one of the Jewish runners' homes, until the Ramadan month of fasting set in.

Avraham Gal, our running lawyer, agreed to take over the court case without cost. To prepare us, he organized several groups of Israeli runners to test the army's response by running in Bethlehem. After the first run, the army seemed to counterattack. Walid's cousin Mohammed was arrested in the middle of the night and charged with having thrown stones several days earlier. After another week, my phone rang at 1:00 in the morning. Walid's voice was shaking. He had been beaten. I drove right over. He told me that soldiers had come in the night and arrested one of our runners, fifteen-year-old Mustafa 'Akel Dar el-Haj, beating him and his father. They wouldn't even let him put on his shoes. Then they went to Walid's house, where they beat him in front of his wife, pointing to the sticker on his wall with our slogan, "We Want Peace," as proof that he was the right one. They demanded to know where our best athlete, Aadel, lived, "the one who runs with you," but Walid refused to tell and got beaten more. Walid and I drove to the army base to look for the officer, but couldn't find him, so in the morning we went to the military police investigation unit's office, where Walid filed a complaint.

Mustafa had been interrogated at length, including having his fingers bent back, but he refused to confess to a false charge of stone-throwing.

Most of our young runners freely admitted to us that they had often thrown stones at soldiers during the intifada, but both Mohammed and Mustafa said that in this case they had not done anything. Faisal Husseini, a very important Palestinian leader, agreed to participate in a press conference for Mustafa, but Avraham, who took on his defense, said it might have a negative influence on the judge. We did, however, get a lot of press coverage, and we wrote to Amnesty International (which distributed an urgent dispatch all over the world) and to the chairs of U.S. congressional human rights committees. Together with Ran Cohen, we visited the families of the arrested, and got more publicity. But this was all negative publicity, exposing the failings of our army, whereas what I wanted was positive publicity that would highlight our ability as Palestinians and Israelis to work together for peace.

Young Mustafa remained in prison for about four months, after which the army offered to release him on a very stiff bail. Leaders in Aideh told us Israelis not to help his family raise the bail, since Israel was using bail and fines to raise money from the Palestinians to make up for the taxes which Palestinians refused to pay during the intifada. The intifada leadership had ordered Palestinians to remain in prison and refuse to pay. However, Mustafa's family felt that their innocent son had suffered enough and they paid the bail, which must have been an enormous hardship for this very poor family. (Had they not paid, Mustafa might have remained in jail another year until his case was heard.) Our failure as Israelis to protect our Palestinian friends from our own army has always weighed heavily on my conscience.

When Ramadan ended, I notified the army that we would be running the next week in Bethlehem according to the court decision. Ze'evi called in Walid and warned him not to run. The colonel called me also, and said, "If the freedom of your friends from Aideh matters to you, you will not run in Bethlehem." We decided that only Israelis would run this time. Ze'evi stopped us and told us that we couldn't run (even though Bethlehem was not a closed military area). We asked according to what regulation we were forbidden to run, to which Ze'evi replied, "You can't run because I say so!" He dragged me to the Israeli police station in Bethlehem but couldn't convince the police to arrest me.

Months dragged on until finally we were ready to go back to the High Court of Justice to fight for our right to run together in Bethlehem. But first I was called in to the military police investigation unit. I answered a series of questions, after which the officer began to talk to me sympathetically, to explain what was happening. The Israel Foreign Ministry had received an inquiry from a U.S. congressman, which had led to the reopening of the investigations of Mustafa's arrest and Walid's beating. The officer told me that Colonel Ze'evi's handling of the affair had been criticized, and he would be transferred to Jericho, the dumping ground for officers whose military careers have ended. For the second time I was amazed that the "all-powerful" military commander could be checked. And within a month a new commander arrived, Colonel Hillel Bar. We delayed our court case, and I arranged to meet with him.

Colonel Bar was very relaxed about our running. I told him that Colonel Ze'evi had limited us to nine runners even though the compromise had not restricted us to any particular number. Colonel Bar stated that he didn't think that some twenty-five runners would enflame the area. And so, with one change of personnel, our tribulations ended and our army, Tzahal, would let us do our thing without military interference.

The next week, we ran in Bethlehem, as free as birds. We had no soldiers guarding us, which is exactly what we wanted. On Manger Street we passed an army foot patrol that paid no attention to us. My mind began racing forward, to a day when all the schools in the Bethlehem area would send their students to run for peace, wearing our shirts—thousands of Palestinians with their Israeli colleagues, showing in a photogenic, action-packed way that the Palestinians wanted peace with Israel.

For the next run we told Colonel Bar that we would have a total of twenty-five runners, and he accepted this without objection. However, he subsequently had to ask us to put off that run because of a security problem that had nothing to do with us. I am convinced that he was being honest, and appreciated the new relation in which the army simply worked to protect people, without trying to repress our political rights. The Palestinian and Israeli runners accepted putting off the run for a week, with complete understanding. Colonel Bar gave us permission to jog with twenty-five runners the next week.

But we never got to take that run. It was September 1990. Iraq had just conquered Kuwait. In the tension that developed over conflicting attitudes toward Saddam Hussein, the leaders of the Aideh refugee camp told our runners that it was inappropriate to hold joint activities with Israelis. We had struggled for a year to create the tools with which to express the forbidden readiness for peace. Now that success was at hand, the Palestinians no longer wanted to send Israel that message.

Personal friendships survived the Gulf crisis, but we never resumed running as a real group. We ran a few times with a Palestinian from Jerusalem, Yihyah Tamimi, and a couple of his friends, but he lacked a community standing behind him, and our runs soon ceased. To simplify organizing a run, I tried to find Palestinians who would join us in some large Israeli popular runs. For example, the Hebrew University has an annual Magnes Run in which the largest group involved receives an award. Why couldn't hundreds of Palestinian schoolchildren take part, wearing the shirts, and bring a message for people to see on T V? I brought my idea to a Palestinian leader, but my way of thinking was too far away from his.

Runners for Peace was a real running club, and not just a publicity stunt. Between 13 September 1989 and 30 April 1991, we ran twenty-five times. We had thirty-five Jewish runners who participated at least once, with about an equal number of Palestinian runners. Most of our jogs included a time for the runners to meet together and talk, followed by our going out to the streets to run, wearing our shirts.

What did the running group teach me? On one hand, even the simplest activities in the occupied territories can be foiled by the army. On the other hand, when the army remains neutral, Israelis and Palestinians can work together safely and productively. But then outside forces, such as Saddam Hussein, can destroy so easily what we painstakingly build up.

When I look back on the many meetings we had in our running group, one experience stands out. Once when I was meeting with the adults, my eleven-year-old daughter, Daphna, popped in for a moment to tell me that she and her girlfriend were going to Mohammed's house to play. I knew sixteen-year-old Mohammed well—he was Walid's nephew and ran with us regularly—and I knew that the girls were perfectly safe with him. Yet I knew that I was experiencing a reality that most Israeli Jews are blind to.

In the hottest times of the intifada, in a Palestinian refugee camp, I knew that our girls were completely safe with a Palestinian youth whom I respected. If only we Israelis could be relaxed with Palestinians, perhaps we could someday agree to compromise for peace.

CHAPTER 14

Dehaisheh and the Settlers

The Dehaisheh refugee camp had a reputation during the First Intifada for being the most active and dangerous Palestinian location in the Jerusalem area. It was situated right on the main Bethlehem-Hebron road, which in those days was the route that all the Jewish settlers from Efrat, Gush Etzion, and the Hebron area drove to and from their homes. Rock-throwing at settlers' cars was so rampant that the army built the highest chain fence I've ever seen, several meters tall, between the camp and the road. This protected the settlers, but made Dehaisheh look like a monkey cage in a zoo.

Our friend Jamil Salhut from Jabel Mukabber asked if we would be interested in starting a dialogue with people from Dehaisheh. We jumped at the idea. We drove with Jamil and waited in a certain store near the camp. A young man named Ahmad Al-Issa came with some friends, and we drove with them to Jerusalem to talk things over. We were all in agreement, so we started a new dialogue group. Because Dehaisheh was almost always under curfew, they suggested we hold the dialogues in our homes in Jerusalem. For planning meetings, we would sometimes meet in Khalid's home in the camp. When we were only a few Israelis, it wasn't hard to sneak us in through a back entrance, cut through several backyards, and reach Khalid's place. His was a simple, bare, gray concrete house like all the houses in the camp. But the people seemed to give the place a warmth and charm by their presence. Army pressure on the people of Dehaisheh was very strong, so we had to keep things as secret as possible. Phones were rare in the camp, and, besides, we worried about being listened to. So we passed messages via one member, Sami, who worked in the Talpiyot industrial area in Jerusalem.

This dialogue group met together for about half a year, with an interesting mix of Palestinians and Israelis. I remember one day when the unified leadership of the intifada issued a statement announcing that Palestinians had the right to kill Israelis. This cast a pall over our relationship. Veronika invited Ahmad, Stephanie, and me to lunch, and we talked together about the significance of the statement. Ahmad said that he wouldn't kill an Israeli, but after all that had happened, he believed he had the right to. I asked what he would do if he saw a settler's car crash next to Dehaisheh. "That's obvious," he said. I pressed him to be more specific.

"Of course I would take him in my car to the hospital. Look, he has stolen my land and I will throw rocks at him to drive him out. But if he is hurt, he's a human being, and there's no question but I must try to save him."

One of the rare times that the Dehaisheh camp got favorable Israeli press coverage was when two little Jewish boys got off a Jerusalem city bus at the wrong stop. Confused as to how to get home from there, they walked all the way through the Arab town of Bethlehem and wound up at the Dehaisheh gas station. There, the workers called the children's parents, gave the boys some hot soup (it was winter), and kept them warm until the frightened parents arrived to pick them up.

All the Palestinians in the group supported peace based on a two-state solution. When we felt sure of our colleagues, we suggested organizing a press-worthy activity. The plan went through several iterations, but finally we decided to hold a press conference in Jerusalem with several members of Dehaisheh who had been hurt by the occupation—one who had been wounded, a mother who had lost a child, a man whose house had been destroyed—but who would state that nonetheless they were ready to live in peace with Israel in two states. After that, we would all drive to Dehaisheh where residents would put our stickers with the slogan "We Want Peace between Palestine and Israel, Each Free and Secure" on their homes in a most public way. We held this action on 13 June 1989, in the second year of the intifada. Such an activity flew in the face of the beliefs of almost all Israeli Jews, who did not believe that refugees from Dehaisheh could publicly declare their support for peace. Despite the opportunity to cover some remarkable behavior by Dehaisheh Palestinians, only two newspapers sent reporters to the press conference. One of them, who was very much on our side personally, described this most unusual convocation with the blasé words, "The forum began predictably enough . . ."

The Palestinians had brought their living examples of suffering, and even introduced one old man who had been imprisoned by the Jordanians because back in 1948 he had supported the two-state solution (which had been the communist position). They also brought a young boy who had been hit by settlers who had entered the camp in a rampaging protest.

At this point it was discovered that several of the Israelis who had come to the press conference were settlers. One of them, Marc Zell, a lawyer originally from America who lived in the settlement of Alon Shvut, called out that it wasn't true: he had organized the settlers' demonstration at the camp, and there had been no violence. The Palestinians disputed his claim, and said that there were many witnesses to the settlers' violence. Ahmad invited Marc to visit the camp with him, offering to introduce him to people who had witnessed the events. Zell was obviously intrigued by the invitation and wanted to accept it, but his wife didn't trust the Palestinians and wouldn't allow him to go.

After the press conference, the reporters had already obtained enough material for their stories and left us. We drove to the camp, where two American television crews were waiting to film the refugees placing the stickers on their homes. But the army wouldn't let us in. We drove around to the back entrance of the camp, but the TV crews had already left. Soldiers stopped us, the Palestinians who had arranged the press conference ran away from them into the camp, and Veronika, Judith, and I were left with a handful of bored reservists who told us that the camp was a closed military area. We had prepared a written statement to read to the military commander before the TV cameras if we were stopped. It was completely inappropriate to read it in this empty setting, yet I was so nervous from the confrontation with the soldiers and the letdown from the press that I began reading the statement to the air, my voice shaking, and once having started I kept on reading it until the end. It was completely incongruous, but thankfully Judith and Veronika were supportive, and the two oldest reservists listened respectfully to my declamation, and might even have agreed with our condemnation of the army's misusing its power for political suppression.

We were adamant about carrying out the sticker action with our colleagues in Dehaisheh. We planned the procedure again, and brought a minibus with some Israeli members of the dialogue group, MK Ran

Cohen, and lots of press. We waited for the Palestinians at the appointed place near the main entrance to the camp. However, there was a curfew, and no one showed up. We then drove around to the back entrance of the camp, near Khalid's house. We waited for a while, and then saw a Palestinian man walking toward the camp. I asked if he would tell Khalid that we were waiting for him outside the camp. "Which Khalid?" he asked. I realized that I didn't know Khalid's family name. I tried to describe him. The man shrugged and continued into the camp. We waited for a while to see whether anyone would come out. I began to wonder if this Palestinian, who walked so nonchalantly despite the curfew, mightn't be a collaborator. No one came, and we had to drive back. Ran Cohen and the journalists were nice enough not to complain—they knew what curfews were like. Unfortunately, the Dehaisheh dialogue group disintegrated before we had another chance to carry out the sticker activity.

One thing that came out of our earlier press conference was the invitation by the Palestinians to the settlers to visit the camp. I felt that perhaps we could organize a dialogue between them. Our Israeli members, many of whom were religious like the settlers, were divided about getting involved with settlers. I called Marc Zell and asked if he would be interested in such a dialogue. Several people said that there was so much bad feeling between Israelis on the Left and settlers that we should first organize a dialogue among *ourselves*. So a series of meetings was held between settlers and Israelis from the peace camp, mostly religious people. Even though I am not religious, I attended, but I felt that the real discussion should be with the Palestinians, and not with us as stand-ins for them.

After several meetings, one of the settlers suggested meeting with Palestinians. Most of his colleagues preferred to continue meeting with Jews, but he was determined to talk with Palestinians. By this time our dialogue with Dehaisheh had ended. This was a phenomenon that occurred in almost all of the dialogues, usually without us Israelis understanding why. Sometimes key personnel on the Palestinian side became too busy with other pursuits, and sometimes perhaps invisible leaders who had backed the dialogue changed their minds. At any rate, we no longer had the Dehaisheh group to approach, but I knew several Palestinians in Bethlehem and Jerusalem who were willing to meet with settlers. We met at my home, then in a settlement, and then several times in Bethlehem.

The first settlers who came to these meetings were an interesting group. They were obviously from the liberal wing of their community. Several impressed me with their sincerity and desire for good relations with Palestinians, without being patronizing or wanting to lord it over the Arabs. One of them told how, when he had graduated from medical school, he had turned to Lova Eliav, a highly respected and liberal Israeli leader, and asked what he could do as a new physician to contribute to Israeli society. Lova had said, "Go to Gush Etzion" (a Jewish area that fell to the Jordanians in 1948 and was recaptured in 1967), which he did. One of the leaders of the settlers in the dialogue stated that if there were a chance for real peace, and it required turning his settlement over to the Palestinians, he would be ready to do so. I was impressed by another settler who drove the dangerous road to Jerusalem daily, but refused to carry a gun, for fear that he might end up killing a human being. As much as I believe that it is wrong for Israel to settle Jews in the occupied territories prior to achieving peace, I was convinced that some of these settlers were more positive in their human feelings toward Arabs than were some of my friends in the peace movement.

The Palestinians who participated in this dialogue were ambivalent about meeting with settlers, and were not themselves a cohesive group. I located some others, and they met several more times, but the group never came together. Finally, it broke up, although the settler who had originally set up the discussions became friends with a Palestinian from a neighboring village, and used his influence (as an Israeli) to help the village in various ways.

Of course, these settlers were not representative of the whole settler community, just as we were not representative of Israeli society as a whole. I have met many settlers who are clearly racist, who believe Jews to be the master race, who have no consideration for Arabs as human beings or for their rights. Other settlers have nothing against Arabs, but moved to the settlements to gain the improved standard of living which Israel awards to those who are willing to live on land taken from the Palestinians. The people who came to the dialogues tended to be willing to have their preconceptions challenged, both by personal contact with those who have been defined as "enemies" and by exposure to world views and readings of history that conflict with their own backgrounds.

One of the criticisms of the Beit Sahour dialogue was that most of the Palestinians were middle-class, educated Christians, so why shouldn't they be reasonable? But in the Dehaisheh dialogue, we had proof that even poor Muslim refugees from the most violent refugee camps were openly seeking a path to peace, and were being blocked by our army at every turn.

Israeli and Palestinian families picnic together in the small
West Bank village of Kafr Ad-Dik to publicize the problems
that the nearby Jewish settlements are creating for the village.
18 September 1995. *Courtesy of Debbi Cooper.*

2005. 10. 13

Jewish volunteers join the olive harvest to protect Palestinian
farmers from physical attack by Jewish settler extremists. On the
left is Rabbi Arik Ascherman, director of Rabbis for Human Rights.
13 October 2005. *Courtesy of Rabbis for Human Rights.*

Jewish volunteer protecting Palestinian farmers (off-camera) from an armed Jewish settler. The settler is seeking to prevent the farmers from picking their olives. Also fending off the settler is international volunteer Angie Zelter. 17 October 2002. *Courtesy of Sharon Abbady.*

Jerusalem City councillors Sarah Kaminker and Moshe Amirav flank
the author in Tunis, after meeting with Yasser Arafat to discuss possible
Palestinian participation in the upcoming Jerusalem municipal
elections. 17 September 1993. *Courtesy of Sarah Kaminker.*

Dozens of Israeli children came to Sheikh Sa'ed to play with Palestinian children. New friends Hadas and Shadiyah pose for a picture in the neighborhood, which is treated by the army as hostile and dangerous. 3 August 2004. *Courtesy of Don-David Lusterman.*

Israeli families being hosted in Palestinian homes in Sheikh Sa'ed, supporting the right of the villagers to remain united, without the Wall cutting the Sheikh Sa'ed neighborhood off from the rest of its village. 25 July 2005. *Courtesy of Flash-90.*

Hundreds of Arab and Jewish neighbors attend a "Concert of Hope" in Sheikh Sa'ed with the Yasmin choir. Their hope was that the Wall would not split Jabel Mukabber, cutting off the residents of the Sheikh Sa'ed neighborhood from their brothers and sisters, from the center of their lives, and from their Israeli friends. 2 May 2007. *Courtesy of Eyal Warshavsky/BauBau.*

CHAPTER 15

Bethlehem, Wadi Fukin, Nahalin, and Husan

In the initial years of the First Intifada, we had many dialogue groups working in parallel, more than the reader would have patience to follow. In Ramallah, a large and important Palestinian city north of Jerusalem, we organized two dialogue groups. The more politically oriented group had all the potential to take off, with an excellent group of people from each nation, yet it quickly ground to a halt for reasons that we could never comprehend. The second took a more personal shape and was active for many years under the leadership (on the Israeli side) of Professor Yoram Bilu, with the closely knit group meeting alternately in homes in Jerusalem and Ramallah.

The leader of the Jabel Mukabber group, Jamil Salhut, introduced us to the journalist Mohammed Manasra, who wrote for the communist paper, and his wife, Najah, who taught psychiatric nursing. They lived in Bethlehem behind the Civil Administration headquarters. Mohammed organized a number of dialogues, including several for high school students, which met in the neutral location of the Tantur Ecumenical Institute on the border between Bethlehem and Jerusalem. Our Danny Orstav, who felt strongly that the most important contacts were between youths, was very active in these meetings. Mohammed also arranged several meetings with young people in Bethlehem who had been badly wounded by Israeli soldiers, yet who maintained a friendly optimism and welcomed the chance to meet, without rancor, with Israelis.

Once we met at Mohammed and Najah's house to plan a dialogue. There were several Palestinian teenagers there who would be coming, with their friends, to Jerusalem to meet young Israelis. We made all the plans: I would come on the day of the dialogue, accompany them on the

Bethlehem-Jerusalem bus, and bring them to the Israeli home. Since I would be coming alone to this meeting place deep inside a Palestinian neighborhood (and from the stones on the street and the graffiti on the walls, we could see that there was a lot of intifada-related activity there), I asked whether the young people could speak to the youths who threw stones and tell them not to throw stones when I would be coming. They answered that there was nothing to worry about. But I was still concerned, and asked them to take it upon themselves to talk with the stone-throwers.

"You don't have to worry; it will be all right," they reassured me.

"But why can't you talk to those youths, to be sure?" I pressed.

"No one will throw stones at you. You see, *we* are the youths who throw the stones in this neighborhood, and we will be waiting to welcome you."

Najah had grown up in the Dehaisheh refugee camp, and had a wide circle of friends from the area. One day she told us that she had spoken to some of them about the dialogues, and they would like Israelis to meet with them. These Palestinians lived in a tiny village of 125 souls called Wadi Fukin. This village lay just on the West Bank side of the Green Line. After the war in 1948, a special arrangement had been made to allow the villagers to cross over into Israel to work their fields, returning in the evening to their homes in the West Bank village.

We organized a group of Israelis and drove out to Wadi Fukin with Najah and several other Palestinians. The entire village attended this dialogue, which was held in the courtyard of one of the homes. The dialogue took the form of questions and answers, with translation, and was thus somewhat cumbersome, but the warmth from both sides and the special quality of meeting with an entire community made it unforgettable.

At one point, our hosts entertained us with a parade of children, their faces masked with *kufiyes*, carrying Palestinian flags and signs in Arabic. It looked exactly like the anti-Israeli parades that appeared from time to time on television, except that the children were not carrying hatchets. Because of the warm atmosphere, we Israelis were not upset by this parade, but I was extremely glad that there was no press with us, for had this picture appeared on Israeli television, our fellow Israelis would have been convinced that we had joined the forces working to throw the Jews into the sea.

On 13 April 1989, I received a phone call from the lawyer Avraham Gal. One of his clients, Nicola Kanawati, a wealthy owner of tourist stores in Bethlehem, had just told him of a terrible massacre in the village of Nahalin, between Husan and Wadi Fukin. Could Veronika and I join Avraham to investigate what had happened? I contacted Veronika, and before I could leave work I received a call from Jalal in Beit Sahour (who was always well informed about what was happening) about the same massacre. Avraham, Veronika, and I went to Nicola's office, where a man from Nahalin was waiting to take us to see what had happened. In the village, people were still in shock, but as we were taken from place to place and heard more and more stories, the picture became clear.

The previous week, there had been a lot of provocations from the border police who were operating in the area. The border policemen there were Druze, who are Palestinians of a religion that broke off from Islam in the eleventh century; unlike virtually all Muslim and Christian Palestinians, they serve in the Israel Defense Forces. Several times during that week, a border police jeep parked on a hill overlooking the village and the policemen broadcast sexual slurs over the jeep's loudspeaker. For example, they called out: "Villagers of Nahalin—bring us your sisters and your wives and we'll f—k them. You're not men—bring us your women and we'll show them what real f—king is. To hell with Muhammad and all your Islam." They also watched the girls of the village through binoculars, and called through the loudspeaker, "Hey you, you with the green dress, come over here so we can f—k you," and similar insults. One of the policemen even punctuated these calls by dropping his pants and exposing himself. Several of the village notables went to the Israeli governor in Bethlehem to complain, but he was too busy to receive them.

On the day before the massacre, the border police told the villagers, "Wait until tomorrow; you'll see what's in store for you."

During the night, border police units positioned themselves at all three entrances to the village. It was the month of Ramadan, so people were rising while it was still dark to eat breakfast, and then would go to the mosque for special prayers, finishing at about 5:00 AM. As they finished, large groups of border police entered the village, from each direction, on foot. They began shooting up everything, wildly. They shot at houses, at water tanks on the roofs; they broke car windows. They shot donkeys, sheep, and dogs. They beat men, women, and children viciously. They ordered a young man who suffered from muscular dystrophy to get out of bed and stand on his feet. When he couldn't, they picked him up off his bed and threw him onto the floor. In at least two cases they dragged villagers behind jeeps, which grated the skin off their chest or back. Near the mosque, two policemen climbed to the roof of a building and began shooting at the villagers, like snipers.

One man who was working in the fields outside the village was beaten so badly that his bones were broken and his stomach muscles were ripped; he required an operation. His wife, who was in their home, was beaten and suffered a heart attack.

Another man was forced into his house where five policemen beat him viciously. They destroyed the furniture, including the refrigerator. They left him wounded in the house, locked the door from the outside, and threw away the key, so that he couldn't get aid until his friends broke the lock.

A seventy-five-year-old woman was beaten on her thigh with a large rock.

Another man was beaten in his house, and policemen threatened to kill him as they pushed a rifle against his rear end.

Avraham, Veronika, and I spent two days collecting data in the village. With our own eyes, we saw twenty-eight people with gunshot wounds, little round scars the size of an M16 bullet, sometimes entry and exit scars, sometimes only an entry scar, because the bullet was still in the body. Villagers were afraid to go to the hospital lest Israeli security forces arrest them, so they walked around with the bullets inside them.

One doctor said that he had personally treated fifty-seven villagers, who were not included in those who had sought hospital treatment. Only about a dozen of the most severely wounded actually went to the hospital. A number of villagers were shot while evacuating other wounded. One wounded man was shot repeatedly as his friends tried to save him, sustaining fourteen bullet wounds, according to the doctor from the hospital. A young woman was shot from behind while she was trying to push her little brother into their house. Border police prevented the evacuation of two of the wounded, who bled to death.

At some point the Druze border police, who are under the command of the army when they operate in the occupied territories, got into a conflict with Jewish army soldiers who had arrived and who would not accept the brutality. Villagers reported on a fight between a soldier and a border policeman, and in the end the soldiers apparently forced the police to terminate their pogrom.

Altogether, 5 villagers died and 103 were wounded. Avraham sent General Amram Mitzna, oc Central Command, a report of our findings, but the report was ignored. The army issued part of the findings of its own investigation, in which it concluded that there were 4 killed and 13 wounded. This bore little resemblance to what we had learned from many different villagers. Instead, the army report looked at the whole incident from the military's viewpoint. It mentioned the beating of a handcuffed prisoner by a policeman, and threats by a policeman against soldiers. It recommended disciplinary action against policemen and transferring several officers from their current positions.

A few weeks later my wife and I were driving in Galilee, where we gave a lift to a Druze border policeman who had been hitchhiking. In the course of our conversation, I asked about what had happened in Nahalin. He told us that the commander of that border police unit was from his village in Galilee. I said that I'd read that he was disciplined. "Not at all," replied the young man. "They told him to take a little vacation, to stay in our village until it all quiets down. But he's not in any trouble. He'll go back to work in a couple of weeks."

One positive thing that came out of our visits to Nahalin was meeting Yusuf Najajara, a villager who took us around to see what had happened. Yusuf was a doctoral student at the Hebrew University's School of Pharmacy, one of the only students from the occupied areas (other than East Jerusalem) studying at my university. Yusuf's family was similar to several others I met. His father was a shepherd. Almost all of his many brothers had gained a higher education, and thus had leapfrogged into the modern world. We visited him in his home in the village, where we disappointed the family by not staying to eat the dinner they wanted to prepare for us. We saw the respect that the highly educated children accorded their traditional parents. We had the pleasure of seeing Yusuf on many occasions thereafter.

I also experienced sad times with him. After a long wait, Yusuf finally received a permit to drive his car to the university campus in Ein Karem, which would save him lots of time compared to taking public transportation, which is not designed for going from Bethlehem to the Hebrew University. But the first day that he parked his car there, with its Bethlehem license plates, someone punctured one of his tires. The next day, he phoned and asked for my help. Someone had punctured all four of his tires. We put his car on blocks and drove the four tires back to Bethlehem in my trunk to get them fixed. I felt terrible for Yusuf, and also terrible for my people, who are cursed to have such racists among them.

I worked at the Hebrew University in the computation center. One day a young Palestinian who worked as a gardener in the Buildings and Grounds Department approached me. His name was Majdi Hamamra. He had heard that I was involved in dialogues. Could we bring Israelis to meet with people in his village of Husan, in the Bethlehem area?

I was pleased with his overture. After a few days, some of our organizers came to the campus and we drove Majdi home. We sat and talked for a while, met a few villagers, and got a good feeling from the people. We gave Majdi one of our stickers, which he stuck on his refrigerator. We made plans for a one-time, large dialogue with press invited. We would sneak into the village in Arab taxis (to get past the army observation towers), come to his house, and then proceed to the soccer field where the villagers would meet us for a major group discussion.

Before the planned date, there was a killing of an Israeli by a Palestinian, and in the aftermath the university laid off most of its workers from the West Bank. Majdi was fired. I had counted on being able to talk with him at the last minute. There were no telephones in the village, and anyway I would never have discussed these plans over tapped phones. We would have to go in blindly. We organized a group of Israelis and some journalists, all without using telephones. The day before the planned activity, a Palestinian who still worked at the university came with a message from Majdi: everything was set from the village's side. I sent back the message that we would arrive as planned.

We Israelis met at the railroad station in Jerusalem. The Arab cabs that were to take us were late. We waited and waited. Finally, we realized that they weren't coming. The Arab dispatcher had no phone, and there was no time to drive over to him. We were already late, so we organized several private cars to go to Husan. There was increased danger of being stoned on the road and of being spotted by the army. But there was no other choice. We drove in a convoy the long way around to Husan, through Israel rather than through Bethlehem, where we might have been stoned. When we reached the village, we drove right past the army observation tower; the soldiers were obviously not expecting us and paid no attention. We drove to the house of Majdi, who had not given up on us despite our late arrival. I remember seeing our sticker on his refrigerator, and feeling that if it was still there, everything would be all right.

I wanted very much to avoid a confrontation with the army. I wanted the press to see only the positive side of the villagers receiving the Israelis, without the distraction of conflict with the army. Most of the adults in the village were concerned about possibly being arrested for meeting with us, so the villagers who came were mainly youngsters and teenagers. But there were plenty of people, and the mood as always was excellent. The Israelis who had made this big effort to come wanted to stay and talk, but I knew that if we stayed too long, an army patrol would come by and there would be trouble. Well before the participants were satisfied, I insisted that we leave. The meeting was reported in the press, with photographs, and this was another contribution to try to correct some of the mistaken impressions that Israelis held. For the villagers, it had been a chance to meet Israelis who supported many of their own goals, and perhaps it gave them some encouragement to seek the peaceful solution.

CHAPTER 16

Nablus (Shechem) I
A Military Alliance

One of the active Jews in our dialogues was Daniel Rohrlich, an American who held a Ph.D. in physics and was working in Israel on a postdoctoral fellowship. An Orthodox Jew, he later immigrated to Israel and married the daughter of the former chief rabbi of Strasbourg, France. Daniel had heard about a Palestinian physicist, Sami Kilani, who had been arrested. They began corresponding, and when the Palestinian was released in 1992, Daniel went to Nablus to visit him. Nablus is not just another Beit Sahour. There are about 100,000 residents and another 100,000 people in the villages and refugee camps in its vicinity. It has traditionally been the leading site for Palestinian nationalist movements. The casbah of Nablus is generally portrayed in the Israeli media as the most dangerous place in the occupied territories, with the possible exception of certain refugee camps in Gaza.

Daniel described the dialogues to his new friend. He then reported to Veronika that Sami was intrigued with the concept and wanted to set up something similar in Nablus. As comfortable as we were in Palestinian areas, the name "Nablus" was a bit startling. Veronika was the only one in our group who had been there. As a member of the Beita support group, she had attended court hearings in Nablus against Beita villagers, hearings that were the result of the settler provocations that had ended with deaths and many homes destroyed.

One of my roles in our dialogue groups was to steer the participants away from becoming "support groups" in which Israelis participated to show sympathy for Palestinian victims of Israeli maltreatment. Support groups are hardly the place for critical discussion, and my goal was to have such discussions. Since I don't believe that the roles of victimizers and victims are always clear-cut, I didn't want to encourage guilt-ridden Israelis who could only blame themselves and see no fault in Arabs' behavior. Of course, we were very sympathetic to Palestinian suffering, and blamed many of our government's actions and aims, but we always felt free to express dissatisfaction with Palestinian actions and goals as well.

Daniel, Veronika, and I met Sami Kilani. There was immediate chemistry among us. He was a very gentle but forceful man, a well-known writer of stories in Arabic as well as a teacher of science education at An-Najah University in Nablus. Twice, Veronika and I had met Palestinians, both lawyers, who had been recommended to us as interested in dialogue, but we had agreed they were not for us, as they had been too slick and possibly devious. But Sami was very straight, thoughtful but decisive. He thought the way we thought, and inspired confidence that this would be a good dialogue group. After our talk, we set up a meeting time in Nablus. I told my friend Jalal that I was getting involved in a new group there, and might have less time for Beit Sahour. "That's OK," replied Jalal. "Nablus is the most important city in the West Bank. If you can get something started there, it's more important than all that we can do here."

We organized several of our Beit Sahour participants (Veronika, Judith, Danny, Daniel, and I) and added some new Israelis for the Nablus group. It was not easy to find Israelis who could take off an afternoon every two or three weeks. (We couldn't hold evening dialogues because the last returning taxi left at sundown, and we didn't want to use our own cars because we risked stonings.) Of our group, Zvi Schuldiner taught at the university, bringing broad knowledge and social commitment. Rabbi Isaac Newman was a retired British Orthodox rabbi and a leader in the group Rabbis for Human Rights. Shmuel Magen, one of Israel's leading cellists, taught at the Rubin Academy of Music and Dance. Gabby Levin was a psychologist turned poet and translator. Betsy Cohen was a young, religious, new immigrant from the United States. Ophir Yarden was a tour guide, fluent in Arabic, who lectured on the Zionist movement. Moshe Landsman came up all the way from the Negev desert; with his wild beard, cap, and general appearance he looked like a settler; indeed, the Palestinians called him "the settler from Beersheva." One day when we got out of a taxi in Nablus a Palestinian saw him and called out, "The Jewish settlers are coming!" but the supervisor of the taxi stand knew us and calmed him down.

The Palestinians had compiled an equally impressive group. Rawda Bassir worked with children with speech and hearing defects. She told us about her eight years of imprisonment in Israel. She had been part of a terrorist cell, but before they succeeded in injuring anyone, one of their members accidentally blew himself up, and they were all caught and sent to prison. The first Israelis she met were the prison guards, some of whom she respected. Her ideas changed until she concluded that violence was not the way; instead, she vowed to dedicate herself to working nonviolently for peace. Her husband, Ibrahim Sheikha, had mastered Hebrew beautifully during his seventeen years in prison, where he had served time for infiltrating with an armed group across the Jordan River and had been captured immediately. The Jordan Rift was where I had done most of my reserve duty, and had he infiltrated a few years later we might have met across gunsights. He too had changed his orientation and was now a peace activist. Both Rawda and Ibrahim had been released in the prisoner exchange of Ahmad Jibril (in which 1,150 Palestinian prisoners were exchanged for three Israeli soldiers on 20 May 1985). Many of the Nablus members had grown up having had no contact with Israelis, and many had served long prison terms.

Several of the members were from the Communist Party and/or from workers unions. Two who spoke neither English nor Hebrew were Hassouna Dabik and Abdel Baset al-Khayat. Hassouna was a serious-minded worker leader with good contacts in the Balata refugee camp, who communicated warmth without words. Abdel Baset had been a member of the Nablus city council. He dressed immaculately without being a dandy, and his open, warm smile inspired trust. Everyone liked him despite our inability to talk with him directly. He lived in a beautiful old house surrounded by a lovely garden, in the heart of the factory district of central Nablus. It was always good to meet in his house, for we'd get to talk with his wife and children, whom we liked very much and who spoke English well. Another communist in the group was Sahab Shaheen, who had returned with her uncle from many years in exile in Jordan, and immediately became active in the dialogue group.

One of the most interesting members, who was with us in the early times, was Samih Ken'an. His father had married a Jewish woman from the coastal strip before 1948, as had several sons of leading Muslim families. Samih was therefore a Jew according to Jewish law, and a Muslim according to Islamic law. He had a great sense of humor and enjoyed kidding with us. After Nablus was turned over to the Palestinian Authority under the autonomy agreement, Samih became head of the police. Several years later, when Israeli soldiers were trapped in what some call Joseph's Tomb in Nablus (during the uprising following the opening of the Herodian Tunnel in Jerusalem, in September 1996), Samih led the successful operation to release the Israelis from the angry Arab mob.

Some members were part of Arafat's Fatah Party. First and foremost was Hilal Toufaha, another former prisoner, who took charge of security whenever we had a major activity and talked to the Israeli military governor when that was required. Hilal was a successful merchant. His family owned a chain of optometry shops throughout the West Bank, and the stores seemed very successful even though I rarely saw a Palestinian wearing glasses. When we would walk about in Nablus, Hilal was always pointing out, "This is also my store" or "This shop belongs to my family." We often met in his large apartment high on Bigar Street, which had an excellent view of Nablus in the valley.

Many other Nabulsis joined us at different times. Samar Hawash was active in a women's organization. Our most regular member in the early days was Mohammed Sawalha; a handsome man with a well-trimmed black mustache, he taught English at An-Najah University in Nablus and was a delegate to the Madrid peace talks. After a few years Mohammed set up another organization, Freedom House, and we lost his participation.

The Palestinians in our group were mainly political activists, including three delegates to the Madrid talks. While people talked about personal experiences, the dialogue was concentrated to a great extent on current events and the political situation. Unfortunately, we had to talk through a translator, which slows things down. My mind would often wander during translations. But the Palestinians were very open with us, and we learned a great deal of what was going on in their world. Similarly, we tried to be as straightforward as possible with them, telling them our personal reactions as well as those of our society to what was going on.

In the early days, before the closure (in 1992), we would alternate the venue of the dialogues between our two cities. When the group from Nablus would drive to Jerusalem, we would wait for them at Ar-Ram junction at the northern entrance to the city, and then take them to Uri Yakir's house in French Hill. Uri was the only one of us who lived in the northern

part of Jerusalem. Almost all members of the peace camp live in the southeast part of the city, nearer to Bethlehem and Beit Sahour. But meeting in
the south would have lengthened the Palestinians' trip by about twenty
minutes. Our Palestinian friends were always on time. Similarly, when we
took a taxi to them, there was always someone waiting for us at the taxi
stand, until we got to know our way around and no longer needed their
assistance.

Riding in the taxis was an experience in itself. The Palestinian taxis
in those days were old Mercedes models that took seven passengers. The
driver would wait at the taxi stand as passengers slowly filled the seven
places, at which point he would drive off. Since the passengers were randomly selected, we got to meet Palestinians who had not chosen to hold
dialogues with Israelis. At times we would talk with people who supported Islamic fundamentalist groups. Many said they were sure that
there would never be peace. But many were friendly and interested in
what we were doing. Never in all the rides did anyone insult us or threaten
us in any way. In contrast to our groups in Beit Sahour, where we used to
drive for just fifteen minutes in our own cars, the trip to Nablus took up
to an hour and a half in a cab, but if our stomachs could stand the constant curves, we were often rewarded with thoughtful conversations with
strangers. Once, we had to change taxis in Ramallah. We asked a college
student, whose hair was covered in Muslim fashion, where the taxis left
for Nablus. She asked where we were from, and we replied "Israel." She
asked us to stop at her home to have a cup of coffee first, but we didn't
have time that day.

One time, I was the only Israeli organizer who could attend a planning
meeting. We sat at Rawda and Ibrahim's house for a couple of hours working on some technical problems. When the meeting was over, I asked who
would give me a ride to the taxi stand. They looked at the time, and told
me that it was too late, the last taxis had already left. I would have to sleep
over in their home in Nablus, and go back to Jerusalem in the morning.
This turned out to be an unexpected pleasure. Unlike most Arab families, Rawda and Ibrahim believe in equality between the sexes. Ibrahim
cooked while Rawda received various youths from the surrounding villages who came to consult with her in those difficult intifada days. Ibrahim
cooked a chicken for soup, then stewed it in an electric frying pan unlike

any pan I had seen in Jewish homes. The food was delicious, the hospitality first class. It was amazing to me that this couple, who had served between them twenty-five years in Israeli prisons, were so committed to peace. Repeatedly, we heard from Palestinians that the most active peace workers were nationalists who had served prison terms for participating in the violent struggle against us.

After we had been holding dialogues regularly, we decided to organize some large media activities. We created a smaller planning group for this purpose. Veronika, Judith, Danny Orstav, and I would meet with several of the key Palestinians. For our first action, we wanted to stage a large march. The Palestinians had no problem calling for an end to violence, so it was easy for us to agree on slogans.

Danny and I went to our friend Ran Cohen, who had been so wonderful in our Beit Sahour activities. But now, in 1992, Ran's party, Meretz (which was a union of the small left-wing and centrist parties Ratz [CRM], Mapam, and Shinui), was part of Yitzhak Rabin's coalition government, and it was complicated for him to get involved with us. When he had been in the opposition, he had been his own boss. He remembered the incident in Beit Sahour when the youth had hung a Palestinian flag above his head. Now, having been the assistant housing minister, he was concerned that if anything went wrong, it might be an embarrassment to the government. He told us that he would not be able to take part in this march, but if it went well he assured us that Meretz would be represented in our second activity in Nablus.

This hit me as a terrible blow. I really liked and admired Ran. He was one of the few members of the Knesset who had no enemies—even those from the right wing could not dislike him. I had felt that his participation would assure our rally's success. But without him, we all decided that we could not hold an outdoor action, which could easily have led to problems with the army. Instead, we decided on a two-stage activity that would both give the participants the intimacy of the small dialogues and provide the demonstrative media picture of large groups of people in one place. We prepared an invitation.

Israeli-Palestinian Dialogue for Peace (Nablus-Jerusalem Group)

In Nablus (Occupied West Bank) there will be an unprecedented joint Israeli-Palestinian call to end the bloodshed on both sides; to end the occupation; and to support peace, freedom and security. Hundreds of Palestinians and Israelis will take part in the activity which includes:

9–10 AM: Nablus families host Israelis in their homes.

10–11:30: Meeting in a hall to sign a joint declaration.

This activity has the support of a very wide spectrum of Nablus organizations and political factions.

The Palestinians found thirty-eight homes to receive us, including some in the Old City (i.e., the casbah), in the Balata and Askar refugee camps, and in a neighboring village. While we would have preferred to concentrate the home visits in a single neighborhood (to simplify the logistics and minimize driving around), the Palestinians said that the refugees insisted on their right to host Israelis as well.

We had no idea how many Israelis would be willing to visit Nablus, as the very mention of the town sounded terribly dangerous to Israeli ears. We placed ads in Israeli newspapers and made hundreds of phone calls to invite Israelis. We spoke to the well-known reporters who covered the territories, explaining why covering the event would be worthwhile even though there would be no blood. The preparations were difficult. Arab bus companies in East Jerusalem refused to rent us tourist buses for the trip to Nablus, fearful that windows might be broken by Palestinians throwing stones. In the end, a company with battered old city buses agreed to transport the Israelis.

In order to reassure and relax the Israeli participants, we decided to take an unprecedented step. We invited about thirty Israelis who had prior experience in meetings with Palestinians to serve as group leaders, to be distributed among the newcomers, to talk with them and make them feel more secure on the trip to Nablus, and to accompany them in the various Palestinian homes. We were convinced that from the moment we arrived, the Israelis' fears would disappear spontaneously, but we wanted to reduce their anticipatory fears. The evening before the activity, we met with a number of the group leaders in Judith Green's home in the Abu-Tor neighborhood of Jerusalem, to explain the day's program and what would be expected of them. Rawda joined us with six young Palestinians from the Nablus area who would sleep over (despite its being illegal for West Bankers to spend the night in Israel), in order to ride with us on the buses and add to our feeling of security. Rawda was well connected with active youths from the villages around Nablus, and had no trouble enlisting several, despite the fact that they knew they risked arrest if caught.

We really had prepared ourselves admirably for this action. But nothing ever goes as planned.

Before we even started our evening meeting, we received a call from Sami in Nablus. There had been an explosion in Balata refugee camp. Apparently, a Palestinian had been preparing a bomb that prematurely exploded—an act that Israelis sardonically call a "work-related accident." The tension was thick, and there was lots of military activity in response. Should we call off our action? It was wonderful having Rawda with us, for she and Sami knew how to talk to each other on tapped phones; they understood each other's nuances in ways which we did not. We updated the group leaders on what was happening, and they discussed among themselves, and with the Palestinian youths, whether the program should be canceled. Palestinians and Israelis were both divided in their opinions, so we continued to analyze and discuss the issue.

But then, there was a new development, one we had never encountered before. Judith's phone rang, and she passed it to me, saying, "It's for you, Hillel. I don't recognize the voice."

I took the phone. A man on the other end said, "I've been trying to locate you for some time. I'm calling from Tzahal. We know that you have planned an activity in Nablus tomorrow. We know your organization, we know that your group is law-abiding, and we have no desire to interfere with your legitimate activities. However, there's been a work-related accident in Balata, and someone blew himself up while making a bomb. We cannot allow you to enter the refugee camps. If you insist on coming, we will have to keep a company of soldiers at the camp to prevent you from entering. If you give me your word that you will not enter the camps, I can send the soldiers home for the weekend."

I told him that I would have to consult with my colleagues, and would call him back. He gave me his name and phone number: he was a lieutenant colonel (I will call him Ari in this book), chief intelligence officer for the Central Command.

Despite the pall that hung over our planned activity, I was overjoyed. In the past, the army had always kept its motives concealed from us; we had played cat and mouse, never knowing whether they would block our activities. In planning actions, we invested the major share of time and ingenuity in finding ways to neutralize the army: we sought not to enter into a clash with them, but to skirt their ability to block us. Now, finally, Tzahal had a name—Ari—and a voice and a telephone number. And for the first time I was hearing that somewhere in Tzahal our activities were viewed as legitimate. I assumed that Ari had read my personnel file from Tzahal, and knew that I had always earned excellent reviews. He was treating me as a colleague, as someone he could trust, whose word was sufficient to release a company of soldiers to a well-deserved rest.

Before we could decide what to do, Sami called again from Nablus. The Israeli Civil Administration (run by army officers) had called one of the Palestinian organizers and told him that because of the tense situation, Israelis would not be permitted to visit in Palestinian homes. Only the large hall meeting would be allowed. We were caught within a bureaucratic lack of coordination between the army (which had notified us that home visits were acceptable) and the Civil Administration (which forbade them). We were also concerned that hordes of soldiers might surround the meeting hall, which would hurt the mood that we were trying to set.

At this point, Rawda, Sami, Veronika, Judith, and I decided jointly to put off the activity for two weeks. I called Ari back and told him he could send the soldiers home for Shabbat. (I also suggested that we meet and establish a channel of communication. He said he'd have to get permission for that.) We divided the list of the 120 Israelis who had signed up for the activity, and gave the group leaders instructions to notify them that the activity would be put off for two weeks. We also notified the press. Six group leaders volunteered to take the Palestinian youths to the leaders' homes to sleep, and Rawda stayed with my family. The next morning, the seven Palestinians reunited at the taxi stand outside the Damascus Gate of the walled Old City and drove back to Nablus. I then went to Liberty Bell Park, the place from which our buses were supposed to leave, to notify any Israelis who might show up without having registered. To my chagrin, I had forgotten to inform one young woman from Tel Aviv about the cancellation, and she had left her home at 6:00 AM in order to take part. Her justifiable anger taught me that we would have to be better organized at canceling planned activities, something that unfortunately happened not infrequently.

Later that morning, tired as we were, Veronika, Judith, Danny, and I took a taxi to Nablus to meet with our friends to soften the blow. One of the leaders of the Balata refugee camp came and apologized about what had happened. He told us that the people of the camp still wanted to host us. He asked us to drink coffee in his home. I felt that we couldn't go after I had given my word to Ari, but I didn't feel comfortable explaining this to a Palestinian who had just met me for the first time. We explained that we were short of time, so he drank coffee with us in our friend's home in Nablus. The organizers then took us to the village of Jneid, where we held an impromptu dialogue with the *mukhtar* and several men in their twenties.

We rescheduled the activity for two weeks later. Everything seemed to be in order, but the night before the action, Prime Minister Rabin's government rounded up 415 Hamas activists and sent them into exile in Lebanon, in retaliation for Hamas having killed an Israeli policeman in the town of Ramle in the center of Israel. Palestinian anger was too great to permit our activity to take place. Once again, we were blocked by circumstances, and we were all pretty discouraged about having again to plan the activity and then perhaps have the situation in Nablus force yet another postponement.

I had invited Lieutenant Colonel Ari to meet with me. He soon received permission to accept my invitation and on 25 January 1993 he came to my office in the Hebrew University's computation center. I explained that I wanted to keep a channel of communication open between the Israelis in our group and the army. I expressed my concern that when we scheduled a dialogue, we might be stopped at a roadblock and prevented from entering Nablus. Ari said he could leave word with the Tappuah Junction checkpoint on such days or, alternatively, if we had any trouble, we could ask the soldiers to call him on his army phone.

At that time, Palestinians were already forbidden entry into Israel without permits, a factor that prevented the group from holding dialogues or activities in Jerusalem (West or East). Among the points we discussed was whether the army would give permits to the Palestinians to attend activities in Jerusalem. This would simplify security arrangements, allow Israelis to participate who might be reluctant to risk going to Nablus, simplify logistics for the press, and relieve the army of its responsibility for the safety of Israelis in Nablus. It would give the army one less headache: security in Jerusalem was the police's responsibility, and the army would be able to relax. After consulting with his superiors, Ari informed me that the army would grant permits to every Palestinian without political consideration, including even people with green IDs (who are generally forbidden any entry) and excluding only those who were considered a real security risk. In addition, we Israelis could submit the list of participants and receive the permits (an important consideration, since the Palestinians would not request permits from the occupying powers).

In response to my questions, Ari said that everything he was telling me had the approval of the OC Central Command and the general staff. He also responded that in case of a conflict between the army and the Civil Administration, the army had priority.

I presented this proposal to the joint planning committee, which was quite skeptical about my assurance that the army was finally on our side and about my desire that we should work together. But finally they agreed to my enthusiastic persuasion. We found seventeen homes in the Talpiyot and Bak'a neighborhoods of Jerusalem to host the Palestinian guests for coffee, and a hall was found that was prepared to receive an Israeli-Palestinian group (several refused) for the large meeting. The Palestinians gave us a list of forty-one families (102 people) with names, ID numbers, ages of the children, and languages spoken, so we could try to match families. I passed on the names to Ari, and happily all the Palestinians were approved for entry permits by the security service.

The meeting was scheduled for 19 February 1993. But on the fifteenth, a Jewish resident of East Talpiyot was stabbed to death at a bus stop, by a Palestinian it was assumed. (It turned out later that the assailant was a Jew who had disguised himself as an Arab, and the motive concerned a romantic triangle—but at the time Israelis assumed it was a terrorist attack in our area.) The residents of East Talpiyot, who, unlike those of Talpiyot, can be quite intolerant, were frightened and furious at this incursion into their quiet neighborhood. Despite the high tensions, we decided not to cancel our activity—which would bring busloads of Arabs into Jewish neighborhoods—but scratched the one home in East Talpiyot from our list of hosts.

We worked very hard organizing the host homes. We meticulously planned the routes of the buses from Nablus so that we could drop off each group with a minimum of lost time. We made endless calls to the press, explaining our planned activity, and followed up with reminders. Everything seemed set.

But then, once again, things went awry. The Civil Administration (whose members are army officers, but who deal with Palestinian civilians) balked at the army's agreement. Two days before the activity, Ari notified me that the Civil Administration demanded that each Palestinian come individually to its office to pick up his or her permit. The head of the Civil Administration told Ari that it would be an "educational lesson" for the Palestinians to come individually, while giving the permits to an Israeli to pass on to the Palestinians would be "undermining the system" (Hebrew: *shvirat ha-kelim*). Allowing the Palestinians to get a permit without personally requesting it from the occupying power would be a "rebellion" against the authority of the Civil Administration. The Palestinians refused to accept this new requirement. Ari did his best to help. He called the head of the Civil Administration at his home at night, and by morning had gotten a very reluctant agreement that it would be enough for just four or five Palestinians to come to the office to pick up the permits for the whole group. But by this time it was too late for the Palestinians to meet to discuss this proposal.

Rather than cancel the entire program, we arranged for four Palestinian leaders, who had permits to enter Israel, to come to the hall to talk with the Israelis, but the impact of the home visits, and the participation of such a large number of Palestinians, was lost. We were greatly disappointed, and my own credibility within our group, after I had supported working with the army against the judgment of all of my colleagues, was a bit shaken. I believe that Ari did all he could, within the bureaucracy, to advance our plans. When reporters asked what had happened, I told them exactly: the army had cooperated with us and promised that I could pick up the permits, but the Civil Administration had later vetoed this agreement. The accounts in the press apparently generated some criticism of Ari. He called me, angry and agitated, as if I had either slandered him or leaked state secrets. "How could you do that?" he shouted. "How could you damage my chances for promotion? A magnificent military past hurt by your hands! I'm finished working with you. I won't be your cannon fodder. From now on, I'll have nothing to do with you." So, on top of everything else, our legitimate connection with Tzahal, which meant so much to me, had been destroyed.

CHAPTER 17

Nablus (Shechem) II
Helping to Advance the Peace Process

We continued our dialogues in Nablus, but it was a long time before we were ready to coordinate a large action again. In the meantime, with Ari refusing to work with me, I managed to get another officer, Major Elise Shazar (the spokesperson for the Civil Administration), to replace Ari as our channel of communication with the authorities. After several months, we planned an activity in Nablus for 25 June 1993. To simplify the arrangements, we called off the home visits and limited the activity to many simultaneous dialogues at the hall of the Friends of An-Najah University in Nablus. We had received a grant from the USAID program, so we took out large advertisements in the newspapers. There is a cliché in Israel (implying that Palestinians don't want peace) that says: "Where is *their* Peace Now movement?" So we countered with our ad.

> *Where is the "Peace Now" of the Arabs?*
>
> *Palestinians from Nablus, who support peace, are inviting us to an open meeting to get to know each other, in order to encourage our two peoples to advance peace.*
>
> *We've waited so many years for such an invitation—is it possible that we won't respond positively? . . .*
>
> *Today, there IS someone to talk to; do WE still retain the desire and the strength?*

࿇

Veronika went to Nablus the evening before to help set things up, and slept over with Rawda and Ibrahim. Eighty Israelis and a large number of journalists traveled in our two buses, and everything seemed to be moving along perfectly. But once again, an action did not work out the way we had expected. When we reached the Tappuah Junction, about twenty minutes from Nablus, soldiers stopped us at the roadblock, told us to park on the side of the road, and said that they had orders not to let Israelis through. I was furious. How could my army be so base as to stop us, when they knew in advance what we were doing, when we had run large public advertisements, when there was nothing sneaky in our behavior? I barely controlled my anger and asked to speak to the commander. The soldiers said that the colonel would come over in about fifteen minutes.

The Israelis started getting off the buses to smoke and stretch their legs. We explained that there was a temporary problem with the army that had to be solved. One well-known activist, who liked to get into the news, spotted an ultra-Orthodox Jew standing and praying incongruously at a bus stop nearby. The activist went over to him and started shouting at the black-garbed settler, blaming him for all the troubles. The TV crews, who love action of any kind, ran over and filmed enthusiastically. I tried to dissuade our man. I told him that we had come to hold dialogues with Palestinians, and he was causing a diversion. He finally relented, but Israeli TV saw fit to waste part of the coverage on that meaningless scene.

After fifteen minutes, the military commander of the Nablus area arrived in his jeep. "What's the problem?" I asked him.

"No problem at all. Nablus is open. You can get on your buses and go where you like."

We shook hands and our people reboarded the buses. It is one of the infuriating aspects of the occupation that the army cannot allow Israelis to visit Palestinians without showing who is boss. There was no need for this colonel to stop our buses and make us wait, with us not knowing whether we would be allowed to proceed or be forced to return to Jerusalem disappointed. It was part of a process of humiliating people from the peace camp, something that is practiced often even against groups that come with members of Knesset. Let them be tense for fifteen minutes. Let them know that we, the army, decide whether Israeli citizens can move or will be stopped. And we had been stopped enough times by the army that the prospect of not getting through was real and present. We had given up our original sneaking around, in which we had outfoxed the army several times. But now that we behaved in a more dignified and open way, the army frequently lacked the nobility to respond in kind.

At the turnoff to Nablus, a Palestinian car was waiting for us. Mohammed and Hilal each boarded a bus. Mohammed welcomed us: *"Ahalan w'-sahalan,* welcome to Palestine. You can all feel relaxed, we are together. Palestinians are waiting to receive you in Nablus. We will be driving together. So follow me." It was a very nice touch. In their place I would have simply led the buses to our goal, but the Arabs, for whom hosting is a cardinal virtue, thought to reassure their guests, and I could see how much this was appreciated by the Israelis.

Another Palestinian touch that took me by pleasant surprise occurred when we got off our buses at the hall of the Friends of An-Najah University. Many of the Palestinians were standing in a long receiving line at the entrance, and we shook hands with some fifty smiling people as we entered. The obvious warmth of the greetings broke the ice and set the mood for the activity.

We began with a minute of silence for all those who had been killed among both our peoples. Then we broke into small groups, around tables, talking about whatever people wanted. At the end, we read a joint statement, which Palestinians view as a necessary part of a politically oriented activity, and people signed a petition.

In all our statements, we pushed to have a call to end violence as the first statement. It was interesting that although violence against Israelis was an important element in the Palestinian struggle to stop Zionism throughout the twentieth century, our colleagues had no trouble publicly declaring themselves against violence, at least from that point on. And we had no trouble condemning Israeli violence against Palestinians, such as the massacres carried out by Ami Popper and Dr. Baruch Goldstein. Our four statements for this activity were:

· End the bloodshed on both sides.
· End the occupation.
· Support peace between Palestine and Israel, each free and secure.
· Support human rights and dignity for all Israelis and Palestinians.

My army behaved exactly as I would have wanted. There was no army presence around the hall. From time to time a jeep drove past unobtrusively. They had the power to destroy the activity, but chose not to interfere, for which I was most grateful and proud. The Israelis and the press could see for themselves that we who came in the name of peace were quite safe in the community of Nablus.

Unfortunately, in bringing such a large group of Israelis to Nablus, we could not be as choosy as we had been in selecting members of the ongoing dialogue group. As I went from table to table to hear how things were going, I was sometimes shocked by the words of some of the more radical Israeli participants, whose venom against anything Israeli turned me off. On the other hand, there were many Israelis who represented the best in our society, and who were exactly the types that I wanted the Palestinians to meet.

When the meeting ended, it was hard for most of the Israelis to leave. But several members of Women in Black—a group that for years has held a vigil every Friday with the slogan "Stop the Occupation"—reminded me that we had promised to get them back to Jerusalem for their 1:00 PM vigil. At the same time, Hilal, who was responsible for security, wanted us to leave before the crowds would be gathering for Friday prayers in the mosques. So we pressed the Israelis back onto the buses and drove home.

While driving back, I was sitting in the back of the bus talking with a reporter, so I didn't notice what was happening in the front. When we reached the Tappuah Junction, a couple of nineteen-year-old paratroopers were waiting to hitch a ride back to Jerusalem. We stopped to allow several of our Israelis to use the phone booth there. The soldiers saw the bus full of Israelis, asked if they could get a ride, and joined us. They had only just sat down when two young men from our group began berating them for serving in the occupied territories, called them names, and said that they wouldn't allow soldiers who serve in the territories to ride on our bus. While I respect soldiers who go to jail rather than serve the occupation, I had no sympathy for those kids insulting our soldiers, who were not part of such a movement. Had I known what was happening, I would have asked the paratroopers to stay with us, and would have pressured the hecklers to shut up. But the soldiers, confused as to who we were and noticing that we were in an Arab bus, got up and left. This was perhaps the single blot on that activity.

It is worth reviewing the newspaper coverage in Israel of this event in Nablus. Such a large meeting of Israelis and Palestinians in a Palestinian town (before the Oslo Accords) was a rare occurrence, and when the town was Nablus it was quite sensational. The liberal *Haaretz* newspaper allocated the story a mere seven lines at the end of an article titled "Two Collaborators Murdered in Gaza Strip." The left-leaning *Hadashot* gave it five lines. The right-center *Maariv* showed a photo of the receiving line with a caption. In addition to these brief reports, three journalists subsequently wrote full-page accounts of the activity. One in *Haaretz* included a lot of good material, but its title was "In the End They Rushed the People to Leave, for Fear of Riots." A long article by Yael Admoni, the daughter of a former head of the Mossad, appeared in the local Jerusalem weekly *Yerushalayim*. After devoting several paragraphs to her fear of going to Nablus and her feeling that she might not return alive, she continued with a good description of the activity. She was surprised to find that the Palestinians, far from being a tiny group of unimportant participants, had included three representatives to the Madrid talks and politically active members of the Nablus community. She closed with the following: "I don't know how to say it without sounding stupid, but it was enchanting. Truly magical. First of all, I returned alive. Second, I didn't see any intifada. Third, I met a group of good people. Their activity is not going to demonstrations, chatting with their [usual] friends, and returning home. Their activity is . . . traveling to a different country, sitting together, talking."

The *Jerusalem Post*'s Amy Louise Kazmin wrote about a former soldier, Dudu Mahanaimi, age twenty-four, who "had never attended such a meeting. 'Usually when I saw these people, they were throwing stones and I was shooting plastic things at them. . . .' Mahanaimi said he hopes to talk more with a young Palestinian man he met there. Most importantly, Mahanaimi said he believed he had gotten past his fear of sitting down and talking to people he had been taught to view as his enemy."

This first successful action in Nablus was universally acclaimed by our group. The Nablus members reported very positive reactions in their community. Once we had recovered from the exhausting work of planning and execution, we wanted to plan another activity. Our new contact person, Major Elise, seemed likely to provide us with permits for the Palestinians, so we decided to plan an action in Jerusalem. We combined the familiar elements of visits in homes and a mass activity that, now that we had some funding, would be a joint dinner in a large hall.

Our first idea for an activity, more than a year before, had been for an outdoor march in Nablus, but we had decided that it would be subject to the army's whims, and therefore rejected the idea. Now I asked our friends if they would like to hold a peace parade in Jerusalem. I explained that unlike the people of Nablus, who lived under an occupation in which there were no guaranteed civil liberties, we lived in a democracy, and it was our right to get a police permit to hold a parade. The idea seemed a bit novel to them, but they had no objection to us, their hosts, turning to our own authorities, and they were even willing for Israeli police to accompany and guard the parade, as was our custom. They explained that they would not apply for a permit in Nablus from the Israeli authorities, whose legitimacy they denied, but they accepted Israeli authority in West Jerusalem, and so there was no reason not to receive local police protection.

We were already experienced at planning these activities, and all went smoothly. We set the date for 29 August 1993, and lined up twenty Israeli homes, all in the same area of Talpiyot, Bak'a, Abu-Tor, and Arnona, to host Palestinians and Israelis for coffee. We rented the dining hall of the Zohar Hotel in Arnona, which was close and offered the cheapest meal, for a communal dinner. We got a police permit to march from Talpiyot to the hotel. The Palestinians found 150 people (including children) to come to Jerusalem and, thanks to Major Elise, the Civil Administration provided permits for everyone, which Hilal picked up. We arranged for three Israelis to act as guides on the three Nablus buses, to lead them to drop-off points that we carefully set up, with maps and written instructions, so that transportation would take minimal time. We rented mobile phones for each bus (cell phones were not yet common). We allowed an hour for coffee, an hour for the march (of less than one kilometer), and an hour for dinner. It was an ambitious program, but it seemed doable.

Unfortunately, the Palestinians had understood that the three buses would all go to the same drop-off place, so the families were not distributed properly among the buses. Veronika, who met the buses, lost a lot of time in rearranging the groups. Then, one bus got stuck—between the high stone walls in the narrow street next to the Greek Orthodox monastery compound—and needed to back out painfully slowly. Poor Veronika phoned me and asked me to come right over to Judith's to help. I agreed, but after hanging up I decided that it was more important for me to wait for the bus that was coming to my house. I called Veronika back, but the battery of her rented mobile phone had just died, so she never got the message that I was not coming.

Somehow, Veronika managed to get things straightened out, but she couldn't understand why I never showed up. Our bus arrived about fifty minutes late, when it was almost time to start the march. I distributed the Palestinians among my apartment and those of three neighbors. We only had a few minutes before we had to leave for the march, but it was hard to get people to leave the homes, since this is what they had really looked forward to. Finally, we sent them by foot to the place where the march was to start, since Danny had to take the bus to pick up the Israelis and Palestinians from Bak'a. I decided to ride with him, but I soon realized that it was very late, so I got off and began walking back to the starting point. It was then that I realized that I'd left the signs for the march back in my garden. There was no way of getting a ride back, so I ran up the hill, in the heat, the kilometer to my home. I reached my garden, panting, but there were no signs to be seen. I could only pray that someone had spotted them and taken them. I turned and ran back down the hill, my throat completely parched.

In the meantime, the police and press had assembled at the starting point and could not understand why there were no marchers. The policemen began to grumble that they were being stood up. Finally, Veronika and the families from Talpiyot arrived. The police officer said it was late and that the march should start, but no one knew the route except me, so Veronika pleaded with him to wait a little longer. The officer gave an ultimatum: either start the march right away or the permit would be canceled. Fortunately, one of the neighbors, who had come outside to see what all the excitement was about, knew the officer, as he played bridge with some of his friends. The neighbor intervened and coaxed the officer into giving us a few more minutes.

I finally arrived, completely out of breath and dehydrated. There was no time to waste, so we started immediately. Fortunately, despite all that had gone wrong that day, the Israelis and Palestinians were in excellent moods, and everyone helped to make the march a success. As we started out, Danny's bus arrived and the Bak'a people joined us. The police stopped traffic and we marched down the main street of Talpiyot. The huge signs miraculously appeared, with our message in three languages: "We Want Peace between Palestine and Israel, Each Free and Secure." Palestinians and Israelis carried them together, the photographers snapped pictures, and we marched together behind a police car while policemen guarded us. For the Palestinians, it was an amazing sight: Israeli security forces were protecting them.

But that was nothing compared to what happened next. An Israeli teenager from the neighborhood, seeing the Arabs and the signs and the parade, tried to ride his bicycle into the group to hurt an Arab. The police officer grabbed the bike before it could do any harm, pushed the Jewish kid over to a wall, held him tightly by his clothes, and told him to get out of there in no uncertain terms. As the kid rode off, the officer returned as calm as could be to lead us on toward the hotel. It pleased me no end to see the looks on the faces of the Palestinian children, who could not believe that Israeli police would support them against a Jew.

We reached the hotel and the Israelis and Palestinians, who had met at the brief coffee visits, joined together at the tables for a sit-down dinner. For the first time, everyone could relax, the time pressure had ended, and the hungry crowd fell to eating and talking. I finally got some water, which was all that I really wanted. A bunch of Israeli and Palestinian kids went off to the side to play card games, somehow explaining the rules to each other without a common language. And then I realized that there was no press covering the event—they had taken pictures of the march and left. How could they not cover this story? Where were the reporters?

The Palestinians, some of whom were delegates to the peace talks in Madrid, knew that something was going on. "Don't worry," they reassured me. "The reporters have a bigger story to prepare. There's going to be peace. There's an agreement today." I had no idea what they were talking about, but on that night the Oslo Accords were first announced in Israel.

Even though no report was published about our joint dinner, the picture of our march accompanied the story of the Oslo Accords in newspapers and magazines all over the world. Completely by chance, it was the perfect illustration for the Palestinian-Israeli agreement to seek a negotiated peace.

The Palestinians' permits expired at 8:00 PM, but they were so exhilarated that they didn't care. It was, as usual, hard to get people to leave. Palestinians and Israelis exchanged telephone numbers. Finally, the three buses started back toward Nablus. We Israeli organizers rode with them to the army checkpoint at the exit from Jerusalem to be sure they would have no trouble, and we heard them singing happy songs all the way. The combination of the announcement of the Oslo Accords and the success of our event gave them hope—a rare commodity in our part of the world.

Things were going so well with the Nablus group (in contrast with the Beit Sahour dialogue group, which had fallen into conflict between the Palestinian members who opposed and those who supported the Oslo Accords) that we went ahead and planned another large activity. During the Jewish holiday of Sukkot (Tabernacles), Jewish kids are out of school and religious Jews are allowed to travel. In the Bible the two mountains flanking Nablus are called the mount of the blessing (Mt. Gerizim) and the mount of the curse (Mt. Ebal). The Palestinians suggested a picnic on Mt. Gerizim.

We organized about 150 Israelis, including many families with small children; the Palestinians did the same. On 5 October 1993 our three buses chugged up the mountain, past the Jewish settlement of Brachah, and reached the Samaritan community atop the mountain. The Palestinians and the Samaritans (who follow an ancient religion akin to Judaism) greeted us, and led us to a wonderful picnic area. While the families spread out food and the kids ran around freely and played, several Jews and Arabs erected a portable *sukkah* (a movable booth) in which the religious Jews could carry out the required prayer for the holiday before eating. The reporters and cameramen could see what we were best at—Arabs and Jews visiting together, without fear, as good neighbors, enthusiastic and filled with hope. The army was decent and didn't bother to visit us at all. The soldiers had apparently learned the strange lesson that Israelis and Palestinians get along fine when they are mutually committed to peace.

The Nablus group continued to be very active. We organized trips to kibbutzim in the area, where the kibbutzniks joined the Nablus residents in large group discussions, and then invited them to drink coffee in members' homes. The Nabulsis, many of whom had grown up in Marxist organizations, were interested in learning about the kibbutz structure.

We sent letters of congratulations to President Ezer Weizmann, Prime Minister Rabin, and Chairman Arafat for their work promoting peace. It was strange getting replies from the bureau chiefs of the Israeli president and prime minister addressed "Dear Friends." We were not used to being on the same side. We also sent a joint letter to the widow of an Israeli officer who had just been killed by terrorists; she had responded to her loss by making a public statement to press forward toward peace.

For all of our successes with the Nablus group, we did not seem to be making a dent in Israeli thinking. I asked my son Noam, who was in the army at the time and was more influenced by general Israeli viewpoints, what the Palestinians could do that would affect his friends' attitudes toward them. He thought a bit, and then replied, "If they would come out for the release of Ron Arad, that would certainly make Israelis more sympathetic toward them."

Ron Arad is an Israeli air force navigator who was shot down over Lebanon and captured by an enemy militia in October 1986. For many years his whereabouts have been kept secret by his captors. Virtually all Israeli Jews identify with Ron and care very much about him being returned to his family. Our concern for him transcends our political points of view, and includes leftists and rightists without distinction.

We talked to our friends in Nablus about making a statement supporting the release of Ron Arad and other Israelis missing in action (essentially, three crew members of a tank that was destroyed at Sultan Ya'akob in the Lebanese war in June 1982, and two soldiers who were kidnapped in Lebanon in 1986). They agreed to do so if the statement also included support for releasing Palestinian prisoners and the dead being held by Israel.

I asked my cousin, who is an air force pilot, to get the telephone number of Ron's family. He got it in order to help me, but told me that he didn't like equating our missing soldiers with the Palestinians, whom he called not soldiers but terrorists. But as our group had studied the subject, we had learned of a parallel that we hadn't considered. During my reserve duty I had often passed a graveyard in the Jordan Rift near the Jiftlik, which I had been told contains the bodies of Palestinian terrorists who were killed in confrontations with us. I had never asked myself why we didn't return these bodies to their families for burial, even as we expect our enemies to return the bodies of our soldiers who fell behind the lines.

Together with the father of one of the missing Israelis, we met with an Arab lawyer, Issa Muhammad Hamad, who was the head of an organization seeking Palestinian fighters who were missing in action. He told us stories of missing people who were seen in Israeli prisons, but whom Israel denies holding. Issa claimed that some 100–180 Palestinians were still missing from the 1948 and 1967 wars and from terrorist actions. In addition, there was a large number of people in Israeli prisons whose release, now that the PLO was negotiating with Israel, would encourage the Palestinian masses to support the peace process.

Ran Cohen organized a meeting for our group in the Knesset (on 9 February 1994) with Knesset members from parties that made up more than half of our parliament. We hoped that our discussion would enable us to make a joint Palestinian-Israeli call to release Ron Arad and the other Israelis and Palestinians. We wrote, "The wars are behind us. Let the prisoners and the missing return home, and let's work together to build the peace."

Just before the Palestinian delegation left Nablus to go to the Knesset meeting, a reporter from an Israeli newspaper reached one of them by phone and asked whether it was true that this would be the first time that Palestinians closely related to the PLO would be visiting the Knesset. Our friends suddenly were struck by the magnitude of their stride forward, and decided that they should really get approval from the Palestinian leadership. However, they could not reach the appropriate high-level official to authorize their participation in a meeting with Knesset members in the Knesset building itself. I was out of the country at the time, so the burden fell on Veronika and Judith to convince the delegation to go ahead with the meeting, even though they could not get the desired permission. After a delay in which the busy Knesset members were impatiently waiting for our arrival, the Palestinians decided to proceed despite their concerns. The meeting went well, and was well reported in the press. The issue of Ron Arad was very much in the Israeli consciousness, and we did what we could to make the Palestinians' conciliatory attitude known to our people.

After the Oslo Accords, the peace process went through many ups and downs. Progress was slow and discouraging. While Prime Minister Yitzhak Rabin had the wisdom to allow the accords to be signed, it took him a long time to become convinced that the Palestinians could be trustworthy partners, and, in my opinion, Foreign Minister Shimon Peres had to pull him along at first. Only shortly before his assassination did Rabin really became enthusiastic about the peace process.

As the first anniversary of the peace process approached, and in light of the fact that many Palestinians and Israelis still expressed their hesitancy or opposition, we decided to organize a large march to support the peace process, down the main street of Nablus. It had already been announced that the large Palestinian cities, including Nablus, would be turned over to the Palestinian Autonomy, so our Palestinian friends were prepared to apply for a permit from the outgoing Israeli administration. We designed signs for the march showing the Palestinian and Israeli flags, with a handshake superimposed on them, and the slogans "Let's Make the Peace Process Work" and "Two Peoples, Two States, One Future." I could picture thousands of Palestinians and Israelis marching together in Nablus to give encouragement to those who were struggling to keep the peace process moving. And finally, we were planning an action to support government policy, so it seemed that we would have no trouble getting approval to march.

We decided to schedule the march in Nablus exactly one year after our successful one in Talpiyot, on 29 August. On the fourth of August, we faxed Major Elise Shazar a request for permission to march, and asked for a meeting with the authorities to plan it out. After two and a half weeks we got the reply that the Civil Administration had no objection, but the army would not grant permission. We then faxed a request to General Ilan Biran, oc Central Command, but never received a reply. On 28 August, with time already having run out, we changed the date of the planned march to 13 September 1994 and faxed Defense Minister Rabin to request a permit. We waited and waited for a reply, but realized that time was again running out. At the same time, things were tense in Nablus, with rival Palestinian groups imposing their rule in the street as the army was getting ready to leave. So we decided to move the activity to Jerusalem, in a simplified repeat of our previous year's activity, but leaving out the march.

We brought about a hundred Palestinians to fifteen homes in West Jerusalem for home visits with coffee and cake, and then moved directly to the Zohar Hotel for a festive dinner. The hotel was decked out with the signs that we had prepared for our canceled Nablus march, with the two flags. In the hope of attracting the press, and to give our activity more legitimacy, we invited the American consul general, Ed Abington, to speak to the group. He gave a very positive speech, but the participants were so busy talking to each other over their dinner that I'm afraid we were a rather rude audience. Virtually no press covered the story, so we were again unsuccessful in getting our message out to the public.

It was good that we had moved the activity to Jerusalem, because on 5 September Haim Yisraeli from Defense Minister Rabin's bureau wrote us that the Central Command would not permit any marches or demonstrations in the occupied territories since such activities might be inflammatory and could lead to disorder and violence. Not only was such a blanket ban excessively broad, but in fact Jewish settlers were allowed to demonstrate in the territories on several occasions. For example, on 14 June 1995, oc Central Command General Ilan Biran gave in to pressure and permitted 300 settlers to demonstrate against the Palestinian Information Ministry in the Palestinian town of Al-Birah. Similarly, on 19 October

1995, hundreds of settlers marched in the streets of Hebron, under heavy protection by the security forces, to protest the government's intention to allow Arabs to drive in Shouhada Street in that city.

As the date for the army's pulling out of Nablus approached, I suggested that once Nablus was autonomous, we could get a permit from the Palestinian municipality and organize a really huge march to support the peace process. We agreed to plan a march of thousands of Palestinians and Israelis down the main street, once everything was calmed down and under control.

The Israeli army pulled out at night and was attacked by the Palestinian citizenry, with the Palestinian police having to hold back their people to prevent a violent clash. Palestinians seized an Israeli flag and burned it on top of the administration building. This was the picture that Israelis saw, giving them that impression of how the Palestinians received our withdrawal. Our counterdemonstration took on increased importance.

We waited several weeks for things to calm down in Nablus. We contacted our friends, but they were busy as community leaders trying to solve local problems. It was not yet time for our large joint march. We waited longer. The control of the streets had moved into Palestinian hands. But Palestinians did not feel a pressing need to use the street to send positive messages to the worried Israelis. For some reason, reassuring the Israelis, who held the keys to freedom, was not on the agenda. So we lost another golden opportunity. The march never took place.

In order to expand the dialogues to villages around Nablus, our friends took us to the town of Salfit, which had been the center of the Palestinian Communist Party in 1948. The communists, unlike most other Palestinian groups, had supported the UN decision to partition Mandatory Palestine, and accepted the idea of a Jewish state beside a Palestinian state. In part, this acceptance was related to the Soviet Union's support for the State of Israel. The communists did not participate in terrorism against us, and were enthusiastic about the peace process that came out of the Oslo Accords.

In Salfit we met representatives from several villages in the area. We discussed the possibility of organizing a joint Israeli-Palestinian activity, such as a picnic, with the press invited. An old farmer from Kafr Ad-Dik invited us to his village. He said that his community had a lot of trouble with the nearby Jewish settlements, and suggested that we combine the picnic with an exposé of settler activities. We set a date to meet to plan the activity at the farmer's home. When we subsequently arrived at his home, we were surprised that our friends from Nablus, who were so experienced in working with us and who had our complete confidence, did not attend. We would have to solo with our new colleagues from Kafr Ad-Dik.

Our new friends had picked out a place for the picnic, next to the highway, with an excellent view of the two settlements, Paduel and Alei Zahav. However, there was no shade, and the proximity to the highway could make it unsafe for small children and might have led to clashes with settlers, who used the highway as well. We asked if there were any places where people usually went for picnics, but I gathered that picnics were not so much a part of the villagers' culture. We had noticed a pine grove at the southern end of the village. At our request, the villagers took us to it. It was one of the most beautiful nature spots I have seen in Israel or Palestine—there were old pines, olive trees, terraces, and a dirt road leading to nowhere. It was absolutely perfect, shady and safe, away from the settlers but with a view of their settlements across the valley. The villagers all knew this place, but it hadn't occurred to them how perfect it was for our needs.

The villagers told us about their problems. Though there were 4,000 residents, the Civil Administration hadn't bothered to connect them to electricity, water, or telephones. They had bought their own generator, which they ran several hours a day for electricity, and they drew water from cisterns. They had no post office or kindergarten, no garbage collection or ambulance. All of these services were provided, they told us, to the two small Jewish settlements nearby, which had been built on land taken from the villagers. They also showed us raw sewage pouring down the hill from the Barkan Industrial Area (for Jewish industries only) into the valley, where they said it was entering the local aquifer.

We organized a group of Israeli families to come out for the picnic on 18 September 1995. I tried hard to get Israeli television to attend this very photogenic activity, but the best we could do was to get a producer from *Good Morning, Israel* who had no experience in the occupied territories, and we got no coverage from prime-time evening programs. We began by driving our bus to an area being prepared for the expansion of one of the settlements. The TV crew interviewed our Zvi, who gave an excellent explanation of the problem. Then we drove toward the picnic site, but the bus got stuck in the narrow village road. The Israelis and Palestinians got off and walked down the dirt road to the picnic area. I helped the bus driver turn around, but then noticed that the TV crew hadn't arrived. I called the producer on her mobile phone to ask whether she was having trouble finding us. "Oh, it's OK," she replied. "I have enough material. After we photographed your group, the head of security for the settlement drove up and I interviewed him. There's no need for any more."

"But the whole point of the activity is the picnic," I protested. "We're holding a picnic with Israeli and Palestinian families, in a Palestinian village, without any army. How often do you see such a thing? There's no problem getting here. I can see your van, and I'll direct you here."

The producer got talked into joining us. She entered the enchanted grove, with the people spread out under the trees looking as if this were the most ordinary thing in the world. She rose to the occasion and began filming and interviewing. While she may have missed a lot of the significance of the meeting, she did get a little of the flavor for those Israelis who would be watching TV the next morning at 8:00 AM.

The picnic was so great that we returned to Kafr Ad-Dik a month later to pick olives with the families. Olive picking was good fun, and was repeated in different villages in the future.

With autonomy came the demise of the large demonstrative actions in our Nablus-Jerusalem group. Judith (with some other Israelis) kept working on developing overnight retreats, tours of Nablus, a program for childbirth education, alternative medicine, group dynamics workshops, and similar activities.

For me, however, there was a great disappointment. I had believed that it was only my government's restrictions that prevented us from broadcasting the Palestinians' message of peace with large joint actions. Yet when left to themselves, the Palestinians did not waste their time with such activity. The opportunity for success seemed to have arrived, yet for reasons that I couldn't really understand, the will to continue in our old ways was no longer there.

CHAPTER 18

Jerusalem Municipal Elections and Meeting Arafat in Tunis

I was always searching for a way in which Palestinians could work alongside Israelis to exhibit their good intentions. While demonstrations were illegal in the West Bank, they were legal in Jerusalem, a city that follows Israeli law even in the annexed Arab areas called "East Jerusalem." Peace Now had taken advantage of this situation in an enormous "Hands around Jerusalem" demonstration where many thousands of Israelis and Palestinians linked hands around the Old City in a human chain for peace. But the police had instructions to find some provocation to break it up. When some Palestinian youths began singing what the police claimed were nationalistic songs, the police charged in, with billy clubs flailing and water cannons blasting, and the press reported the event as one more example of Palestinian violence.

Palestinians in Jerusalem were reluctant to ask for police permits for demonstrations, because they felt that asking would indicate acceptance of Israeli sovereignty over East Jerusalem, the part of the city that had been captured by Israel in 1967 and was now annexed. In addition, there was a good chance that the police would turn them down, and in any event the Shabak would photograph the participants and get its revenge later. With municipal elections coming up in 1988, I talked to my old friend Sarah Kaminker, who was running for city council on the Ratz (CRM)-Shinui ticket, asking if Palestinians might use the framework of the elections to present their ideas for peace and independence.

All Palestinian residents of Jerusalem, including the vast majority who are Jordanian citizens, have the right to vote in municipal elections (but only those who hold Israeli citizenship may vote for the Knesset). Nonetheless, virtually none of the Jordanian citizens vote, because the Palestinian leadership has told them that doing so would weaken their claim for Palestinian sovereignty over East Jerusalem. The only significant exceptions are among the Palestinian municipal workers, most of whom work in menial jobs, who were bused to the polls under the watchful eyes of their Jewish supervisors in order to vote for Mayor Teddy Kollek and not risk losing their jobs.

Sarah agreed to organize an election march in Beit Safafa, an Arab village in Jerusalem where half the residents have been Israeli citizens since 1949 and the other half are Jordanians. We met with Fuad, who was born in the Israeli side of the village and was married to a woman from Sharafat in the formerly Jordanian side of the village. Fuad had achieved the highest rank of any Arab bureaucrat in Israeli Jerusalem. He was interested in organizing villagers to vote for Ratz, which had a pretty good record regarding Arabs. We met several times with Fuad and his wife in their home in Sharafat, and he told us he could get about 300 villagers to participate in a march through the village, supporting Ratz and an independent Palestinian state.

I submitted to the police the request for an election march and rally. Our route would be from Sharafat, on the formerly Jordanian side, to the soccer field on the Israeli side of the old Green Line. But a funny thing happened. Even though the Green Line had been removed from all maps, and Israel considered Sharafat to be as Israeli as Tel Aviv, the police would not allow us to march there or in any of the villages that had been annexed in 1967. I assumed that the police wanted to avoid setting a precedent of allowing free demonstrations in the annexed Arab sections of East Jerusalem. In addition, they specifically prohibited "nationalistic slogans, displaying Palestinian flags, or any other national symbol *expressing hatred to the state*" (emphasis added). It was therefore unclear to me whether the police would ban some of our slogans, which had been agreed on by Fuad and the party leaders:

- "Equal rights for Arabs and Jews"
- "⅓ of the budget for ⅓ of the population" (One-third of Jerusalemites are Arab, but only a small part of the budget goes to Arab areas.)
- "Keep the schools open" (There was concern that because of the intifada, schools might be closed down.)
- "End the bloodshed"
- "From occupation to freedom: Two states for two peoples"
- "Peace talks between the State of Israel and the PLO"

I wanted the party to take the police to court over limitations on the route and possibly on the content of our electioneering slogans. We had a final planning meeting at Sarah's house. Fuad excused himself to the bathroom, and after some time came back, sweating profusely. Sarah and I exchanged glances. Fuad was high on drugs. We sensed that something was terribly wrong with the arrangements, but it was too late to cancel the demonstration. We dropped any complaints against the police.

Our plan had called for speeches by three candidates from the party and a member of the Knesset. Fuad was to represent the village. But instead of 300 villagers, the only Palestinians who showed up were Fuad's family and a dozen children whom he had managed to round up. It was tragic that a man with his talents had gotten hooked on drugs. In the Gulf War, three years later, he even spied for Saddam Hussein in order to get money for drugs. He was caught and spent some time in prison.

For Sarah and me, the lack of success was one more discouragement. I had thought we could find a crack in the government's defenses against Palestinians voicing independent peaceful ideas. But we hadn't succeeded in finding a partner who could utilize this tactic.

Ratz-Shinui did quite well in the elections, and Sarah won a place on the municipal council. She was an extremely effective member of the council (a position without remuneration). We frequently talked about the Arabs of East Jerusalem. She explained to me how, after the conquest of the West Bank in 1967, Israel decided to expand the city to include not just Jordanian East Jerusalem (including the Old City) but as much surrounding land, with as few Arabs, as possible. Land was taken from twenty-eight villages and towns, and Jerusalem's area increased threefold. The Israeli town planners marked a blue line on their maps around the built-up area of each annexed village, and would not allow any homes to be built on the village lands beyond that blue line (i.e., the residential areas could never expand). A series of severe measures was taken to grab land from the Palestinians for Jewish use and to prevent the Palestinians from building on the land that they still owned. Huge portions of the Arab lands occupied since the war were expropriated under Mayor Teddy Kollek, on which were built high-rise, dense neighborhoods for Jewish use only. Much of the Arabs'

remaining private lands were zoned as open green areas or were reserved for public purposes, designations that prevented the owners from obtaining building permits. Even when permits were issued, they were always for low-density building, usually only one or two stories high. This policy was intended to prevent landowners from building and thus, because of the overcrowding in Arab areas, to force young Palestinians to leave the city so that there would remain a "demographic balance" of no more than about 24–28 percent Palestinians within the municipal borders. Housing was probably the most severe problem facing the Arabs of East Jerusalem. Many who could not get building permits tried to build anyway on their privately owned land. Subsequently, the municipality tore down many of these structures.

Since the Palestinians would not vote, their numbers did not give them any political clout in the municipality. Sarah favored keeping Jerusalem open as a single urban unit, but with Israeli sovereignty over the western portion and Palestinian sovereignty over the Arab sections. In this plan, Jerusalem would serve as the capital of both states (to be). But Ratz would not express such a stand, out of fear of alienating the Jewish voters who wanted all of the expanded "Jerusalem" to be retained by Israel, so Sarah had to keep her views to herself.

Despite her popularity, Sarah had been squeezed out in the primaries, which took place several months before the 1993 municipal elections. Her work as a municipal councillor would be ended after just one five-year term. I called her on the night of the primary and could hear her great disappointment.

"Thanks, Hillel, for calling to console me. It's good of you," she said.

"I'm not calling to console you," I answered. "I'm calling to congratulate you. You've finally gotten rid of that party yoke that held you back. Now I have a proposal to make to you. You start a new party, a party that calls for two capitals in Jerusalem, with the Palestinians sovereign in their own part of the city. We'll talk to the Palestinian leadership in Jerusalem and offer them a joint party, which will give them power in the municipal council without giving up their claim to their own sovereignty. Once Palestinian nationalists are firmly established in the Jerusalem municipality, they can carry out their campaign for sovereignty, for housing, for budgets, for schools—all from the powerful and legitimate position of elected officials of their community. And, if they are willing to have Jews run with them, they will give added legitimacy to their cause by showing that their nationalism is not anti-Jewish."

Sarah was dumbstruck. She had always wanted to take a strong stand on Palestinian rights in Jerusalem, but could not go beyond what her party would permit. My idea came at just the right time to keep her from dropping out of politics. She thought it over, and finally her answer was positive.

Sarah decided to bring in another municipal councillor, Moshe Amirav, who had also lost in the latest primaries and was outspoken in his support for Palestinian sovereignty in part of the city. Moshe had started his political career in the right-wing Herut Party of Menahem Begin, but had moved around a lot politically. The other founding members of the group were the following:

- Dr. Veronika Cohen from the dialogue groups
- Dr. Lotte Salzburger (now deceased), a social worker who had been a deputy mayor in previous councils, who established an agency providing legal protection for Arabs who fall victim to governmental abuse
- Dr. Gershon Baskin, the Israeli co-director of the Israel-Palestine Center for Research and Information
- The late Dr. Shlomo Elbaz, born in Morocco, who had founded a peace movement for Jews from African and Asian countries, called East for Peace

In the way I viewed our task, the Palestinians constituted about one-third of the city's eligible voters. Since few of them had ever voted, they were not divided between several parties. I assumed that just as the *haredim* (ultra-Orthodox Jews) vote as a bloc the way their rabbi tells them, the Palestinians would vote as a bloc for the new party when so instructed by the PLO. I envisioned a joint party of Arabs and Jews as ideal, because we could help them to fight the Israeli system, and our presence would give a positive message to the Jewish population—that Palestinians are willing to try to find an end to our conflict. I was equally willing to have a party with only Arab candidates if that was their wish. In any case, it was clear that virtually no Jews would vote for this party.

I envisioned possible attempts by Jewish politicians to place obstacles in the way of Arab voting—for example, they could pass a law stating that every candidate must sign a document declaring that he or she supports Jerusalem's remaining under exclusive Israeli sovereignty. I also anticipated problems after our candidates got elected—perhaps all the Jewish parties would agree never to form coalitions or make deals with our party, effectively destroying the Arab councillors' power to affect conditions in Jerusalem.

My principal reasons for recommending that Palestinians enter the elections was for them to gain an enhanced platform from which to tell Israelis and the world the solution they wanted for Jerusalem, and for them to gain access to information (from municipal records) about discrimination against Arabs in Jerusalem, which they could use to prove their need to get out from under Jewish domination. Sarah and the others were more concerned with the continuous loss of Arab lands to Jewish building projects, and they considered the main goal of Palestinian participation in the council to be the acquisition of political power to block land expropriations and house demolitions.

My colleagues were concerned about funding for the election campaign. It seemed to me that there was no need for costly advertising. I envisioned the campaign as helping Palestinians to develop a mostly volunteer network and to pressure their community to get voters to the polls. Once at the polls, they would presumably vote for the only party supporting Palestinian sovereignty over part of Jerusalem.

It seemed like an excellent opportunity for the Palestinians. We Israelis were a group who had proven ourselves to be reliable partners in various struggles. As Zionists, we could help them avoid the many possible tricks that Israeli politicians would use to prevent Arabs from taking a larger slice of the municipal pie. We could also make the contacts with the municipal and state authorities that the Palestinians might find repugnant. The deal seemed so good that I could not believe that the Palestinians would not welcome it with open arms.

According to Israeli law, Sarah and Moshe were allowed to leave their party in the municipality before the end of their term and start a new party. The Ratz-Shinui coalition was furious with them for creating competition for the next elections, but was even more furious when we threatened to take a big chunk of the governmental funding (which is based on the number of party members in the outgoing council) for running the election campaign. Mayor Teddy Kollek's "One Jerusalem" slate of candidates (who were mainly from the Labor Party) also felt threatened that we might take away the few Arab votes that Meron Benvenisti was trying to organize for Teddy.

We named the party, in Hebrew, Shlom Yerushalayim (which means the Peace, or Welfare, of Jerusalem) from the biblical passage "Seek the welfare of Jerusalem . . ." In Arabic it was called Salaam min ajal al-Quds (Peace for the Good of Jerusalem).

We met with Faisal Husseini and other Palestinian leaders. They were interested in the idea, but were very worried that participation in the municipal elections might look like acquiescence to the annexation of East Jerusalem by Israel. We tried to convince them that running on a platform calling for two sovereignties in Jerusalem would prove that they reject the annexation. I asked the Palestinians, "When the municipal trucks come to take away the garbage in your village, do you lie down in front of them and say 'Don't touch our garbage. You are occupiers'? If you pay taxes to the municipality without accepting Israeli rule, why can't you put your representatives in the council to decide what's to be done with the tax money?"

The political leaders set up meetings for us with a wide variety of community leaders in Arab Jerusalem. In virtually every discussion, whether our interlocutors agreed with us or not, they told us that what was important was what Yasser Arafat would say about it, and we should go to Tunis (where he was in exile) to talk to him directly. If Arafat sent the word to vote, the Palestinians would come out in large numbers. But if he said to boycott the elections, virtually no one would vote.

In those days, before the Oslo Accords, it was illegal for Israelis to travel to Tunis or to meet with PLO representatives. Nonetheless, we decided to send a delegation to Arafat. We waited patiently for the invitation from him to come. Finally it arrived, and luckily for us, just at that time the Oslo Accords were announced and the regulations against meeting with the PLO were rescinded.

Sarah, Moshe, and I flew to Rome, and from there to Tunis. We were assured that our visas would be waiting for us at Tunis. While I have an American passport in addition to my Israeli passport, I felt that as a representative of an Israeli party I should use only my Israeli passport. When we landed in Tunis, we were whisked aside to a room in the airport which belonged to the PLO. The PLO official took our Israeli passports and gave us visas that we could use to identify ourselves. I had always been extremely careful when traveling not to lose my Israeli passport, lest it reach the hands of terrorists. And here we simply turned them over to the PLO. It was a very strange feeling.

The PLO men drove us to a hotel and told us that we would be contacted when Arafat was ready to receive us. We had been told stories of people waiting several days to gain an audience. We had some delicious Tunisian couscous, then tried to relax in the lobby, but suddenly an official told us that we could proceed now: we had an appointment for eleven that night. The driver and the armed escorts reminded me of our own Shabak bodyguards in their appearance, dress, and mannerisms. As we drove into a lovely residential neighborhood, we noticed that on every corner stood a soldier with a Kalashnikov. We were getting closer. Finally, we saw a private home surrounded by barricades and lots of young, armed men. The car could go no farther. We walked with our escort to the building. Interestingly, we were never searched; the Palestinians apparently trusted us. The PLO men were without exception friendly and relaxed with this trio of Israeli visitors.

We were taken past guards upstairs to Arafat's office. It was a very simple room, with an old-fashioned writing table, the kind that does not hide your legs. On the wall behind it was a large picture of the golden Dome of the Rock in the Old City of Jerusalem. The only other furniture was a couple of couches and a place for Arafat's secretary. Chairman Arafat greeted us warmly. He did not sit behind his desk, but moved his chair in front of it so that there was less distance between us. Sarah and Moshe gave an excellent presentation about the pressing danger—soon, there would be no more Arab lands to struggle over in East Jerusalem. Gaining power in the municipal council might help the Palestinians hold on to what little was still left.

At one point the chairman was called away to the phone, and his wife, Suha, entered and chatted with us. In the end, Arafat told us that he would have to think over the suggestion for Palestinians to vote, and would let us know in a few days.

We spent the next morning touring Tunis. When people asked where we were from, we answered "Israel," and everyone took it in stride, even though we must have been among the first Israeli tourists to visit the town. I liked everything about Tunis, its Mediterranean character, its flatness (great for jogging or biking), the bustle of the street life, the friendliness of the people. We rode in a taxi and the driver pointed out a kosher butcher and every Jewish shop along the route.

We flew back to Israel and waited for an answer from Tunis. We considered some new proposals—what about having only Israeli Arabs (who happened to be living in Jerusalem) run for the council, but encouraging all the Arabs in Jerusalem to vote for them? I was getting less and less enthusiastic about the situation. My original idea of utilizing the city council for educational (or propaganda) purposes had never caught on. If the Palestinians would not vote in tremendous numbers, I felt that the project would be viewed as a failure.

While we were waiting to hear from Tunis, I posed a hypothetical question. What if we succeeded in capturing one-third of the municipal council and had a chance to make a coalition with the ultra-Orthodox Jews? They, like the Palestinians, are anti-Zionist and oppose the State of Israel. Suppose they would agree to no more expropriations or demolitions in exchange for having more power to coerce us secular Jews and to inflict their way of life on us. Would the Jewish members of our party agree to such a deal? Sarah said definitely not: How could we destroy Jerusalem for secular Jews? This answer made me wonder whether the Palestinians wouldn't do better with an all-Arab party, so they could seek out the best deals possible without worrying about our needs. After all, we are free to move to Tel Aviv if Jerusalem becomes fundamentalist like Tehran.

Among the seven Jewish members, only Sarah, Moshe, and Gershon wanted to run for office, so for the rest of us the subject was not personally pressing. A new issue concerning financing for the election then came up. We could get NIS 500,000 (Israeli new shekels, equivalent to about $170,000) from the government, because Sarah and Moshe were currently on the council. But we would have to give guarantees that if we didn't get enough votes, we would return the money. I felt that the Palestinian leadership should give the guarantees, since they would be responsible for getting out the vote. Otherwise, we should give up the right to get government financing. I also felt that if we did take the money, we should spend almost all of it on community needs, and not waste any on advertising or on paying people who would promise to bring out their families and friends. But I was afraid that if we did receive the money, it would lead to corruption, and we Israelis would find it hard to tell our Palestinian partners how to spend the funds.

With only a couple of days left until the slates of candidates had to be submitted, I felt that the time needed to organize things properly was running out. I also felt that it was a mistake for us to enter such a major undertaking with such ambivalent and uncertain partners. Then, we got a message, from an Arab member of Knesset, that there was a particular Israeli Arab living in Jerusalem who could be the head of the slate, but it was not yet clear whether Palestinians (other than Israeli citizens) would be allowed by the PLO to vote. And the Palestinians were not in a position to give bank guarantees.

We also heard criticism of this particular Palestinian; some said that he had served in a certain community function without doing any work. He was not a well-known leader who could rally Palestinian enthusiasm. He would not have been our choice, but if we had felt that we had real partners in the Jerusalem Palestinian leadership, we might have accepted him anyway. We held a vote as to whether to accept what was offered and hope for the best, or throw in the towel. Some of our members felt that we should stick with our plans, but I had become determined to dissociate myself from what I now saw as a losing cause. We decided to pull out.

My image of the campaign had been of a cause that would bring the Palestinian villages and neighborhoods, the *hamoulas* (clans), the different illegal political parties, and the competing leaders into one united struggle that would use Israel's democracy to push forward the rights of the Palestinians for sovereignty over parts of Jerusalem. For the Palestinians to enter the campaign without enthusiasm seemed to me to assure the defeat of the opportunity, and more harm than good would come from it.

The Palestinian leadership in Jerusalem and in Tunis invested a good amount of time and energy in struggling with the question, but they did not choose to establish a joint Palestinian-Israeli leadership that could have worked together to build a party. The one exception was journalist Daoud Kuttab, Jonathan's brother whom I had met in the streets of

Ramallah when I was a soldier. Daoud joined us in the very last days, he had no trouble working with Jews, and he immediately won our respect. He supported the idea of entering the council and tried his best to save the project, but to my thinking he came too late and without enough Palestinian backing.

If I try to summarize what I learned from the experience of Shlom Yerushalayim, it is that it is much harder to find Palestinian partners who think as I do than I sometimes have believed.

CHAPTER 19

Jericho IV

The Tourist Board

The Oslo Accords meant that the kind of activities I believed in—joint activities that would influence public opinion by giving each people a new way of looking at the other—would be easier, since they would no longer be blocked by the Israel Defense Forces. I believed that the power of the Palestinians, once they could show themselves to be a peace-loving people, was unstoppable.

The first step of the new peace process was to set up autonomous areas in Gaza and Jericho. I immediately went to my old friends Yusra and Sa'ed Sweiti in Jericho with an idea. Why shouldn't Jericho develop as a tourist center for Israelis? Many Israelis were panicked by the new peace process. They couldn't believe that we were going to allow a Palestinian police force to be armed. They couldn't believe that Jews would ever again move about in Jericho without being killed. Why not show them that Palestinian independence would not push them out of large parts of the Holy Land, but that the Palestinians would welcome them as tourists, just as Egypt welcomes them in Egypt and Sinai?

Before the intifada, Israelis had loved Jericho. Whether on their way from Jerusalem to the Sea of Galilee, or simply to spend a few hours, Israelis would drive to the desert town, sit in the garden restaurants, eat Arabic food and sip Arabic coffee, shop in the little *suq*, and visit the antiquities. Jericho was known then as an extremely moderate town that welcomed Israeli tourism. With the intifada, Israelis were missing this part of their Middle East experience.

Yusra was willing to try. She organized a group to meet with us to discuss the idea. The head of the group, Ibrahim "Abu-Amar" Jadallah, was a senior officer from the Palestinian army who had fought in Lebanon, and now had been allowed to return as part of the peace process. Abu-Amar had been given the function of head of tourism in the Jericho Autonomy.

Others in the impressive group were the head of archaeology in the autonomy, a young archaeologist from Bethlehem, two teachers (one from the Aqbat Jaber refugee camp), a journalist, and a woman who worked in tourism. On the Israeli side we had some of our veteran dialogue organizers, including Danny Orstav, Uri, and Shraga, along with several new but committed members.

We met at a new restaurant that had just been completed in the flurry of activity with the coming of autonomy. We talked about bringing groups of Israelis, first and foremost to make them feel welcome in the Palestinian-controlled area. We would include some meetings with Palestinians, and would drink coffee in Palestinian homes with Jerichoans who could present Palestinian thinking in a positive way. We would tour the town with Palestinian guides, and eat in the lovely garden restaurants. While tourism brings in money, we presented it mainly as a plan to affect public opinion. The meeting went well.

Afterward, Yusra took us to the office of Jibril Rajoub, the new head of the Palestinian security apparatus. He had moved into the old Israeli security headquarters. He greeted us warmly, and after we drank coffee together, he assured us that our project would have his support. "Just notify me whenever you bring a group of Israelis, and I'll look after their security."

At that time Israel had not yet built a road to bypass Jericho, so all traffic up the Jordan Rift passed through the Palestinian-run area. The newspapers were full of debates about whether it was safe for Israelis to drive through Jericho. MK Rehav'am "Gandhi" Ze'evi, who advocated "transferring" the Arabs out of the West Bank, was seen on television saying that he would shoot any armed Palestinian policeman who tried to stop him. We brought Abu-Amar the large colored signs we had made for the Nablus march (which never took place), with the two flags, the clasped hands, and the slogans "Two Peoples, Two States, One Future" and "Let's Make the Peace Process Work." We offered to provide him with even larger signs that he could hang over the main highway, at each entrance to the Jericho autonomous area, so that Israelis could see that Palestinians were seeking peace with them. We said that the highway was affording Palestinians free advertising to put across their message. If he put up the signs, he could also invite the press to come and film them, so the message would get to all Israelis and the world.

Abu-Amar was interested, and passed all our ideas to his superiors. When we didn't hear from him, we called his office and were told that he was in Jordan. We waited longer. We realized that the Palestinian Authority was busy with many projects and couldn't do everything at once. Our Palestinian friends from the West Bank told us that the new authority, whose members had returned from lengthy exile, were not used to working with Israelis, and it would take them some time to get used to the idea.

We are still waiting.

CHAPTER 20

Jerusalem Information Center

Sarah Kaminker and Daoud Kuttab set up a nongovernmental organization called the Jerusalem Information Center; it would make information available about the situation in East Jerusalem. My role in this center was primarily to help organize and guide, together with a Palestinian guide, trips through East and West Jerusalem to show groups of journalists, consular workers, and others the comparative conditions in the Jewish and Arab parts of the city.

I remembered from one of our dialogues in Jabel Mukabber that Jamil had said there were people in the village living in caves. I asked him if this was really true, and he said he would take us to see them. We drove down to the Kidron Valley to the subneighborhood of Sall'a, which, like the rest of Jabel Mukabber, is part of the Sawahre al-Gharbiyye village. There, we met Samih, who spoke perfect Hebrew, owned a garage, and taught automotive mechanics in a vocational school. He showed us the beautiful stone house that his family had built before 1967.

Sawahre, like many Arab villages in East Jerusalem, had no sewage system. Each house had its own cesspool. The bordering Jewish neighborhoods did have sewage systems, and in order to expand their systems a pipeline was laid through Sawahre to take the Jewish sewage to the Kidron Valley, where it was dumped untreated between the last Arab houses of the village and into the valley. The pipeline ran beside the foundations of Samih's house, which had begun to sag. Samih's engineer said the city was responsible, but the authorities denied it. He lacked the funds to enter into a long lawsuit with the city. The city engineers condemned the house as unsafe, so Samih's family had to find a new place to live. Fortunately, they owned some private land close by. Unfortunately, the city had never given out a single building permit for residents of Sawahre. So Samih began to build without a permit on his own land, resulting in the city inspectors issuing a stop-work injunction. He showed us the single wall he had put up before he was forced to stop.

Next to the sagging house were two large caves, which Samih's elderly parents had converted into their home, with doors affixed and a kitchen and furniture. It was startling to see that in this modern, "united" city, people were literally living in caves, even though they owned land in a sparsely populated valley. We asked Samih if we could bring the press to see this. He said that he knew that he would get into trouble for it, but he agreed.

On our next tour we brought a busload of journalists to see the caves. They were shocked to hear the story. Israeli television was doing a special show on Jerusalem and included the caves in its story. Cave dwelling is not common in Jerusalem, but this was certainly not the only case, and it illustrated, by being so extreme, what was happening to Arab housing needs throughout their neighborhoods and villages in "united" Jerusalem.

After several tours had visited the caves, Samih's parents decided that they were being treated like monkeys in a zoo. This was their home, and they wouldn't have any more people coming around to stare at them. But before that happened, the municipality decided that this publicity was undesirable. They warned Samih. They sent him a bill for municipal property tax to be paid for residing in the caves. One morning, Samih called me to say that his garage had been broken into and all the tools had been stolen from it. Ordinarily, thieves would sell the tools far away, but Samih was told that the thieves were selling them right in his own village. The significance was clear. They were collaborators who had been sent by the authorities to force Samih to stop working with our center.

The Sall'a neighborhood concentrated many problems into one small area. Since no one could ever get a building license, many people built illegally on their privately owned land, so there were lots of destroyed houses and lots of homes threatened with demolition. We located several families with large numbers of children (birth control seemed to be unused, especially in the poorer and Muslim families) who were forbidden to expand their tiny homes, and who were willing to be visited by our groups. In poor Arab homes, there is always a niche piled high with mattresses that are spread out at night, completely filling the floor space.

Once, we brought a tour from the U.S. consulate, and this crowdedness (which the family demonstrated by spreading out the mattresses and the kids) had a strong effect on the visitors. But other times we would come during the day, when the children were away at school, and the mothers would get tired of displaying their poverty to strangers. Even though these tours were designed to gain sympathy for the Palestinians' plight in East Jerusalem, it was hard to find enough people in the community who were willing to be available for a busload of strangers—who never quite made it on time.

Our route passed a spot where on our right was a beautiful, modern playground, protected by a high steel fence, for the Jewish children of East Talpiyot, and on our left were poor Arab homes where kids played in the street. It was clear to those members of our tours who looked out the windows of the bus (rather than chatting with their neighbors or reading) that there was an enormous discrepancy in the allocation of municipal resources to Arab and to Jewish neighborhoods. Scarce funds were not "wasted" on the Arab villagers, who were viewed as enemies and rivals, and who did not vote anyway.

The Arab village of Issawiyeh, which was annexed (de facto) to Jerusalem in 1967, is blessed with an active village council led by Darwish Darwish. Darwish was excellent at organizing tours of his village. Once, our tour visited a member of the village council to sip Arabic coffee in his home. He told us that his married sons and their families lived with him, twenty-two souls in all. He had applied to the municipality for a permit to build a second toilet room, but had been refused. He was a polite and courteous man, and spoke of the embarrassment and difficulties caused by the need for such numbers to manage with just one toilet when all had to get ready for school or work in the morning. Similarly, other parents spoke of the lack of privacy when a married couple had to sleep in a single room with all their children. The people owned enough land to expand their homes or build new ones for their grown children, but the municipality, in its attempt to hold down the Arab population, refused to grant them the permits.

The tours were eye-opening for many of the participants. For me, as an Israeli who acknowledged my share of the responsibility for the appalling conditions, it was hard not to get overly emotional in my condemnation of what we were doing to the Palestinians. This was inappropriate for a guide on a fact-finding tour, so in the end, recognizing my own deficiency, I left the guiding to other members of our group. It was hard for me to find the balance between coolly presenting the facts and responding personally to what we were seeing.

CHAPTER 21

Ibrahim and Isma'il

In 1999 I studied Arabic with Noha, a private teacher from the Beit Hanina village in Jerusalem. Very well educated, she was from an elite family in Jerusalem. Noha also had opened a shop selling high-quality Arabic furniture near the Jerusalem municipality. Since customers did not come into the store too frequently, we would sit in the shop and she would tutor me. From time to time, Noha's two nephews, Ibrahim and Isma'il, aged eleven and nine, would come by and she would have me talk with them in simple Arabic. They were very accepting of my many mistakes, and it was good to talk with different native speakers. Their biblical names are, in English, Abraham and Ishmael (the latter was Abraham's first son, the forefather of the Arabs).

The two boys were obviously very bright and were fun to talk to. One day, Ibrahim suggested I come to visit them at their home in the Old City of Jerusalem, and they offered to take me to see the Haram a-Sharif (where the Temple had been and where the Al-Aqsa mosque and the Dome of the Rock stand today), very close to their home. They were both enthusiastic, but then Isma'il began looking worried. "What if our neighbors see you and think we are collaborators?" But Ibrahim had a solution: "We'll tell them that you are a Hebrew teacher, and that you've come to give us a lesson."

One day, their father stopped in. He had been to the Education Department in the municipality to register Ibrahim and Isma'il for a municipal school for the next year. He explained to me, with my teacher's help, that originally his sons had gone to a private school because the public schools for Arab children were so poor. But he'd had a heart attack and could no longer work, so he tried to transfer the boys to a free city school. At the municipality they told him that there was no room and that he should come back next year, when perhaps there would be room. But he had been turned down for three years, and so he sent the boys to a school of the Islamic Waqf.

I told the father that he was living in a democracy. In Israel we have a compulsory education law guaranteeing free education to all residents of Jerusalem. We could get him a lawyer who would be able to place the boys in public schools, and it would not cost him any money. But the father was afraid to antagonize the authorities; he had lived under occupation long enough to believe that suing the authorities could get him into a lot of trouble.

I told this story to a friend, and was amazed to learn that thousands of Palestinian children in Jerusalem are refused entry to public schools, in violation of Israeli law. Their families must pay to send them to private schools or else they do not study at all. This is because there is a shortage of more than a thousand classrooms in the public school system for Arabs, while every Jewish child who asks to study in public school is accepted.

I consulted with my friend and neighbor the lawyer Danny Seidemann, who became very interested in this problem. He took the case pro bono, with the help of an organization he had established, Ir Amim (City of the Nations). Danny set up a working group to ensure free public education for all who wanted it. The group included one member of the Jerusalem municipal council (initially Dr. Meir Margalit, later Pepe Alalu); the director of the Beit Hanina Community Center, Hussam Watad (a Palestinian Israeli); the head of the Parents Committees for the Arab schools in Jerusalem, 'Abdel Karim Lafi; a lawyer from the Association for Civil Rights in Israel, Tali Nir; Sarah Kreimer and Haim Erlich (the latter had been the principal of my children's school) from Ir Amim; and others. When the authorities refused to accept every child, we turned to the High Court of Justice.

The High Court of Justice is a uniquely Israeli institution. Just as kings in biblical times would sit at the gate of a city and hear appeals from any citizen, including the most humble, so did Israel set up a special court, making use of justices from the Supreme Court, who would deal with petitions from any citizen or organization that had a complaint against governmental actions and policies. This highest court has frequently made brave decisions against unfair governmental actions, including decisions that have protected Palestinians from the Israeli government's excesses.

Unfortunately, this court didn't rule that building settlements in the occupied territories is illegal (which it is in international law, but not in Israeli law, as the latter does not consider areas conquered in 1967 as "occupied"), and so it could not always rule against unjust situations, which were created by Israeli law.

Once, while waiting to hear a case that interested me, I listened to one that illustrated the specialness of this court. Two Ethiopian *olim* (new Jewish immigrants), a man and a woman in their early twenties, had petitioned the court. They had no lawyer. The man explained to the judges that they were in love. The woman was studying to be a nurse in Jerusalem, but the only job the man could find was near Haifa. They were Orthodox Jews, so they could not drive on the Sabbath, the only day that they were free to be together. The woman had asked to transfer to a nursing school in Haifa, but there was no room there so she was turned down. The couple asked the High Court of Justice to get her into the Haifa school.

This is not the kind of case that usually gets to the court, which hears lawyers pleading for government ministries, banks, villages, and large nongovernmental organizations. This petition, by contrast, verged on *hutzpah*. But the three judges took it seriously. They questioned the couple, then turned to the lawyer for the nursing school and asked whether an exception could be made for them. Life for new immigrants is always hard, and these young people who had found each other should not be blocked. The lawyer consulted with the school's representative, then told the court that the woman would be accepted. And so, the highest justices of the land intervened to help a simple couple fulfill their love for each other.

Our coalition of Arabs and Jews went to the High Court of Justice again and again, but we could neither get all the needed classrooms built, nor get the state to reimburse the Arab families who had to pay for private school. All sides agreed that the petitioners were entitled by law to receive free education. But there was always a catch, a legal hindrance that the court accepted, that blocked implementation of the children's basic right to free education.

Why did the Jerusalem municipality and the national Ministry of Education not build and lease more classrooms so that all the children could get the free education promised by the law? I assume that most of these civil servants would have been proud to provide all Arab children with a superior education. But there was an economic consideration. For many years we had gotten used to the idea that Arab schools get minimal budgets, and therefore thousands of Arab children in Jerusalem get no public education. To change the status quo would cost millions of dollars, which would lower the budgets available for our Israeli children.

The Ministry of Education admitted this concern to the court: "Requiring the Ministry of Education to pay 100 percent of the educational expenses of the students who are learning in [Arab nonpublic] schools . . . would be a most heavy burden on the Ministry of Education's limited budget. . . . When we speak about a limited budgetary 'pie,' requiring the Ministry of Education to fund the full educational expenses of the approximately 40,000 East Jerusalem students who are not studying in public schools is liable to damage the Ministry's ability to [build additional public schools]." In other words, those children refused admission to public schools would have to finance their own educations.

When we decided to take our case to the High Court of Justice, I was convinced that the problem would be solved forthwith. One of the first laws passed by our Knesset was the Compulsory Learning Law, which included the right to free public education. How simple it should have been.

On 17 July 2000, we submitted a petition for 117 Arab children who had been refused entry into public schools for the following school year, against the municipality of Jerusalem and the Ministry of Education (petition number HCJ 5125/00). But the municipality outwitted us: it jumped our petitioners to the top of the waiting lists of the schools, allowing our children to be accepted while other children who had applied to the schools much earlier were rejected in their stead.

We decided that in order to succeed, we would need to bring enough petitioners to the court so that the municipality would be unable to accept all of them in place of other students. In a major effort, we managed to round up 905 children who had been refused entry to the public schools for the coming year. On 30 June 2001, we submitted petition number HCJ 5185/01.

In what seemed like a partial victory for us, the authorities agreed to build 245 new classrooms over four years. However, our 905 children would not be accepted to public schools. On the issue of refunding their tuition, the court would not rule but said that we could go to the lower courts with the particular cases. I asked Hussam if we could find parents who would sue in a lower court for reimbursement of their tuition, but he said that the parents were furious that their children had been rejected by the highest court. They were no longer willing to work with him, nor would they take the risk of suing the municipality.

The case dragged on for years. The president of the High Court of Justice stated that she had never sat on such a frustrating case. The authorities promised to build hundreds of classrooms, but would pretend that they were working on them while dragging their feet. Some new classrooms were built (even to Israeli standards), but the building rate lagged well behind the birthrate.

I was growing more and more discouraged by our High Court of Justice. Much as the justices believed in free public education, they could barely budge the authorities to build the required classrooms, and the high cost of refunding the tuition that parents were paying to the nonpublic schools probably frightened the court. And then, something happened that gave us a new direction. On 4 May 2006, Yuli Tamir was appointed minister of education.

Professor Yael "Yuli" Tamir was a champion of the peace movement. In 1978, she had been one of the founders of Peace Now. Among other accomplishments, she had been chairperson of the Association for Civil Rights in Israel, had been on the board of the Israel Institute of Democracy, and was one of the Israeli figures behind the Geneva Initiative for peace. She held a doctorate from Oxford and was a professor of philosophy and education at Tel Aviv University. We felt that finally we had a solution. By law, Yuli could sign an order that the children who were rejected would have their tuition at nonpublic schools refunded by the treasury.

I wrote and asked for her intervention, but she never responded. I tried again and again. I could not believe that Yuli would not agree that it is unacceptable to deny free education to Palestinian children in Jerusalem. I wrote to her friends and colleagues, hoping they would influence her, or shame her, into doing her duty. But Yuli would not intervene. She was working on an important reform to give schoolchildren a "new horizon," and probably could not spare the funds or afford to make new enemies. But if this exemplary person would not put an end to this travesty of justice, who would ever help us?

It seemed to me that the state would never build enough classrooms for all the children, so the more important issue was to get a ruling obliging the treasury to reimburse the parents' tuition expenses. But no families were willing to sue. It occurred to me that perhaps we could initiate a class action in which families would not have to endanger themselves, but could reap the rewards if we won. I went to one of our leading civil rights lawyers and learned of the likely technical problems. He recommended a different path, but then finally in 2008 attorney Tali Nir managed to find several families willing to sue for their tuition expenses, so I dropped this tack. I was convinced that now it would be clear sailing. This case was HCJ 5373/08.

Once again, I was amazed that the court did not jump at the chance to redress the wrong. The Ministry of Education claimed that the "nonpublic recognized schools" (where several of the children had studied and paid tuition) receive almost as much money from the state and the municipality as do the official public schools, so there was no reason for them to demand tuition. The president of the court was quite hostile to the petition, and asked whether Tali might prefer to withdraw it altogether. But what did the court want these families to do? There was no way they could get their children educated without paying the required tuition.

We were all upset, and we were still waiting for a court decision that might take months or years to come. But then I managed to get the statistics (which had always been kept secret) showing the funding totals for each school in Jerusalem (a freedom-of-information bill that had recently passed the Knesset allowed me to obtain these numbers). It turned out that our petitioners' schools cost the state only about 40 percent per pupil of the state funding received by the average public school, and none of them had ever received any funding from the municipality. Even if the state reimbursed our petitioners' tuition, the authorities would be expending less for them than they spent on the average public school student. In addition, a telephone survey we conducted showed that virtually every Jewish or Arab nonpublic recognized school charged tuition. The ministry had purposely misled the court. There was no way that a decent nonpublic school could survive financially without charging tuition.

Finally, on 6 February 2011, the High Court of Justice ruled that the authorities would have five years in which to achieve a condition where every child who applied to public school would be accepted. At the end of that five-year period, any child rejected by the public school system would have his/her tuition in a private school paid by the state. Unfortunately, the decision left the parents paying tuition for another five years. But it was a great step forward—after eleven years of repeated petitions, the court finally accepted that the state would have to provide free education, in practice as well as in theory, to all the Arab children in Jerusalem who requested public education.

CHAPTER 22

Olive Trees and the Wall

At the end of September 2000, after the failure of the Camp David peace summit and after Ariel Sharon's visit to the Temple Mount/Haram a-Sharif (on 28 September 2000), the armed, bloody Second (or Al-Aqsa) Intifada began. The Palestinian leadership then forbade Palestinians to engage in joint Palestinian-Israeli activities (which were labeled "normalization"). This brought our last dialogue group, in Beit Sahour, to an end. And my own peace movement activity, which had always involved joint actions with Palestinians from the occupied territories, also seemed at an end.

But two developments soon permitted us to work together again: settlers began attacking Palestinian olive groves, and Israel began to build a security barrier, or "the Wall."

In the autumn olive-picking season of 2002, settler extremists significantly increased their attacks on Palestinian olive groves and farmers. The former Sephardic chief rabbi of Israel, Mordechai Eliyahu, ruled that "since the land is the inheritance of the People of Israel, planting on this land by gentiles is planting on land that does not belong to them. If someone plants a tree on my land, both the tree and the fruit it yields belong to me." Settlers stole Palestinians' olives and even built a professional olive press to turn them into oil. They attacked farmers and destroyed thousands of trees. I heard about problems that were occurring in the Palestinian village of Yasouf, and went to see for myself.

I arrived in the evening and found a remarkable British woman, Angie Zelter (one of the founders of the International Women's Peace Service), sitting with dozens of villagers and a few IWPS colleagues and Israelis like me. They were discussing how they would act on the next day. Next to Yasouf, Israel had built the settlement of Tappuah, which was known to be a center for supporters of the late Rabbi Meir Kahane, whose racist policies had caused him to be banned from running for the Knesset and whose group was listed by the United States as a terrorist organization. Tappuah was a magnet for disturbed young men, providing them with an opportunity for violent acting out.

I learned that the settlers had established a new illegal outpost on a nearby hilltop, and were using a dirt road between the outpost and their official settlement. This road ran perpendicular to and cut across the dirt road the Yasouf villagers used to get to their olive groves. The army had decided that the villagers could no longer use their road, since it would endanger the security of the settlers.

The evening meeting in Yasouf was a kind of town meeting. People discussed different options. It was decided by consensus that the villagers would walk en masse along their road, and if stopped by settlers or the army would all sit down together, while the internationals would try to stay between the Palestinians and the potential enemy. Meetings of this sort took place almost every evening, with Angie and her colleagues making sure that the village was really prepared for nonviolence. Angie had wide experience with nonviolent actions in England (e.g., against nuclear armament); she was quiet, open to hearing other viewpoints, self-assured, fearless, and an accepted leader.

We slept over in the village, and the next morning started walking toward the olive groves. Settlers blocked us and the villagers all sat down in one group. I stood next to one young settler of American origin who talked nonstop into a walkie-talkie, speaking complete nonsense. He claimed that villagers were attacking the settlers, carrying clubs, and getting ready to attack Tappuah from three sides. At one point, this settler began to point his M16 assault rifle at the villagers. I saw several soldiers standing nearby, so I ran to their officer, a man in his forties, and told him that the settler was pointing his weapon and should be removed. In response, the officer growled, "Don't give me orders!" and walked away. I went back to the disturbed youth and stood in front of his muzzle, between him and the villagers. He pointed the gun at different angles to aim around me, but whenever he changed position I stepped in front of his muzzle to prevent him from shooting a Palestinian. Finally, another officer came and separated the settlers from us.

Angie and her IWPS colleagues worked hard, day after day, to help the farmers use tools of nonviolence to counter the settlers. My government finally ruled that Angie was a threat to Israel's security. On a trip back from England she was stopped at the airport by security agents who wrapped her up in a blanket, carried her off screaming, and deported her.

I then began working in the olive harvest with Rabbis for Human Rights and their indefatigable leader, Rabbi Arik Ascherman. We would accompany Palestinian farmers whose olive trees were in areas that the settlers wanted, and where violent settlers might threaten them. The Palestinians go out to their groves as families—husbands and wives, children and grandparents. We would help pick olives while keeping an eye out for marauding settlers. Many of the young Palestinians had never before met Israelis with whom they could talk, or at least smile. In the middle of the day, we would all sit on the ground and eat together. Our hosts would bring out home-baked flat breads, olive oil, and, depending on what they could afford, sometimes salami, tuna, cheeses, peppers, and pickled vegetables. This was our real reward, sitting together amicably while the rest of our nations were fighting it out. Sometimes at the end of the day's work, we would go to one of the homes to drink coffee or tea together. While this contact was very different from our dialogues, in which we talked with politically knowledgeable people about the situation, it still had the important effect of reminding us all of the humanity of the other.

Most settlers are not ideological, but simply take advantage of the low cost of living in the occupied territories. We, however, would go to the most ideological and vicious areas, where the farmers had been terrorized to the extent that without our presence, they could not reach their fields. Once, near the settlement of Yitzhar, shots were fired and one of our volunteers took a rock to his head from a settler, requiring stitches. Nonetheless, the chance to renew friendly contact with Palestinians made the activities positive in my eyes, despite my disappointment at the behavior of some of my fellow Jews and some of the soldiers.

The war to defend the olive trees was so important for Palestinians that their leadership could not prevent the farmers from accepting Israeli help. A second area where the ban on Palestinian-Israeli cooperation could not be enforced was the campaigns to fight against the harm done by Israel's separation barrier, known as the Wall.

At the end of September 2000 Palestinians began the Second Intifada, a struggle against Israel which turned very violent. A new tactic of suicide bombings proved very effective in killing large numbers of Israeli civilians. Israelis were extremely threatened by this method; it seemed impossible to defend against it.

A group of Israelis from the peace camp came to the conclusion that peace could only be achieved after Palestinian terrorism ceased, and they called for building a wall around the West Bank that would effect an end to the repeated bombings. In February 2002 the Movement for Unilateral Separation was founded, initially by the Israeli Council for Peace and Security, which comprised more than a thousand reserve generals, officers, and former senior members of Israel's police, Shin Bet, and Mossad security services, who were seeking a peaceful solution. (Just as many of the leading Palestinian peaceniks had previously engaged in violent activity and served prison sentences, so also many of our retired security people actively pursued peace.) The idea was for the Israeli army to withdraw from areas behind the Wall, and to evacuate some 20,000 Jewish settlers from about forty settlements. Support for this movement came from the moderate Left, while the Right was completely opposed to any wall that would limit Israeli expansion and interfere with the settlement project.

I opposed this plan, feeling that separation was not the right solution, and hoping that there was still a chance to negotiate a peace which would end the violence. My daughter Daphna, on the other hand, believed that the Wall was the only chance for peace, for two states for the two peoples. She became active in this movement, serving as chief organizer for the Jerusalem area and for university students. She worked hard with the managing director, Shaul Givoli, who was both a retired brigadier general from the army and a retired major general from the police. (Shaul and I would meet several years later when we both would try to prevent the Wall from dividing a village, as I'll discuss below.) Despite my reservations, my wife and I helped Daphna organize a meeting at our home. A leader of the movement tried to convince our guests of the wisdom in this approach.

Eventually, the government headed by Prime Minister Ariel Sharon gave in to the concept of unilateral separation. But in contrast to the movement that wanted the Wall to be along the Green Line, the right-wingers drew the path inside the West Bank, causing a swath of destruction, separating Palestinian farmers from their fields, and even worse, grabbing land that would de facto be joined to Israel for enlarging the settlements.

Palestinians fought the Wall, often with the help of Israelis and internationals. As with the olive-tree issue, the Wall was such a pressing matter that Palestinian leaders could not prevent villagers from inviting Israelis to join forces with them. I was personally not very active in these struggles, until one day Veronika called me. She told me that Rabbi Arik Ascherman had sent an e-mail stating that the village of Jabel Mukabber was about to be split by the Wall—part would be on the Israeli side and part on the Palestinian. Arik was calling on Israelis to help. Jabel Mukabber was next to our neighborhoods, and we had Arab friends there, so Veronika and Elliot Cohen, Professor Sidra DeKoven Ezrahi and I, together with others, decided to see what we could do. We teamed up with the neighborhood council, led by Daoud Awisat from the Sheikh Sa'ed neighborhood, which was threatened with being cut off from the rest of the Jabel Mukabber village.

We met with people from the village, and learned more of Sheikh Sa'ed's history. In June 1967, immediately after the Six-Day War, Israel decided to expand its borders around Jerusalem to prevent that part of the West Bank from being returned to Jordan (which had been occupying it). A rather arbitrary line was drawn, based on annexing the maximum land with a minimum number of Arabs. The village of Jabel Mukabber consisted of seven neighborhoods. Six of these were annexed into Israel (and became part of East Jerusalem), while the easternmost neighborhood, Sheikh Sa'ed, a hill surrounded by extremely steep *wadis* on three sides, remained outside Israel in the West Bank. The residents of Sheikh Sa'ed had only one land connection to the rest of the world—through the remainder of their village and from there into the rest of Jerusalem. From 1967 until the first Gulf War in 1991, there were no checkpoints and no restrictions on Palestinians traveling in Israel, even in their own cars, so the residents managed to travel freely without difficulty. Even after 1991 (when more and more restrictions were placed on West Bank Palestinians entering Israel), since there was no fence and since Israel realized that the Sheikh Sa'ed residents had no alternative but to enter the Israeli side of their village, they were basically allowed to travel freely. Most of the Sheikh Sa'ed residents worked in Jerusalem; they were known as skilled building trades workers. Many of the residents had family on the Israeli side, and they received almost all their services—health, education, shopping, even burial—from the Israeli side. Were the Wall to be built separating them from the rest of their village, they would lose all connection with the center of their lives.

Through lawyer Ghiath Nasser, the residents turned to the Israeli courts to appeal the path of the Wall, and recommended an alternate route that would not cut them off. They also sought help from their Jewish neighbors. We met the members of their neighborhood council, who were very easy to work with. Most of the men knew Hebrew from working in West Jerusalem.

Our first thought was to have a joint Arab-Jewish demonstration. But many of the Palestinians were not allowed into Israel, and we were concerned that Israelis might be afraid to go to the West Bank. So we decided to have a march along the Jewish street closest to Jabel Mukabber, and then walk back on the Arab street closest to the Jewish neighborhood (known as Armon HaNatziv). I went to the police to get a permit. The permit said that no nationalistic slogans or flags could be displayed, a stipulation that didn't bother us since we only wanted to carry signs calling for the Wall not to split the village. On 23 May 2004, I got to the starting point of the march early, and saw that the police had come out in force. There were a couple of officers, an armed personnel carrier, a motorcycle SWAT team decked out in their scary black outfits, and lots of border police. They looked as if they were expecting a large-scale riot.

Since this was our initial activity, only about a dozen Israelis turned out. We waited and waited for the Palestinians to arrive. Finally it became clear that they were afraid of the enormous police presence. One of their leaders, who didn't have a permit to enter Jerusalem, came anyway, and pulled half a dozen of his friends out of their homes, making them participate. An officer sent the troops home, and he and one border policeman accompanied us on our march route. We even got a lone TV crew to film our tiny procession, which was more press than we'd be able to get in our future activities.

For our next action, on 2 June, we got Israelis to sign a petition to move the Wall eastward, beyond the Sheikh Sa'ed neighborhood, so that the Sheikh Sa'ed residents would be united with the rest of their village. Some Israelis refused to sign because they wanted not just to move the route of the Wall but to take it down altogether. Others said that the new route would take land from the West Bank and move it de facto into Israel. But the residents didn't care about these fine points. They wanted to continue working to feed their families and to be part of their village, regardless of where it was. This time, we worked together, Israelis and Palestinians, in explaining the petition to potential signatories.

We found that Israelis were not too frightened to go to Sheikh Sa'ed, so we were able to organize a series of events together. One was a class in playing the *darbooka* (an Arab drum) for Israeli and Palestinian children, in Sheikh Sa'ed (3 August 2004). In March 2005, we hiked the streets of Sheikh Sa'ed overlooking the gorge of the Kidron Valley and the beautiful olive groves, ending up with refreshments on the porch of one of the villagers. On 25 July 2005, we organized a large meeting of about 200 Israelis who visited in several homes in Sheikh Sa'ed for coffee and hospitality. Another activity, on 2 May 2007, brought the Yasmin children's choir from the Old City's Magnificat Institute to sing Hebrew and Arabic songs to a large mixed crowd.

We invited the press and the television stations to all of these activities, but with few exceptions they were uninterested, even though it was most unusual to see such assemblages of Palestinians and Israelis during the Second Intifada, especially in the West Bank. Since the media would not come to us, we went to them, paying for advertisements that included photos of our previous events while inviting Israelis to the next event.

In 2006 the court decided to move the route of the Wall to keep the village together. On 26 March we held a joyous victory party in Sheikh Sa'ed with several hundred Israelis and a similar number of Palestinians, including all the *mukhtars* from the other neighborhoods of Jabel Mukabber. But our joy was premature. The army appealed the decision, and on 15 March 2010, the High Court of Justice ruled that the Wall would in fact divide Sheikh Sa'ed from the remainder of Jabel Mukabber. As a compromise, a gate would be available twenty-four hours a day, allowing those, with permits, to enter Israel (on foot).

Unlike the olive-picking activities, in which we generally met Arabs for only a few hours and then moved on to another village, in Sheikh Sa'ed we worked together for about six years, and had the chance to forge real ties with our colleagues. I can only hope that our work together may have helped to leave open the gate linking most of the residents with the rest of their village.

CHAPTER 23

From Dialogue to Strategic Community Activation

Some Reflections on Technique

My thinking regarding Israeli-Palestinian dialogue went through several stages. At first I felt that a single positive experience, like that of Jericho, was a sufficient goal. I believed that such actions would let Israelis overcome their fears of Palestinians: they would visit in a Palestinian home or town, and meet people who could give them a measure of optimism about the chances for a peaceful future. Veronika taught me that there is also a need for ongoing dialogue, in which questions can be discussed in depth and participants can learn if they really trust their colleagues. This type of dialogue also offers more symmetry, since Palestinians learn about Israelis while showing their own peaceful face.

From the Beit Sahour dialogue, I learned the tremendous importance of a dialogue group composed of highly respected members of their community, respected as leaders of their national struggle but with roots in the local community. Unlike a dialogue of individuals, which may be enlightening but does not affect more than the participants, the Beit Sahour dialogue led to large, press-worthy activities that could carry the message of peace far beyond the confines of the dialogue room. These dialogues differed from the meetings of national, rather than community, leaders, such as those between members of the Knesset and members of the PLO, or between national leaders of Israeli peace movements and of Palestinian organizations.

The highly integrated community of Beit Sahour accepted the leadership of those Palestinians most involved in the dialogues. The Palestinians learned a great deal about Israeli thinking, and the group achieved a high level of trust through working together in the tough days of the intifada, so that it was possible to embark on ambitious activities, such as bringing Israeli families with small children to sleep overnight in a radical Palestinian town during the hottest days of the intifada. To this stage in our development I gave the name "dialogue-action group": the dialogue leads to community action.

It should be noted that there is a certain contradiction between *dialogues* that are open to people of all points of view, and *action* that is designed to affect public opinion in a particular direction. How could we invite right-wing Israelis to participate in a dialogue run by a group that in its community activities advocated territorial compromise? I believe that we were cognizant enough of this inherent contradiction, and dedicated enough to the positive aspects of dialogue, that it was not a problem in practice. There are many good arguments that rejectionists, both Israeli and Palestinian, can put forward, and in general we were supportive of the right of participants with differing points of view to make their views, or doubts, heard. Much more difficult to deal with were the abrasive personalities of some participants who, regardless of their views, could create anger and unproductive tensions in the group. In the Jabel Mukabber group, for example, as long as the organization was strong it tolerated a religious Jew who enjoyed attending and who declared that he favored transferring the Arabs out of the country, but as the group began to fall apart the Palestinians complained about having to receive in their homes someone whose ideas were insulting to them.

I personally feel that people with any point of view should be able to participate in dialogues, so long as they can talk respectfully with the others. Sometimes, too many forceful speakers with a single, party-line point of view can hurt the dialogue, so it is helpful to have a variety of opinions. In some dialogue groups, it is possible to limit membership to well-informed individuals, or to people who agree to meet regularly.

In the course of the dialogues, I sometimes tried to imagine the minimum common agreement that I would like to see in a group working together for a long time. In the end, I decided on four points.

I would like Palestinians to accept:

1. The Jewish people, over many centuries of exile, have been repeatedly persecuted, so there existed a "Jewish problem" that eluded solution.
2. It is a historical fact that the Jewish people lived in Israel/ Palestine in ancient times. Jews' emotional and religious attachment to this land persisted during their dispersion.

I would like Israelis to accept:

3. It was perfectly natural for Palestinians to feel threatened by the Zionist movement. Zionists hoped for an influx of more than 10 million Jews, largely from imperialist Europe; these numbers would have reduced the Palestinian Arabs to less than 10 percent of the population.
4. Regardless of the relative responsibility of each people, there is no question that the Palestinian people suffered greatly during the twentieth century.

It was always difficult to get Israelis from the Right or the center to attend the dialogues, and we frequently criticized ourselves for preaching to the converted. Nonetheless, for the small groups of peace supporters who overcame their fears and participated, the dialogues were often energizing experiences that helped participants to be more committed to their peace-related activities.

Within our groups there was a marked asymmetry between Palestinian and Israeli members. Whereas the Palestinians generally organized around an individual or small group of people with influence in their community, and represented the majority point of view of their people, we Israelis were a powerless group from the small percentage of Israelis most trusting of Palestinians. We Israelis could not claim to speak for our communities. However, we came from the much more powerful nation and, though our fellow Israelis considered our views extreme, we were still from the mainstream Zionist group. Unlike the more radical Left in Israel, we were generally accepted as legitimate, pro-Israel citizens. The fact that many of our members were religious and many were involved in Jewish studies gave us added legitimacy. We also brought useful contacts with Israeli journalists and foreign correspondents, as well as contacts within parties such as Meretz and Labor. We frequently could provide easy contact with human rights groups and Jewish lawyers. Through our relation with Peace Now, we were able to connect our Palestinian colleagues with the mainstream of the Israeli peace movement during the First Intifada.

Once I had seen the power of the dialogue-action group, I could scarcely be satisfied with a group whose only goal was to influence the few people who attended, even though such groups are so rare that they should be treasured.

I also didn't personally care for groups that came together solely to draft a joint statement, get it into the press, and then disband. This for me was a kind of gimmick, and while it took less effort than dialogue and was often more effective in getting press coverage, I tried to avoid its temptation.

Until the Oslo Accords, our groups seemed to intuitively find activities that supported our long-term goals. After Oslo, though, it seemed to me that in Beit Sahour we continued more from inertia than from any considered strategy. With the grinding down of the peace process under Netanyahu (beginning in 1996), I felt that one of my basic beliefs was being undermined, namely that if the Palestinians could only reassure Israelis of their peaceful goals, and stop terrorism, our own desire for peace would lead us to reasonable compromises. This change made me think that it was more important to affect U.S. and European opinion, because Israelis were ready to follow Netanyahu, regardless of what the Palestinians did. During the First Intifada, I had denigrated the importance of foreigners who would attend our dialogues. I had felt that they detracted from the Israeli side of the dialogue. But now I began to wonder whether we didn't need to consider energizing foreigners to work in their countries to support our goals.

This made me feel that we needed to add another dimension to our dialogue-action groups: strategic thinking. What were our long-term goals? Whom did we need to influence? How could we reach those people? How could we assess the results of our activities, including the effect on participants and the effect on their work to advance our goals? People who had the background and abilities to organize dialogues did not necessarily have the information and ability to analyze strategic goals. It seemed to me that we needed some better-informed consulting group to help us, perhaps made up of academics, journalists, and political leaders. I began to think in terms of strategic community activation dialogue groups, which would use the tool of dialogue to activate a community to act in ways that would help achieve strategic goals, and that would provide feedback for us to see if we were succeeding.

During the First Intifada, a secret, unified Palestinian leadership existed on both the national and local levels. Their acceptance was necessary for an action to take place, and their support was important if a program was to succeed. With the end of the intifada, there was no longer an organization respected by the community to push people to abandon their lethargy and come together for large, demonstrative public activities which could help to achieve strategic goals. The Palestinians finally achieved their own leadership in the Palestinian Authority, but unfortunately they found that the exiled leadership returned to milk the people, to lord it over them, to introduce corruption worse than what Israel had employed in its bald-faced occupation, to deny civil liberties, and to torture their own people to death at a higher rate than Israel had done. So the Palestinian Authority was not the unifying and activating force that was still needed.

Another weakness of our groups was our limited self-assessment of our activities. If an Italian television crew came to an event, we did not know whether they actually broadcast a report, nor to what extent there was some influence on the Italian masses and on people with the power to affect our situation. What kind of activity would give the best payoff toward achieving our long-term goals?

The ideal group, as I see it, is one that combines dialogue with activities whose planning is assisted by expert consultants analyzing strategic goals.

The actions tap into the strengths of the community, which are activated by the dialogue group, which is given legitimacy by a local leadership that has the long-range national goals in mind. Finally, there should be a way to analyze the success of each action in terms of audiences that view or read about the activity, and the extent to which this media exposure produces a positive effect on the ultimate decision makers. The linking together and coordination of many such groups would be important for amplifying the effect.

Needless to say, our small, isolated, voluntary organizations were far from meeting such an ideal, yet they managed to accomplish, for their size and resources, a lot of good, with real enhancement of the image of the Palestinians and of the possibility of our living together in peace.

Conclusion

Is There Hope?

My years of intense activity with Palestinians taught me several things that many of my fellow Israelis seem to have missed.

First and foremost, I am convinced that the Palestinians were ready to make peace with us long before we suspected it. We Israelis grew up with the belief that Palestinians would never accept a peaceful solution. At best, we supported giving the West Bank back to the Jordanian monarchy so that Jordan would suppress the Palestinian troublemakers for us.

In truth, there were several cases of Palestinians who were assassinated by fellow Palestinians because they worked for peace—just as happened later to Yitzhak Rabin, who was assassinated by a fellow Jew for pursuing a peace policy. In all these cases, the killings did not prove that there was not a willingness for peace.

My personal contacts with Palestinians in a dozen communities—Muslim and Christian, wealthy and poor, educated and simple, refugees and old-timers, urbanites and peasants—convinced me that by the start of the First Intifada in 1987 (at the very latest), most of the Palestinian leadership and most Palestinians favored a peaceful settlement with Israel based on two states for the two peoples.

The second point that I came to realize was that we Israelis were largely ignorant of this readiness on the Palestinian side. I felt at the time that if the Palestinians could but convince us of their sincerity, our overwhelming desire for peace would lead us to the peace table. Unfortunately, the Palestinians did not view proving their readiness for peace as a top strategic priority, or else they did not know how to get that message across to us.

Part of our problem was certainly our Israeli leaders' ambivalence toward a peace that would permanently block our chances for territorial expansion. We were taught the axiom that a Palestinian state was synonymous with throwing the Jews into the sea. Palestinians who refused to live under Israeli or Jordanian rule seemed to us unreasonably rebellious. In this atmosphere it could not have been easy for Palestinians to convince us of their willingness for peace.

A third problem that I saw was the concerted efforts of my government's army and security services to prevent any joint action by Israelis and Palestinians in support of peace. Our general conception was such that even those public servants who sincerely supported a true peace felt called upon to block such actions. Perhaps they wished to protect us from being duped by the Arabs. Or perhaps they saw no contradiction between their sincere desire for peace and their need to block activities that might lead to our giving up any land.

Fourth, our press and education system, despite the many journalists and educators who supported a peaceful solution, failed to give us the true picture of where the Palestinians stood vis-à-vis an end to the conflict. Our children were poisoned against Arabs from the cradle; our adults had their fears reinforced daily. Even the left-wing papers joined the rest of our press in giving enormous coverage to any Arab violence against Jews, while offering minimal reporting of conciliatory moves by Palestinians.

A fifth issue was our view of the Palestinian community. Some Palestinians' violent resistance to us led most of us Israelis to view their community as a vicious, hate-filled jungle. Even if we were lucky enough to meet a decent Palestinian in our world, we believed that at night he returned to the murderers' den in which he lived. Most Israeli Jews were afraid to come to dialogues in the West Bank, including East Jerusalem, for fear that the Arabs would slaughter us. It is terribly hard to overcome fears that have been taught since childhood, and that are reinforced with each terror attack. These fears prevent the mutual trust that is so important for advancing the peace process.

During the years of the First Intifada, I told my Palestinian colleagues what I really believed: we Israelis would agree to a reasonable peace if we could only overcome our fear and distrust of Arabs. The agreement by Shimon Peres and Yitzhak Rabin to embark on the Oslo peace process supported my beliefs. Unfortunately, as I am writing this book in 2011, during a period of almost no Palestinian terror, ongoing demographic changes make us more religiously fundamentalist, expansionist, and anti-Palestinian. This casts doubt on our long-held belief that we are the forces of peace while the Palestinians are the sole rejectionists.

I know that meeting Yusra and Sa'ed, and becoming drawn into the dialogues, radically changed my approach. But why? After all, I was always identified with the Israeli peace movement. So what changed?

I grew up, like most Israelis, viewing the Palestinians as *rivals* and *enemies*—as rivals for the resources here, especially the land, and as enemies who dragged us repeatedly to the field of battle. Perhaps what distinguished me from my right-wing Zionist colleagues was my insistence that we fight fairly and decently, and that we be willing to yield some of the resources in order to achieve peace with our rivals. I believed in the basic purity of our Zionist movement and was ready to forgive the Palestinians if they were ready to live with us in peace.

I was brought up with the belief that the essence of being a Jew is in living for social justice and decency. I was named for one of our great teachers who, when asked to define all of Judaism while standing on one foot, replied, "Don't do to others what you would not want done to you. This is the whole Torah. The rest is simply commentary."

The dialogues and activities with Palestinians changed something inside of me. I spent many, many hours with Palestinians who were not my enemies, who shared my goals, and who were definitely my friends. I wanted their children to get decent educations, not only because that is a right of all children, but because their education was important to my friends, their parents. I opposed their being degraded by my soldiers at checkpoints not only because we Jews should not behave that way, but because their pain would hurt me as well.

They challenged my way of thinking, they challenged what I had been brought up to believe. Despite my commitment to Zionism, I began to realize how reasonable it was that they had opposed us. I began to see the contradictions between the Palestinian society which I had imagined—the jungle of primitive villains—and the society which I actually visited. As I became friends with people who had engaged in the violent struggle against us, I was forced to adapt to new contradictions.

I think of my parents' friends the Soifers, whose children were blown up in Zion Square by a booby-trapped refrigerator. I think of our close friends Betty and Burt, whose daughter was blown up by a suicide bomber. I think of the bomb that exploded at the bus stop on Leib Yaffe Street, where our daughter Daphna would catch the bus to ride to school (fortunately, no one was hurt). I think of the suicide bombers, and the rockets fired into our civilian neighborhoods. I cannot avoid the truth that within Palestinian society there are people ready to kill us in order to push us out of this land which they, as we, want.

But I have also seen how some of my fellow Jews have treated my Palestinian friends, how we have destroyed their lives. I have detailed much of the mistreatment in these pages. I see the terrorists on both sides: our Jewish underground, Baruch Goldstein, Ami Popper, Rabbi Meir Kahane, and the settler extremists, and their Hamas and Islamic Jihad.

This is a book of contradictions, for our conflict is filled with them. The same army that carries out sadistic oppression of the Palestinians is led by officers committed to a decent end to our conflict. The same Israeli who supports driving the Arabs out of Palestine insists on connecting them to the water network. The Palestinian who claims the right to kill settlers insists that he would save an injured settler. Those who fight each other the hardest may be those most willing to compromise for peace.

For generations we believed that we were the seekers of peace, that the Arabs were the obstacle. It's time we realized that peace is achievable, Palestinians are willing, and it now requires our commitment to make it happen.

ACKNOWLEDGMENTS

This book would never have been written but for the enthusiastic encouragement of my friend Professor Michael Zuckerman. I e-mailed Mike the first chapter I wrote, and got a positive response. I then e-mailed him each chapter as I completed it, and his response would give me the strength to write the next installment.

My thanks to the many Palestinians and Israelis who created the activities described in this book, with special thanks to Dr. Veronika Cohen.

Thanks to Dr. Joyce Rappaport, who edited the manuscript, and to copyeditor Merryl Sloane; to my sponsoring editor at Indiana University Press, Rebecca Jane Tolen, and to IUP staff; and to Judy Labenson, who got me on the right track after my first forty rejections.

My thanks to Danny Orstav, who was always ready to help when I needed it.

Thanks to my wife, Anita, who was always encouraging, and accepted the many, many hours that I spent hunched over the computer.

I feel the need to acknowledge my many mistakes in our dialogues and activities. I often was filled with such self-assurance—as though I knew better than others—that I'm afraid I sometimes behaved haughtily, hurt others' feelings, and missed using better ideas just because I had not initiated them. My special apologies to those who participated in the meeting to set up a network of dialogue groups, and to those who participated in a bus trip through East Jerusalem that I guided unforgivably.

The adventures described in this book gave us all a chance to work together, to try to make this land a better home for both Jews and Palestinians. For this, I am forever grateful.

GLOSSARY

aba': Bedouin cloak (Arabic)

ACRI: Association for Civil Rights in Israel

ahalan w'-sahalan: welcome (Arabic)

Civil Administration: part of the IDF which deals with the occupied population's civil needs

CRM: Citizens Rights Movement; political movement of the Ratz Party

debka: Arab men's line folk dance (Arabic)

dir balak: take care! (Arabic)

doubon: a cozy, hooded, quilted coat, which makes the wearer look like a bear (Hebrew)

faqqous: delicious member of the cucumber family (Arabic)

falafel: deep-fried ball of ground chickpeas (Arabic)

Green Line: 1949 armistice demarcation line between Israel, the West Bank, and the Gaza Strip

haadis: incident or accident (Arabic)

hamoula: clan (Arabic)

hamsin: dry, hot, dusty wind (Arabic)

hutzpah: nerve, brazen audacity (Yiddish)

IDF: Israel Defense Forces (Israeli army); also called by the Hebrew acronym Tzahal

ILA: Israel Lands Authority; in charge of most of the land in Israel

intifada: lit. "shaking off" (Arabic). The First Intifada was a mass uprising by Palestinians in all the occupied territories, beginning in December 1987. A second uprising, much different from the prior one, began at the end of September 2000 and is called by some the Second, or Al-Aqsa, Intifada.

IWPS: International Women's Peace Service

jalabiyye: an ankle-length shirt which traditional men still wear (Arabic)

JNF: Jewish National Fund; among other tasks, it plants forests throughout Israel

Kalashnikov: AK-47 assault rifle

kiddush: Jewish blessing over wine; also a reception after morning prayers (Hebrew)

kufiye: an Arab man's headdress (Arabic)

lijna: council (Arabic)

MK: member of Knesset (i.e., parliament)

moshav: cooperative farm (Hebrew)

mukhtar: the chosen leader of a village or clan (Arabic)

narvaze: nervous, or angry (Arabic)

olim: new Jewish immigrants to Israel (Hebrew)

Ramadan: the month when Muslims fast from sunup to sundown (Arabic)

seder: Jewish ceremonial meal at Passover (Hebrew)

Shabak: acronym for the General Security Service, i.e., the security police; also called the Shin Bet

shabab: young men (Arabic)

sulha: traditional Arab way of preventing blood feud between clans (Arabic)

suq: market (Arabic)

tel: mound covering an ancient town (Arabic)

Tzahal: Hebrew acronym for Israel Defense Forces

wadi: valley (Arabic)

Born in Mandatory Palestine, **Hillel Bardin** is an Israeli Zionist who has been working since 1985 to improve Jewish-Arab relations. Bardin served as a squad commander in the IDF reserves and was one of the founders of the civil guard in his neighborhood in Jerusalem.

He is a founder and former board member of the Association for Civil Rights in Israel, the Rapprochement Dialogue Center, and the Jerusalem Information Center, and has served on the board of Defense for Children International. He was a founder and served as the authorized representative of the Shlom Yerushalayim Party in the Jerusalem municipal council.